Last Train

to

St Tropez

Phil Jeremy

DEDICATION

Sue, Alexander and Jane.

LEGAL NOTICE

CONTENTS

CHAPTER 1

WHITE LINES

"Dream as if you will live forever, Live as if you will die today"

James Dean

"You should have taken it," these words filled my head as I stood on the slip road to the A6 auto route in Paris at 7:00 am on a sunlit morning in May 1978. I had a rucksack, a croissant and a thumb shoved forcefully into the heart of the Parisian rush hour. A mass of students, travellers, immigrants, loners and weirdos were all trying to hitch a ride onto the auto route south. This baffling array of competition for the one car that would stop was daunting but I knew luck was shining like a beacon in my head and I was a lighthouse to fortune. It was warm. I felt a breathtaking sense of release from all things familiar whilst relishing a future unknown. This exhilarating detachment from normal life was my understanding of freedom. Emotionally I was a bundle of calm, cool excitement as thousands of cars sped by. In France, ignore at your peril the unwritten rules of hitch-hiking:- The poor pick up people with no money, usually in a deux chevaux. The wealthy with a social conscience, pick up the aspirational looking traveller. Cool drivers in cool cars pick up girls. Gay guys in cool cars pick up guys - and lorry drivers pick up anybody.

Appealing to the broadest cross-section possible is the goal. Sometimes they will take you 10 kilometres to the next exit and sometimes a lot, lot further to places you've never dreamed of.

I arrived here after sitting in my parents' cottage in Cheshire, England just two short weeks ago. I had just returned from a short break in Europe and whilst there had accidentally bumped into a group of young people who were living a very different life to me. Being a typical ex graduate in seventies Britain meant I had no idea that another sort of life existed, gap years had not been invented. I was heavily involved in establishing my career and I already owned a car, a mortgage and an overdraft facility. But whilst on this vacation I met people who were travelling, hanging out and searching for something different. They had no interest in careers, their passion was living. A yacht broker had offered them, and by accident me, a job on Robert Stigwood's yacht sailing around the Greek Islands, the only condition being that you had to be able to tie a Bowline. Robert Stigwood was head of RSO music responsible for Saturday Night Fever with the Bee Gees, and they and other alumni would be on this three month cruise. I had reservations. First, Robert was a well known philanderer of young male crew members and second, what the fuck was a Bowline!

Well I solved the Bowline knot, hardly the Gordion, but an indispensable skill when working on board a boat and was promptly offered the job. I found the whole idea faintly ridiculous and consequently refused the offer and returned to England believing that I couldn't possibly be so reckless when busy forging my career back home. And it was then that my father, with his paper and pipe in hand, slippers and log fire crackling away, looked up from under his spectacles and mused. "You should have taken it." This unexpected statement threw me completely, I presumed he would have said the opposite and accused all these young travellers as wayward losers. He continued. "You're only 24, forget the car, forget the job, forget the mortgage, go out and experience life." He promptly went back to reading his paper blissfully unaware of firing a starting gun in my head. I believed my reaction had been sensible and mature and he thought I'd been an idiot. For a middle class, middle aged businessman with a lifestyle to match this was heady stuff, it was the year of the 'Winter of Discontent,' strikes and industrial disputes were a weekly event. Inflation had hit 26%, jobs were hard to come by; life wasn't easy in Britain in the Seventies, it was a bleak place and to me always seemed grey and full of drudgery. The people I'd met had cast off these chains of an ordinary existence and were looking for something else in life. The effect on me was deeply pervasive and I thought about it constantly.

Although my father had inadvertently given me 'permission' to go, it wasn't quite that simple. Leaving would mean no income, my parents couldn't and wouldn't support me, there was no hidden trust fund; I didn't even know what a trust fund was. I had been brought up, originally in Yorkshire, to be fiercely independent and what you chose to do with your life was your decision and the consequences of those decisions were yours alone. I asked my best friend Bob to come and he thought it was a great idea but not the right time for him. Also his parents were vehemently against it, as in fact most parents were. The social mores of 1978 were very different to today, nobody just quit their job and took off, it just didn't happen. I remember a story he told me of a guy we knew at school who was 23 years old and who'd been offered a job as a trainee manager at the Leamington Spa Building Society and when asked why he had taken it his reply was, "they have a very good pension plan"…. and he was serious. The thought of planning your whole life on that basis was an anathema to me yet this sort of belief was quite normal at the time. I wasn't running away from an un-happy childhood or social life, on the contrary I couldn't have been more fortunate, it was just a burning desire to see the other side of the fence. I remember one ac-quaintance sagely announcing, as if her idea,

"Ah Phil, be careful, perhaps you think the grass is greener on the other side?"

Well I've got news for her, quite often it is.

Anyone can always find a reason for not doing something and mine was simple, beautiful and called Jane. We had been together four years and with me leaving for an unspecified period, to go who knows where, was not part of the plan. We talked for many hours, argued, cried and laughed but in the end she knew I had to go. We both were aware that a young guy on the road was going to have temptations. Could our relationship withstand this lengthy separation? We would find out.

My decision was made. I was fully committed and within two weeks of my father's words I had quit my job, sold my car, rented my house and with £85 in my pocket had bid farewell to Jane, friends, family and set off, Dick Whittington style, to London. It was a typical summer's evening in the capital city - freezing cold and wet. I trudged along through the ever busy underground arriving late at Victoria train station and sat myself down to await the train to the Dover. This was a ritual for all young people travelling to Europe in the seventies; it was a kind of rite of passage, wandering about for hours until the Boat-train arrived. There were no reservations so it was every man for himself. The only café shut at 10:00pm, café being a rather loose term, as a grotty sandwich and two day old bun were the only choices available. God knows what the Frenchies must have thought arriving from Paris - probably not much different to what they think today. It was a strange feeling sitting there on a cold draughty concrete floor, reflecting on my recent decision. I sensed the same degree of trepidation and excitement as I wondered what the coming months would bring. There was an odd kind of peace in this old relic of Victorian times, it was a crumbling smelly depressing place but to me it represented the springboard to excitement.

After a wet sleepless night on the car ferry floor I arrived in the Gare du Nord and blinked as the day unfolded before me. The whole world was going one way and I was heading the other, I loved it. I jumped on the metro to the Porte d'Italie station and then emerged into the Parisian sun, which was already warming the cool air off the pavement. That unmistakeable aroma that only exists in foreign countries arrested my nostrils; I felt awake and alive as I followed the throng of young people to the spot where I now stood.

My rucksack was neatly packed and for a hitcher I looked quite smart compared to my fellow travellers. I smiled at every passing vehicle trying to establish eye contact with the driver or co-pilot. My whole shtick was my attempt at bagging the aspirational vote in the auto stop stakes. Unfortunately my plan and enthusiasm were to be severely tested as my thumb went out at 7:00 am and I got my first lift at 5:00 pm … 10 hours later. It was a severe wake up call to the ups and downs of life on the road. Whilst waiting for my first lift I chatted to some of my fellow travellers in my bizarre French which consisted of an extensive vocabulary joined together by about the only ten verbs I knew.

" Vous avez un Pan Bagnat sandwich, J'ai un Coca, partage?"

To me this meant I'll share my coca cola with you, if you share your sandwich with me. I have existed for many years on the back of this quite extraordinary command of a foreign language and, as a result, have often gone days without eating. I would wander 100 metres up the road one way and then 200 metres back down the other, sit, sing and then contemplate my navel for two hours.

As the hours and cars rolled by I met an ex student called Graham, a Brit with a tent, which was very classy as I only had a sleeping bag. But, I did have something that was unique; years before Walkmans or iPods I'd got hold of a small battery operated cassette player which fit snugly into my rucksack, it was about 7 inches in length and shaped like the shuttle craft from Star Trek and believe me was the height of cool for a guy on the road. This music kept me sane throughout my various travails and I would happily sacrifice a sandwich for batteries, if it helped to retain my karma. My state of mind always took precedent over anything else; still does. Graham was a dark haired Brummie, short, with a mass of stubble; he was easy going and had a killer high pitched snigger that reminded me of Mutley in Wacky Races. This, combined with the typical Brummie twang just made me laugh.

"Hey Phil, it seems to me that the only people getting rides today are girls."

"Spotted Graham and why do you think that is?" I asked in mock confusion.

"Maybe they've got better legs than us, *tee hee hee*."

"Speak for yourself Mutley; I only waxed this morning."

Realising that two guys hitching together were never favourite for a lift, we split up but committed to looking out for each other whilst on the road.

Suddenly a car stops, this is it, a ride at last, I run … is it for me? Yes. Go! I had to be quick or I'd get bumped, so bag in one hand I am at the car door in microseconds.

"Bonjour, vous allez ou?" the customary greeting delivered in immaculate French. Where are you going? A totally meaningless question because whatever the answer your response was always the same "Parfait", anywhere was better than staying here. As Thom Gunn put it, "One is always nearer by not keeping still."

The abrupt change in atmosphere and situation is both instant and startling after hours waiting helpless at the side of the road. I am now in a comfortable car speeding away from my little two foot square piece of ground that's been home for the day. The feeling is strange as I look back at the other stranded travellers disappearing out of view. Do I feel a hint of guilt? Nah, I'm gone and my adventure unfolds before me.

I introduce myself to Henri and describe my long wait in the heat, the traffic and the boredom. He listened intently and gave his considered reply with a shrug, "boff"; a fabulous expression of complete indifference. Brilliant. He looked like a typical French intellectual, the type you see in those sixties French movies, black specs, long hair and Gauloise in hand. He clearly wants to improve his English and he witters on about how there is a "musical crisis in ze world today." Lets bear in mind this is a guy whose been brought up to believe that Johnny Halliday is a bonafide rock star and on that evidence alone I was inclined to agree but to the French this is a gross insult bordering on the sacrilegious. However let's face it Johnny Halliday is crap; he can't sing, can't dance, wears ridiculous leather trousers and looks like a Muppet who's overdone the botox. Get over it. France is the most beautiful country, with the finest food and wines, diverse culture, artists, philosophers, an unbeatable way of life, superb health care and stunningly beautiful women but Johnny Halliday is quite simply crap. I recalled a quote by the author AA Gill 'The seriousness with which the French take their pop music is overshadowed only by its hysterical awfulness' It was impossible to translate all of this, so I just said,

"Oui."

We chatted away about nothing, in that over animated, over friendly way you do when attempting to convince someone that their choice of hitchhiker was correct. I'm desperately willing the car to eat up as many miles as possible before we reach our next destination.

"Your car is très cool."

"Oui, c'est une Citroën."

"Ah, superbe, très confortable, bonne vitesse." I say in a flattering tone.

"Ah qui, très quick."

"Cool."

"Vous habite Paris?" I enquire.

"Non Fontainebleau."

"Ah mon père habite Fontainebleau après the war ... la guerre, oui"

"No?"

The conversation is quite clearly a complete mystery to both of us but I persevere in the hope of a translation breakthrough.

"Oui, c'est une belle cite, he adoré Fontainebleau, how long avez vous habite there ?"

"Three years"

"Vous work in Paris et habite Fontainebleau, that is un belle commute, vous comprend?"

"Bien sur."

"Your car has very comfortable seats." (It's pathetic I know).

"Oui, c'est la cuir, you say leather, yes?"

"Ha-ha," I chuckle, "that is a word for a gay man in English."

"Really, in England you use the word 'leather' for a homosexual?"

"Oui, exactly. You speak tres bien Anglais"

"Merci Phil, you speak tres bien French."

This shit can go on for hours.

Fortunately time passes quickly as we speed south out of the suburbs of Paris and into the beautiful forests of Fontainebleau and besides, having been stood by the roadside for ten hours, I was quite happy to warble on about anything. Unfortunately the ride only lasts 45 minutes as our discussion turns to where I wished to be dropped off … either this was his exit or I was more boring than he was. The choice was a 'Peage' toll stop or a service station, I plumped for the latter, I was starving, plus it's a nice place to rest in the sun, its easy for hitching and if you become really desperate you can cadge a lift from people returning to their parked cars who either say 'yes' or the French equivalent of 'piss off'; usually the latter. The other excellent place to stop is an 'air de repos', there are no services, its just a place for drivers to rest, hang out, sleep, picnic or kids to play. It's terribly Gaelic, pointless and brilliant at the same time. After a steak hache - a posh French burger without the bun - chips, and an ice cold beer I was completely chilled and the adjustment from exhilarating car journey to a charming spot in the French countryside was perfect.

Most French cars in the late seventies were, contrary to my earlier compliments to Henri, falling apart. This is not as a result of sub-standard construction it's because they've owned them for about a thousand years. Food and wine is everything and the car was always last on the list. Everyone smokes and I mean everyone, you were offered a Gauloises or Disque bleu the moment you got in. Now I don't smoke but to keep up good international relations I would accept but not inhale. (Yes, I realise I was way ahead of my time). They had a wonderful musty smell, the cars not the fags, but were essentially nostalgic death traps. They somehow could reach speeds of 100 mph and in that time honoured traditional way of French driving, would try to mount the car in front. Ah, those sex mad frenchies they just can't resist a shag whatever the situation.

Now, as I lay on the lush grass in the afternoon sun, peace and calm descends into a post coital haze. I listen to the birds chattering away covered by an umbrella of Pine trees. All around nature was doing its thing, the aroma of the pine circulating in the breeze, squirrels chasing each other along the branches and a stunningly clear blue sky. Perfect. There were little wooden tables and benches scattered around in the shade and in some parts pine needles formed a golden brown carpet. This whole area was surrounded by the forests of Fontainebleau, it has a wonderful sense of history, and you can feel it. Louis VII and later all the Kings of France hunted wild boar in these woods right up to the time of Napoleon and was often used as a summer retreat away from the capital. Locals still hunt here and as my mind wandered of into visions of the King and his entourage tearing through the undergrowth I heard someone call out my name,

"Phil, Phil!" Who could possibly know me in this place?

It was Dick Dastardly's sidekick who I had met in Paris at 7 o'clock this morning- it seemed a very long time ago. I had stood for 10 hours and he got a lift just a short time after we'd met but had been stuck here ever since. Christ! this was not going to be easy. It had been a long day and it was good to see him, we were sharing a similar adventure and that laugh was great to hear and... he had a tent! We chatted about our various reasons for leaving the UK,

"After graduating I decided to just travel and see the world," said Graham.

"Me too, although my girlfriend's not to keen on the idea."

"Well you're lucky in some respects; I mean, at least you've got a girlfriend, *tee hee hee*."

Darkness fell and as it became surprisingly cold and windy we pitched the tent. It's illegal to camp in a rest area but what the hell. It was so windy that night I hardly slept at all, the tent helped but it was bloody cold.

We arose early. The cars in the evening had been a faint distant hum but now we and the nation, were on the move again. After the ubiquitous coffee and croissants we got a ride with an Irish lorry driver whose only subject of conversation was the girls he saw on the roadside. "Mother of Mary, would you look at the arse on that?" He wasn't the most discerning purveyor of beauty and I suspect he would have been happy with any arse on any woman if he'd got the chance.

Later on, after briefly meeting some fun girls from Holland, we were forced to split up and I continued my journey south past Auxerre. I was now entering the wine regions of France near the town of Chablis. This is the true Chablis made entirely from the Chardonnay grape not the Chardonnay served in your average Diner - if you catch my drift. The fields and valleys stretch away for miles in every direction. I had travelled through Europe before but always on summer breaks in-between studies, this was very different. I had no idea how long I would be away for and there was no real plan other than to go with the flow, the experience was the goal and the excitement of freedom, of not knowing what the day would bring. Today things are very different, there are so many distractions, mostly due to advances in technology but in the seventies it was far easier to live in the 'now', to appreciate the quiet and to understand the value of the moment.

My next ride suited my mood perfectly, the guy didn't want to chat he just played cool music; it was very Zen- like and my thoughts drifted off as the temperature rose. I thought of Jane and how she must be feeling and what she would do whilst I was away? It was terribly emotional when I left, tears were streaming down her face as we kissed goodbye. She held me close and then looked straight into my eyes, "Go, go and get it out of your system but whatever happens and whoever you meet, promise you'll come back to me." I promised I would.

My preparation for this journey could be considered reckless; I had no tent, few clothes, a sleeping bag, no credit card and my precious £85. Mobile phones were some crazy future fantasy. I had never stayed in a Youth hostel, it was not my style. I believed, naively perhaps, that something would always turn up; when necessity takes hold it's amazing what can happen, of course it doesn't always work out but that's the buzz, the uncertainty. I imagined people scurrying to work and the frenetic nature of everyone's lives back home and I marvelled at the lack of it in mine.

We eventually arrived at the Rhone-Saone corridor where the rivers have cut their way between the Massif Central in the west and the Alps to the east. Vineyards cascade off the hillsides down slow inclines to the river floor and it's here that the motorway shoots off the Massif plateau and drops dramatically as it turns south, it's exhilarating as you leave one area of central France and begin the long journey to the sea.

Two hours later, having sliced our way through the vineyards, we pass Villefranche and I smile with anticipation as we enter the Lyons tunnel. It find it thrilling to pass under this fabulous city at high speed and then 5 minutes later pop out the other side in glorious sunlight right next to the huge river Rhone -it's breathtaking. At this confluence of rivers, roads and railways is a mass of fellow hitchers and I was deposited right into the middle of them. This is the Grand Central Station of European hitchhiking, the competition for a ride is huge but the supply of cars and trucks is equal to it. There is a strip of land between two busy roads enabling you to get a ride from either side. Everyone is travelling quickly, stopping suddenly to pick up a hitcher and shooting off. It's frenetic, the screeching cars, the hitchers jumping in and out, everyone shouting and running, it's exhilarating and dangerous all at the same time.

As a driver, one of the worst times to come through here is the Bastille Day holiday in July but conversely it is great for hitchers. All of Paris for some bizarre reason seems to leave for the Riviera at exactly the same time arriving at the Lyons tunnel entrance 5 hours later. Huge traffic jams ensue; I have never understood why people don't leave the night before or a few hours later, it's one of those strange French traditions. This exodus is then repeated at the end of the holidays in August, when they all return. Years later they would build a huge ring road around Lyons to avoid this mayhem but I've heard it makes no difference.

My luck holds and I'm off to Avignon in another dodgy Peugeot, who cares, I'm moving and the white lines roll out before me. I have two favourite road signs in the World and one of them is coming up, "Bienvenue aux auto-routes du Soleil," say no more, the other is near Lake Tahoe "Welcome to California," but that's another story.

My mind drifted back to a time many years ago when I travelled through Avignon with my friends, Bobby and Chapman and I remember being deliberately stopped at a large flight of steps by the bridge - not the one in the song that fell down in 1633 - the other one. It was going dark and suddenly, a voice below demanded,

"Donnez mois un franc!" We were all startled by this ghostly command,

"Donnez mois un Franc!" it came again - this time with aggression.

My friend Chapman, who's French, is worse than mine said,

"Frank, there's nobody here called Frank."

"Non, give moi un franc, English." As he blocked our path with his outstretched arms, we all stood there trapped; he refused to let us pass. It was now pitch black and it all started to get a bit tense. A stand off began, we were travelling rough and there was no way Chapman was going to give him anything. He then asked again, Chapman turned to us all,

"If he gives us any trouble lads, kick him down the stairs!"

The ridiculousness of the situation soon became apparent, there were three of us, all over six foot and this little guy below who was clearly drunk - If we'd kicked him down the stairs we would have killed him. The naivety of youth, luckily Bobby, always the diplomat, took charge of this threat to the "entente cordiale" and offered the guy a smoke. It worked, he let us pass and relieved we all shook hands and bid farewell.

I'm still convinced to this day that Chapman would have loved to kick him down the stairs.

By 5:00 pm I am stranded at another service station. The Mistral was blowing and there's only one thing to say about this fierce wind from the Alps, its bloody freezing! I spend nearly two hours jumping in and out of a café trying to get a ride and keep warm at the same time. I'm concerned, if I have to stay here tonight I'll get hypothermia and they'll be chipping me out of a block of ice in the morning. It was a dilemma but I could only hitch for five minutes at a time. As I stood there stuck to the floor, a van speeds past on the motorway and suddenly stops on the hard shoulder and then reverses illegally back up the on ramp towards me, what is going on?

Then, for the second time in two days I hear a

familiar voice shout, "Phil!" followed by a high pitched laugh, it was Mutley and the two Dutch girls from the ride this morning and having spotted me, asked the driver to stop; grateful, does not describe the feeling. I hardly knew these people but we all had a bond, born out of our shared experiences and this act of unexpected kindness made all the difference. In hitchhiking these moments are precious and must be appreciated because the ride will come to an end and your situation can easily change. But for the moment there we all were, huddled into the back of a warm van, our little European group debating how to sort out the world and all its problems in the summer of 1978.

Evening draws on and we split up once more. I find myself wandering near a peage in the middle of nowhere. A swarthy French guy asks me for a light; his hair is long and straggly and clearly hasn't been washed in about a year and his finger nails were bitten down and filthy, he looks like a tramp. It was bizarre, he had no pack or sleeping bag either; I felt distinctly uncomfortable. A VW stops to pick us both up. Pierre, the driver, is a really nice bloke and keen to talk to his new mates about our life stories but it turns out that Swarthy has just got out of prison; Pierre assumes that both of us are mates and is now scared shitless. He stops the car and proceeds to drop both of us off in a place more in the middle of nowhere than before. I'm pissed off for several reasons; if I'd been on my own it would have been a pleasant ride to Marseilles but this other guy really screwed it up, I mean its one thing to go to prison and quite another to boast about it. The problem is I am now stuck with Swarthy at 11 o'clock at night in the cold and dark - and I ain't sharing a park bench with him.

Human nature is a funny thing, this guy just gives off danger and I am on red alert and alone. The rustling pine trees that the day before were so beguiling now form a dark brooding mass of fear and trepidation. I give him some pathetic excuse that I will try hitching further down the road and Swarthy slinks off into the night. Next, I do that fast walk thing that's supposed to look like walking but looks pathetically like you're running away. I didn't give a shit. I figure if it comes to legging it I am sure I can outrun him, especially if panic is involved. All I could hear were my footsteps and breath but the further I walked the better I felt. As calm returned I looked up at the night sky and in the distance I could just make out the shape of mountains, this was the area of Aix-en-Provence, Cezanne country.

I had studied the artist Paul Cezanne when I was younger; he is one of my favourite painters and worked all over Provence and in particular the mountain I was looking at, Mont St Victoire, which he painted over 60 times. He was always trying to capture this rugged, beautiful place in his work. I have read a story, which may be apocryphal, that after he had finished a painting he would just leave it in the field, either because he was not interested in the finished work or he didn't feel he had captured the subject. Hortense, his wife would then collect these valuable masterpieces at the end of the day with a view to selling them. No Hortense, no Cezanne's in the Louvre.

I was now lost in my thoughts of this rebellious artist wandering around this very same countryside with his friend Emile Zola discussing art, poetry and philosophy - much as the young Frenchman of today still do. As Cezanne once said, 'Painting from nature is not copying the object; it is realizing one's sensations.' This is a magical place that stimulates all my senses at once, the beautiful vineyards, the smell of pine trees after a rainstorm, the taste of olives, the crickets chirping on a warm summer night, the impossibly clear blue sky in the day and the millions of stars of the Milky Way so dominant in the darkness of the countryside at night.

I may have been lost in my thoughts but now I was well and truly lost in Provence. I kept walking for as Sundance said "I'm better when I move". The motorway had gone; I was on 'route nationale' road, a Napoleonic concept - who else? And eventually I noticed a sign stating it was the RN8 to Marseilles. I could just pick out the white lines in the centre of the road as the headlights of the odd car passed by but other than that it was pitch black. There was no moon and although the stars twinkled brightly in the sky I could not see a thing on either side of me. It was somewhat unnerving so I just sang out loud to keep myself company.

Many French travellers prefer night hitching because a different type of person stops; they're friendlier and more understanding and as there was nothing to lose, out went the thumb and sure enough at around midnight, a 'car wreck' pulls up and a young couple both in bare feet open the door.

"Vous allez Marseille?"

"Oui. "

"Allez, let's go"

She had long black hair and smoked a Gauloises, he was cool and she was a babe. They were really friendly and fun and would constantly take the piss out of each other;

"Natalie, my angel, I think you smoke too much"

"Piss off Freddy, you drive like old fart. Phil, he drive like a poussy, no?"

"Maybe he's just being careful" I said.

"Thank you Phil, you see Natalie he understands it's dark and dangerous driving at night."

"No, he is English and polite like the Queen"

"Ma cherie, je t'aime, but you mustn't be so rude to our guest"

"I *lurve* you too Freddy but now I think you are both old farts"

As far as I was concerned she could say whatever she wanted, she was gorgeous and I was quite happy listening to this banter all the way to Marseilles. They rightly presumed I had nowhere to stay and kindly invited me to their friend's apartment for the night. We arrived at 2 am but although their friends weren't there the door was open and the three of us just waltzed in, I slept on a mattress in a spare room and after my long day on the road this was pure heaven and I went out like a light.

Morning arrived and shattered the nocturnal calm.

"*Bang !* … Ah merde! … Idiot! … Bonjour Jaques … *Clang!* … ca va?"

A cacophony of sound burst through my window as the city of Marseilles exploded into life. I awoke instantly from a deep sleep and lay there listening to all this madness, it was fun. I was in a strange city of noise and bustle and such a contrast to the silence of the night before. The room was quite bare, apart from an old lampstand in the corner, on the wall opposite hung a faded 60's poster of Jean Paul Belmondo looking cool, white voile curtains billowed in the soft breeze as the sun and sounds flowed in through the open window. It seemed a bit quirky but who was I to judge, it was a palace compared to yesterday's tent on the roadside. Eventually the cool couple awoke and after a quick coffee we were off, I never did meet their friends, maybe they were part of some mass national student squatting association - it certainly wouldn't have surprised me. They dropped me off on the outskirts of the city, well 'dropped' is not quite the right word, basically their car engine started smoking and the 'car wreck' refused to go any further.

"Freddy my angel, we should have got ze car fixed in Avignon"

"Oh fuck off Natalie, you sound like an old fart"

I had a great big smile on my face as I wandered off down the road, pack on my back and following a line of beautiful 'platane' trees directing me towards Aubagne. It must have rained in the night because the smell from the wet pine drying out in the morning sun was overwhelming, I loved it. In the distance were mountains with what appeared to be snow topped peaks but are actually the white limestone on the barren ridges. I didn't care if anybody stopped or not.

Provence is quite an easy place to hitch because the side of the roads just runs straight off into trees or fields. When it's hot the cars and lorry's can kick up a lot of dust but I didn't care I was doing exactly what I wanted to do in exactly the place I wanted to be, I could have walked forever with no thought for the future, I was elated.

In this state I must have walked for about 2 hours, but all good things must come to an end and I was offered a lift, at least I think it was a lift, because it was two gendarmes in their odd little blue van.

"Am I under arrest?"

"No no Monsieur, it is very hot and so we thought to give you a lift to the peage."

"Merci. In England it is unusual for Police to give lifts."

"Ah but we are Gendarmes."

"I don't understand, what's the difference?"

"We are separate to the Police but are also Police! And," he said proudly, "we are administratively part of the Armed forces and the Ministry of Defence but are operationally part of the Ministry of the Interior, in France."

Blimey! I wish I hadn't asked.

This still didn't really explain why they would offer me a ride. Maybe they were being kind or maybe they were moving this 'vagrant' out of there as some locals had complained about a nutter wandering along the road, singing out loud, with a big smile on his face in 80 degree heat. The moment they realised I was a Brit all had become clear.

Later on I took a bit of a detour to Cassis. I had caught glimpses of the bay in the distance during my brief mobile incarceration courtesy of the Fifth Republic and decided its time to hit the ocean. It's quite a walk into Cassis but luckily its all down hill, on either side are huge white limestone cliffs, it is stunningly beautiful. I felt an adrenalin rush of excitement as I passed a parade of shops, a little port and onto the small sandy beach and then in one movement peeled off and ran directly into the clear blue sea. Fabulous! Splashing about in my seventies equivalent of Calvin Klein boxers making lots of whooping noises I must have appeared to be some bizarre tourist attraction. The cool water washed the day's exertions from my parched skin and the sand was warm as I let my body dry out in the hot sun of the Cote d'Azur. In the distance the sky and sea just melted into each other. I had arrived; this was going to be fun.

Although it was nearly June it wasn't terribly busy so I hung out for awhile catching the rays and watching the boats glide across the bay whilst listening to Joni Mitchell and the Doobie Brothers. I was nearly asleep when I remembered I had no sun tan lotion and though I'm naturally quite tanned it was probably tempting fate a bit to stay here too long. Travelling around the South of France looking like a bloated lobster is definitely not cool so after a delicious Chef's salad in a café by the beach it was time to move on. I now had to hike out of Cassis but I felt up to the challenge and had climbed half way out of the village when a car stopped. This guy was obviously gay and after about 2 minutes of chat realised I was just a hitcher and that his luck was most definitely not 'in.'

"I have a problem."

"Oh, what's that" I enquire in mock surprise,

"I am 'omosexual," he said sheepishly.

"Ah I see, well congratulations but I'm not into leather"

"I don't understand, what do you mean, into

leather?" Clearly this conversation was heading in the wrong direction.

"It's just a joke, you see in English 'queer' sounds like ... oh never mind, I can't go through all that again."

"I don't understand." I must admit at this point I began to feel a little bit sorry for him.

"Look I tell you what, why not just drop me off here and we'll put it in the Guinness Book of Records as the worlds shortest ride." Total bemusement fell across the poor guy's face; I bet he never picked up a hitcher again.

I continued on, heading for the autoroute to Toulon and it was early afternoon when I realised I had to answer the call of nature and being an experienced traveller I had all the necessary personal items I needed- except the toilet and kitchen sink. Now taking a pee at the roadside is a way of life in France but anything else is a completely different story. But, I was in the middle of nowhere so feeling relaxed I wandered into a wood on the edge of a small vineyard. It was an idyllic country scene with a cloudless sky. I dropped my trousers and squatted by a tree with one hand on a low smooth branch for support. Apart from a skylark singing in the warm breeze it was quiet and calm and I felt at one with nature figuring if its good enough for wild bears its okay for me.

I was just getting comfortable when I detected a small humming sound. I ignored it at first but very, very slowly it grew louder and as it did I began to get a little nervous and felt unable to move. Hoping the sound would go away I tried to remain calm but it continued and then slowly I detected an odd cutting, thrashing noise of heavy machinery somewhere behind the trees extremely close and getting closer. My mood intensified and I became anxious, realising I was in an extremely vulnerable position.

Within seconds it was a deafening sound but I still couldn't see anything and by now my mind was racing; imagining the possibility of an old Napoleonic law on the legality of making deposits on small plantations. The sweat was pouring off me I just couldn't believe this was happening in such a remote place. Suddenly this enormous machine that resembled a combined harvester is nearly on top of me and in the cabin is the driver, wrestling with all sorts of gears, on his way to the next field. As I look up he spots me, this young, blonde, blue eyed, Englishman taking a dump in his vineyard. The tension was unbearable and at that precise moment I lost all control and crapped on his grapevines! He stares at me, startled, neither of us knowing what to do or say and then, reverting to time honoured tradition, he shouts,

"Bonjour, ca va?"

In my current predicament, trousers around my ankles how am I supposed to reply to the question, 'Am I okay?'

"Yes," I said, "it's a beautiful day"

"Oui, c'est incroyable"-indeed it was incredible. God knows what he was thinking as we both managed to completely ignore the blindingly obvious. Mercifully he kept moving and leisurely chugged away into the next field. I felt quite literally an enormous sense of relief ... and release and, as I got myself together I mused where one *could* take a dump and never be disturbed. I suspected the desert but knowing my luck, Lawrence of Arabia would probably appear out of a bloody mirage and squat down beside me - Salam! I have often wondered how my farmer friend would retell this tale in his local café that night,

"Hey, Jacques, how was it today?"

Well Pierre, I saw *zis* English guy crapping on my vines and ..."

"Ah Jacques, you have been smoking that funny pipe again."

So ended our rather personal 'brief encounter' never to be repeated and for me and probably Jacques, never to be forgotten.

Later, after I had calmed down, I arrived in Toulon which is one of the most difficult towns to get through when hitching, the roads are complicated, it's noisy, dirty and dangerous so I got in and out as quick as I could. It's an old naval port and home of the French Mediterranean fleet and it may be loved by many but I have always considered it to be a complete dump.

My aim, if there was such a thing, was to hitch-hike all along the Cote D'azur to Monte Carlo and once you hit the coast road just past the town of Hyeres, at Le Lavandou, it's possible to stay on it all the way, about 200 kilometres. I believed there would be a lot happening at this time of year as the road meanders past sandy beaches and small rocky coves, through beautiful little towns and picturesque bays, with the lush green hills on one side and the sparkling blue ocean on the other. I knew it would be fun hitching rides from bay to bay and if not then it would be a breathtaking walk - albeit a long one. But, what I didn't know then, was that a few miles away there existed a life that I couldn't possibly have imagined in those early summer days. For the moment I was heading East oblivious as to my future and what it may hold.

I walked for about an hour into the old town of Hyeres and it was dusk when I came across a small park and a quaint turn of the century covered bandstand, the type you only ever notice in France. Its ornate decorative metalwork and circular vaulted roof conjured up images of Victorian days of music and dancing that you often see in old brown stained photographs. The smart women of the day with large white hats and the men sporting straw boaters and soft flannel trousers.

As I stared at this marvel, an old lady with weathered dark brown skin and piercing blue eyes began talking to me. She was leaning on the railing watching the children in the park. Her name was Monique, I guessed she was about 85 years old, she had a timeless simple quality about her and I had the impression nothing would faze her; she'd seen it all. We conversed in a kind of broken French which was difficult for me to understand. It was peppered with the local Provencal dialect which has many 'dang' sounds on the end of words as well as other slang phrases or 'argot' as it is known here. She spoke of the time she had danced to the music and played in the village square as a little girl - at least I think that's what she said. I told her of my little adventure which she thought very exciting having lived here all her life.

"I once went to Italy but I didn't care for ze

food."

"You are lucky you've never visited England then." At this she nodded sagely,

"Someone once told me that it was, 'degueu-lasse', you say disgusting, yes?"

"We do, yes, you're right."

We both laughed as she continued in her odd dialect,

"Where are you from in England?"

"A place called Yorkshire." I said proudly, and at this her eyes suddenly lit up.

"What is the pudding from Yorkshire?"

"Excuse me, did you mean Yorkshire pudding?"

"Yes, I have been told that you eat *zis* pudding with your main course?"

"Well, actually, the correct way to eat it is *before* your main course, as a starter"

"You eat a pudding *before* your main course?" she looked horrified.

"Yes and you put gravy on it."

"Pas possible!"

At this last comment she didn't laugh she just looked at me, pulled a face of disgust and then politely expressed her sympathy. I then asked why she had never visited any where else and then came her fabulous reply;

"Pour quoi? J'habite au paradis.'

There's not a lot you can say to, 'I live in paradise', and I nodded in agreement as I surveyed the idyllic scene before me. The platane trees were now full and thick with leaves providing shade to the square. The colour of the bark on these trees is a mosaic of grey, purple, brown and lilac and is simply stunning. They are not exclusively indigenous to the Mediterranean but to me they are part of the soul of southern France. All throughout this region they decorate village squares and line the avenues and pathways. In the autumn they are aggressively cut back and remain bare all winter with odd branches protruding out resembling bizarre modern sculptures.

In this square, as in many village squares in Provence there was a 'Petanque' pitch made of flattened sandstone and gravel. Although the Ancient Greeks in the 6th century played a game that was similar, it was introduced into France by the Romans and is best described as a French version of English Bowls. The word 'Petanque' derives from the Provencal dialect meaning 'feet together', which is how you stand when throwing the boule. It is quintessentially French, full of history and charm. I watched as the shiny metal boules gave a loud thud as they hit the ground followed by much animated arm waving and chatter. It sounded as if they were arguing but considering the point of the game is simply to get the large boule as near as possible to the small one I just couldn't figure out what exactly they were arguing about.

It was late as I lay on the bandstand floor and most people had drifted off home by the time the crickets began their mating calls. The only sound now was of a few old villagers playing their last game of the night. The warm air enveloped me as I remembered this wonderful day; it was a magical feeling of calm as I melted into a restful sleep.

My dreams were always full of the day's events and by day, as I walked, I would dream about my future. Sometimes when a smart car passed with a young couple I would think of Jane. I missed her terribly but knew this was my future for now and it's what I had chosen. I always believed I could go into a myriad of different careers if I put my mind to it and was neither afraid nor concerned about what I would do and I never felt burdened or regretful about the choices I made. However, I did feel guilty about just taking off and leaving Jane behind. I knew she wanted to get married and have a family but I did not feel ready. My desire was to see the world and discover different people, living different lives and then if the time was right and Jane wanted me back, we could make the decisions on our future together. I knew I was being selfish by just doing my own thing but the alternative of living in England and having a normal life was both boring and dull.

I was 24 years old and unusually for a young man, had always listened to the counsel of people much older, judging that at 50 or 60 years of age they had been around the block more times than and so it was a good idea to listen to their guidance. I could then make a better and more informed decision on the choices that I may have in my life. Every person I ever asked about travelling said, 'do it when you're young because it's not the same when you get older, you feel different and will not have the same experience'. I took their advice and that was the reason why I was now sleeping happily on the floor of an old bandstand in a village in the South of France.

CHAPTER 2

LAST TRAIN TO ST TROPEZ

"Only dull people are brilliant at breakfast"

Oscar Wilde.

France has supposedly more festivals than anywhere else in the world and the next morning I awoke to discover that today was one of them. Lying there with my eyes closed I had a sense of movement and strange noises that I could not recognise - was I still dreaming? It sounded like music or to be exact musical instruments. I looked up, and was surrounded by strange metal tripods and odd looking cases. It dawned on me as I scrunched my eyes in the bright sunlight that I was slap bang in the middle of a 10 piece band setting up for the day's festivities. Should I feel embarrassed or amused? I was not sure as I lay there in my sleeping bag accompanied by my new musical friends. No one had disturbed me or asked me to move, they were polite and courteous and going about their business as if I was invisible, tuning their flutes and horns focused on the day ahead. It was all terribly gentile as I slowly packed my things and bade them "adieu." I left a scene from a bygone age as the old lady from the night before just smiled as I passed her by.

Many times I have pondered on the magic of

the Cote d'Azur, trying to find the essence of this wonderful place. I believe it is a subtle combination of the light, the crystal clear ocean and the deep azure sky that is unique to this part of the world. If I then add to this cocktail, the mimosa, pine, olive groves and vineyards thereby creating that distinctive aroma and mix it with the quiet majestic mountains and the rugged stunning coastline, it stimulates a melange of emotions and fires my senses. I breathe in the clear morning air and I'm already gone.

Heading for the coast road at Le Lavandou a gorgeous French girl stops in a tiny car, I squeeze in, with my pack on top of my knees; she is just on her way to the shops. My mind begins to race at the thought of the mad affair we are about to begin, the romance of the place has grabbed me and I am crushed when she drops me off 15 minutes later with a smile and a wave. Such is life but what a babe.

Walking parallel to the sea, I stop every 10 or 20 minutes to swim or look out over the ocean, it's fabulous. I love it. At lunchtime, always an event in France, I stop for a sandwich, a sun bathe and a chill out to the sounds of Stevie Wonders, 'Fullfilingness First Finale,' heaven, pure heaven. A group of Swedish students stroll over. Of all the nationalities I meet when travelling I find the Swedes the most amusing, their command of English is perfect but they have this strange habit of trying to be cool when they swear, they do this by placing the right words in the wrong place.

"Hey, how are you doing?" I said.

"Cool, that Stevie Wonder is the shit. I'm Lasse, this is Anna and these are the following."

"Excuse me?"

"Oscar, Erika and the arse short guy is Bjorn."

"Hi," I said laughing, "I'm Phil."

"Okay man, you want smoke," he said offering me a cigarette.

"No thanks, I don't."

"Shit man, really, not even grass?" said the surprised Swede.

"No, my body is my temple."

"Cool, that's bloody fucking man … hey Anna!" he shouted. "Phil doesn't do drugs." She looked over with an expression of total amazement.

"Wow, piss me, you're kidding!"

"No really, besides I thought all you Swedish kids were into healthy living and sports and shit"

"Yeh but fucker crap man, c'mon."

They are hilarious and they all do this other weird thing of putting their cigarettes and lighters in the turn ups of their jeans. I have no idea why, but as the guys are friendly and the girls are babes, who cares. I've learnt a lot from hitching with them, they are neat and clean, look good and always get lifts. I am 6 foot 2 insches and in the sun my hair goes quite blonde and I tan easily so if I can do a good impression of Lasse and his mates and get a ride then that's fine with me.

Today has been fun just hanging out meeting people on the roads and beaches and on the road to Cavalaire-sur-mer I got my next ride. It was an old classic Bentley with two guys, Edward who was Scottish and his friend Jacques, who was French - surprisingly. They were really funny and we had great chat about my travels and their life in France. Edward was about 35 years old and Jacques a little younger. They had just come from the beach, which was interesting, because there clothes looked as if they had just stepped out of Armani. They had a villa in Cavalaire and invited me for a drink, it was pretty hot and as I had no other engagements, I accepted. Their house was immaculate; we just hung out on the patio drank and chatted all afternoon. Edward puffed away on a giant cigar; he had a ruddy complexion with auburn hair and a strong accent and was basically ... a Scotsman. Jacques was more studious, younger and slightly overweight, a point that Edward constantly ribbed him about it.

"*Pheel*, would you like some more olive cake,"

"No thanks,"

"Phil for Christ's sake have some fucking cake or my French friend here will eat the lot." Jacques feigned a look of hurt.

"Eddy is always very rude to me but I think he is jealous because I am younger and more handsome, no?"

"Absolutely Jacques - and he is Scottish," at this Jacques laughs and Eddy responds with a long slow draw on his cigar followed by,

"Ah yes Phil and you are young and handsome - and English, so nobody's perfect."

This banter continued as I surveyed their lush, almost tropical garden which concealed an aromatic mixture of lavender and jasmine. It smelt as beautiful as it looked and was a perfect setting with the bay of

Cavalaire stretching away in the distance. These guys were obviously doing okay and adored living here; they had a small fashion business in the local area and were quite clearly as bent as nine bob notes. As we were sitting in the afternoon sun I felt completely relaxed, they seemed to have no desire to 'come on to me' it was just guys having a laugh. Edward explained to me some local facts, "You know Phil this is a well known cruising area where guys drive along looking for anyone who might be inclined."

"Does this mean I look inclined?" More laughter.

Jacques continued. "Who would you rather give a lift to, a pretty interesting girl or an ugly boring one? It's the same with the guys."

"Does a lot of this go on?"

"Yes, it's called dragging"

I leaned forward enthusiastically, "Does this mean if an absolute babe stops to pick me up it's the same set of rules."

"You wish," laughed Jacques. "Anyway how would I know I am a poof!"

The light was beginning to fade when Eddy, in a casual and nonchalant way, invited me to dinner and proposed I stay the night as they had a plenty of room. They were both sophisticated guys and I felt in no way threatened and genuinely enjoyed their company. Edward explained, "You will not be surprised to learn that my rotund friend is an excellent cook." He smiled, "otherwise how could I possibly have stayed with him so long?"

"I'd love to and I appreciate the offer" and then as tactfully as possible I said, "I guess you guys realise I don't swing both ways or 'putt from the rough', so to speak."

At this they both cracked up with laughter having never heard that expression before,

. "Phil, I understand completely and would not want you to feel uncomfortable, besides, if it makes you feel any better I already had three guys on the beach earlier today."

Now this statement *did* shock me and certainly *did not* make me feel any better but he said it in such a nonchalant way I thought, well, whatever and in the same vein I replied; "Slag!" Jacques laughed so hard he nearly choked on his olive cake. "Is it normal in for a gay couple to shag around as well?"

"Well it all depends on the relationship but yes, it's fairly common," replied Eddy completely at ease with the concept.

"Yeh, well it's not normal in straight relation-ships."

Eddy jumped on this. "Bullshit! You just don't admit it," and thinking out loud I said,

"Yes I guess you have a point but three girls in an afternoon, that's a whole different ball game … if you'll pardon the expression."

Jacques, with an understanding smile said "Phil, it's a pleasure to have you stay with us, and by the way if you want to have a shower before dinner, the bath-room's down the main hallway."

As I walked down the corridor I kept thinking of

my best friend Bobby back in England and how hilarious he would find this whole situation or Chapman, who would probably be shouting - "Run!"

I then entered the world's most fabulous bathroom. It was immaculate with a stone floor and pebble inlay, one side a mirrored glass wall, paintings, a carved white wooden surround in the ceiling, luxurious folded towels and a bath tub sunk into the floor resembling a stone Roman bath with a fountain for a shower. At one end the bath appeared open to the garden because a piece of glass went from the ceiling right down to the base of the bathtub itself. This allowed the array of fauna in the garden to feel as if it was actually cascading into the room. The 'piece de resistance' was as it grew dark the lights automatically came on in the garden and were projected into the room in such a way that they actually lit the room from the outside in. Couple all that with a wonderful aroma and the sounds of Verdi seeping through the walls and it was quite simply the most extravagant shower I have ever had.

Dinner, as promised, was a delicious feast and our conversation ranged into a myriad of topics, it was great fun and later, when I relaxed into a huge outrageously comfy bed, I pondered on my four days on the road. It seemed a lot longer. Here I was in the lap of luxury when last night I had been lying on a bandstand floor. They were both completely different experiences and what my journey was all about.

The next morning Edward awoke me with a gentle knock on the door; I slipped on a robe and joined them for breakfast on the terrace. You had to hand it to these guys they certainly knew how to live. They had been incredibly kind to a complete stranger and later when we said our farewells Jacques smiled and said,

"Have a great time Phil but be careful."

"Jacques, you sound like my mother." He replied warmly,

"Good."

I literally skipped along the seafront and just kept repeating to myself 'this is great'. The world of cosseted security had gone and it was back to living on my wits again, I loved the paradox. Morning drifted into lunchtime as I moved past palm trees and golden beaches finally ending up in a car with a guy, a girl, a bottle of wine and a spliff. I did my usual and took a few drags without inhaling but the car was so full of dope I'm sure it affected me. As the journey continued, the countryside appeared even more stunning than normal and by the time we stopped at the beach I felt completely 'out of it' as all around me were beautiful women who appeared entirely naked! It took about 20 minutes to figure out that this was a nudist beach and I was 100% sober – Vive la France.

I arrived in St Tropez with the sound of the David Gates song, 'Last train to St Tropez' drifting out of my rucksack. I have lost count of the amount of times I have had to explain to my fellow travellers that there is no train to St Tropez, never has been, it's just a song. Sitting in a shaded café on the port I did my posing bit as I watched the world go by. This is a prerequisite of visiting this old fishing village so if you don't know how to pose, don't go. It really is full of all the 'beautiful people', cool shops, cool people, cool yachts, cool cars - just cool really. However there is only one problem, when carrying a rucksack and possessing only £85; you definitely do not fit in, so I quit town and headed back to the beach.

The weather turned dodgy for the first time on my trip and I felt the clouds descending on me, this was an uncomfortable feeling and not what I expected. Maybe it was the contrast of the high life of St Tropez to my current predicament but as night fell I started to get very down, I felt poor and alone and strangely vulnerable. The rain began to fall near St Maxime and I began to feel very sorry for myself, Jane's radiant smile and sparkling green eyes drifted into my head and I began to cry, I doubted what I was doing and where I was going. This was unusual and deeply unnerving. I have always been a very confident person and I believe if you lose your confidence things can go badly wrong.

I began night hitching in the rain hoping some kind soul might take pity on this bedraggled young guy at the side of the road, it had worked well before so why not now but to be truthful and in my present state, I wasn't very hopeful. It is one of life's cruel ironies that if your desperately wishing for things to get better then I can guarantee they're going to get a lot worse and sure enough a car stops.

I could hardly make out who was in the car in the pouring rain so I just jumped in.

There were two guys in the front seat but I instantly felt uncomfortable, the atmosphere felt very different to anything I had ever experienced before. The car stank of alcohol and stale sweat, it was filthy, the seats were ripped and there were old cans of beer and cigarette buts all over the floor, it was disgusting. The guys were big and burly, rough looking, built like wrestlers and strangely nasty from the very first moment. I was feeling vulnerable before I got in but now I became distinctly nervous. It was dark, the roads were deathly quiet and my mind started racing as soon as one of the guys began to speak;

"So you're on your own tonight?"

"Yes"

"It's late, where are you staying?

"Oh, St Raphael with friends"

"Really, where in St Raphael?"

"I'm not sure exactly."

As we drove off the guy in the passenger seat then turned and looked over his shoulder at me,

"Ever been fucked by a guy before?" at this, his lip curled up into a false smile and my blood really did run cold. It is an expression you read about but when you actually feel it, it's a visceral, physical state. They both began laughing in a weird scary way when I replied pathetically,

"No I am on holiday, I prefer girls."

"What's wrong with guys, don't you like guys?"

He was now looking straight ahead but I could tell he was smiling and enjoying my sense of unease.

"No, it's not that. I'm just not gay." At this he quickly swivelled in his seat,

"Are you accusing us of being queer?" His tone was now truly aggressive.

"Well ... no ... it's not that but you asked about

guys." I was saying all the wrong things in a weak and pathetic way which only made my situation worse.

"I have a good idea, why not come and meet some of *our* friends?" By this time I was so frightened I didn't know what to say.

"Can you drop me at the next lights?"

"Why? You said you were going to St Raphael." There followed an embarrassing silence until the other guy who was driving and who had not spoken until now, slowly looked over his shoulder and in a very quiet voice said,

"No."

They began talking French in a highly animated fashion, arms waving, spitting invective and clearly discussing me. Time began to move at a snail's pace as I just lay back on the seat feeling helpless and unsure of what to do or say. Looking out at the driving rain I needed time to think, stay calm, don't panic, I knew I had to do something but what? Twenty minutes ago I'd felt sorry for myself but now I was in serious shit. When they spoke I just tried to ignore them or nodded or just said "Je ne comprends pas," with a fake smile, anything to avoid inflaming the situation. I was living in my own version of 'Deliverance' and I was terrified, they would not stop and were driving incredibly fast, in the dark, in the rain. Was I going to be robbed, beaten, buggered or worse? My stomach felt like mush, 'Shit!' I thought to myself, 'Do something!' I had to act and whatever I did it was clear I'd only get one chance and … it had to be very soon. I avoided eye contact and decided on a plan.

In the distance I detected lights ahead, we were nearing St Raphael. I carefully put my arm around the strap of my rucksack and waited. A roundabout loomed out of the darkness, they would have to slow down, they *must* slow down. I waited and waited. I was sweating profusely as the primitive instinct of fight or flight engulfed me. I was silent apart from my own breathing which was racing as fast as my heart was pounding. A few more seconds passed. The car slowed a little and then a bit more and just before we reached the roundabout the car in front slowed dramatically, it was now ... 'GO!' I screamed to myself. I flung the door open and dived out of the car, dragging my bag behind me all in one movement. The momentum of the car and the swinging door made it swing back and slam shut with a loud bang as I fell onto the roadside.

They were caught by surprise, other cars were behind them sounding their horns urging them to keep moving - thank God for French impatience. Passers-by were startled by the sudden appearance of myself onto the pavement next to them. I was sitting in a puddle and they all carefully stepped around me assuming I was some kind of weirdo.

My lasting memory of this whole incident was the two guys swearing and shaking their fists as they drove off into the night. 'Fucking hell' I uttered to myself, 'shit!' I could hardly get my breath. "Fucking hell ... Fucking hell!' The adrenalin was pumping around my body and it took me quite a while to calm down; 'So much for night hitching.'

The rain had stopped by the time I had crawled out of my puddle, still wary I walked on into St Raphael. Soon there were hundreds of people walking, sitting in bars, music playing, just people on holiday in the cool night air. Slowly I calmed down; it was exactly what I needed, just normal people having a good time oblivious to my recent experience. I felt protected and inconspicuous in this mass of happy positive energy. I had survived a terrifying ordeal and my mood had changed completely from the guy crying in the rain feeling sorry for himself to feeling extremely grateful just to be safe. It was somehow ironic that security to me now was a strange town at night and alone but that's how I felt - maybe my confidence was returning.

I desperately needed to unburden myself to a willing listener and as I perched on a low wall by the ocean, two English girls asked me where I was from. I introduced myself and then unfortunately for them, blurted out my recent tale in a torrent of grateful relief. They understood completely and then I realised my selfishness.

"Listen I apologise, obviously for girls travelling in Europe this type of thing is a daily occupational hazard."

"Yeh, that's why we always go by train and never hitch due to the dangers," said the blonde with the kindly face. Maybe I had been quite naive but up to this point all had been well and I had no reason to think otherwise, still, it was a wake up call to tread more carefully in future. With this in mind I asked the 'careful twosome' where they were staying and they both replied simultaneously,

"Here!"

"Yes but *where* in St Raphael?" and once again in unison.

"Here, we're sleeping on the beach, everybody

does." I just burst out laughing and so did they. "Hang on a minute, what happened to all the dangers and being careful?"

"Oh Phil, don't be such a wet, everyone sleeps on the beach," by now all of us were in fits of laughter,

"So one minute I'm a wuss for being too naive and now I'm a wuss for being a wimp."

"Yep, you said it"

I was really fortunate to bump into these two they were really friendly and a laugh and they succeeded in putting Dumpty here, back together again.

So began my first night ever of sleeping on a beach; it definitely would not be my last. We went down onto the sand chatting away; I glanced up at the stars and could hear the sea lapping onto the shore. The beach was quite protected by the promenade wall as we lay in our sleeping bags on top of the soft sand and although I couldn't see them I could hear many other young people doing exactly the same thing. I felt like some latter day hippy, it was cool. I switched on my tape player and as Marvin Gaye drifted across the sand, a bottle of wine appeared out of the shadows in appreciation. Later, as one of the girls closed her eyes I cuddled up to her blonde haired friend; she smiled. I was feeling calm and chilled, my earlier experience a distant memory, we snuggled for a while and later fell asleep in each others arms.

I was in a deep sleep when something suddenly disturbed the state of my comatose slumber.

"Ow, shit, Ow!" I screamed as a sharp pain shot

through my leg.

"Levez vous. Wake up!"

"Ow … What the fuck is that?" I half opened my eyes and could just make out two dark shapes.

"It's the Police" said last night's blonde haired companion. I turned to face her,

"What! What's wrong?"

"Get up, wake up" came the command. I thought to myself what the hell have I done now. "Get up"

"Shh, don't make a fuss" she whispered softly, I scrunched my eyes open and squinting, saw two policemen standing on the end of my sleeping bag.

"Passport! …. Passport!"

"What time is it?"

"6 am, just give them your passport." Finding your passport at 6am, half asleep, in a panic and with two Policemen standing over you is not easy.

"Allez, go." I looked around to see two more policemen kicking some other unfortunate bleary eyed beach residents. We slowly got up and began rolling up our sleeping bags whilst discussing the dramatic alarm call.

"What do they want?"

"It's illegal to sleep on the beach," she said apologetically.

"You're kidding, thanks for the heads up" I said with a wry smile.

"Well, I didn't want to mention it last night. I thought it might, you know … spoil the mood, sorry."

"Hey that's okay."

As the sun began to rise above the ocean the sky was a vivid melange of bright yellow, red and orange This slowly melted away to reveal a mass of stirring bodies lying on the sand in the crisp morning air. I had no idea I had slept with so many people in one night, it was quite an achievement; so this is where all the young people disappeared to at night.

"Check your wallet too"

"What?" I said startled.

"It might have been stolen during the night."

"Look, don't take this the wrong way but are there any more nasty surprises?"

"No." she said with a sheepish smile,

"I mean you're not pregnant are you?"

We both laughed as we finished packing up our stuff, I donned a rather smart pair of trousers, white shirt and yellow V neck sweater, and she wore a cream blouse and tight jeans.

"You know for two people sleeping rough on the beach I think we cut quite a dash."

We arrived at a lively café for breakfast and positioned ourselves in a sunny corner under the dappled shade of the leafy surrounding trees. We sat down here for hours talking and meeting young people from every corner of the world. I began doing a few pencil sketches; I used to draw a little at University and thought, why not? I then pronounced to my new friends, "I tend to draw an outline in pencil and then use my fingers to shade and create depth in the composition, this way I can bring more life to my work and give it a more vital and realistic feel." This was uttered with a straight face and with no hint of affectation; they just pissed themselves laughing. Despite all this bollocks the girls quite liked my stuff and asked me if I would do some portraits, so, whatever it takes.

St Raphael centre is quite small and is flanked by the beach on one side, the railway on the other side and the port and main road opposite. It's quite understated apart from an enormous 19th century church, Le Notre-Dame de la Victoire which appears to be completely out of place in such a small town. For me, it's main claims to fame, perhaps surprisingly, are the train and bus stations which are close to the sea and adjacent to each other. The geography of this explains why students and young people who are travelling all over Europe alight here, as a kind of staging post to the Riviera; Germans, Americans, Irish, Brits, Danes, Dutch, Australians, Italians and of course the bloody fucking shit man Swedes all come through here.

My thoughts, once again, meandered off to a time when I passed this way with my friends Bobby and Chapman and I smiled to myself as I recalled our encounter with the irreplaceable, 'Steven the arsehole.'

Waiting outside the station in the midday sun, sitting on our rucksacks and watching the world go by, we noticed a group of very cool, tall, blonde good looking Swedes and in the midst of them stood a short fat guy with thinning straight greasy hair. He wore a pair of thick rimmed NHS spectacles and had a strange penchant for talking in a pseudo mid Atlantic drawl that bore no relationship to where he was from in southern England. He too had his fags tucked into his turn ups in a desperate effort to look cool but he was so short, it just made him look ridiculous. For some bizarre reason he was travelling around Europe with this group and to this day I have no idea why. Unfortunately, the first person he chose to speak to was the ever cynical Chapman and his modus operandi in travelling, unlike most people's is, 'speak to no one,' - Steven also lacked perception.

"So where you headed?"

"What?" said Chapman annoyed at the interruption.

"Are you chilling out here man ... or are you gonna split west to St Trop?"

"What!" Chapman's clipped tone was accompanied by a withering stare.

"You know, St Tropez man"

"No, I'm going to Italy with my mates tonight."

"Maidstone? Shit man, what a coincidence. I'm from Maidstone,"

"What!"

"Hey man, that's really cool ... Wanna smoke?" now bending down to take a lighter out of his turn ups. Chapman just looked at him.

"No, I don't smoke. Why are your cigarettes in you turn ups?"

"Hey man ... like where else can I put them?"

"In your pocket perhaps."

"Ha-ha cool, I like that, that's good man." Mercifully one of the Swedish cool crew comes over,

"Hey Stephan where's Inga and Trudi?"

"Peter, cool it man, I'm rapping with my friend here from Maidstone,"

Bobby and I walk up and introduce ourselves and Chapman, with perfect timing, turns to Steven and announces,

"These are my mates."

"Maidstone? …. man that's incredible, you too." Bobby and I look suitably bewildered, Chapman just turns away sniggering.

"So how's it going with the French chicks, they're really up for it yeh? You know the other day I'm with my chick and I open a brand new pack of condoms and three of them just burst, like unbelievable you know … just burst on me man and I'm like, shit and my chick is like … shit! So I get out the rest of my box of 144 to check them."

This guy is totally serious and we are creased up laughing, I mean what's he doing with even one condom let alone 144? The Swedes are laughing too, they think he's hilarious and so do we but for completely different reasons. However he's on a roll and there's no stopping him.

"So I check out these skins yeh and 144 have got holes in, you know, like I can put my finger right through" he says sticking his finger in the air. "… 144, right through man! and my chick, she's crying, 'Steven what are we going to do?'"

Chapman can't help himself,

"Gosh Steven how awful for you, what a blow,"

"Hey man, that's good, I like that. Peter, ha ha ... that's English humour man, cool - but guys can you believe it, 144 right through, new pack, you know."

The babes, Inga and Trudi arrive,

"Stephan the train is shit late, shall we just stay here and have a fucked lunch?" Jesus, this loser is the leader of the group and they think he's cool; how is this possible? We are all mystified and then suddenly across the station concourse the crowds part and striding through comes Steven's girlfriend. Now I have seen many beautiful Scandinavian women in my time but without doubt she had to be the ugliest Swedish girl in existence. She was short and fat with close cropped hair, white skin and a spotty face and as she waddled up to us - the recipient of 144 disappointments - she shouts,

"Hey Steven you *arsehool*, where are we going?" He slowly wraps his arm around his 'chick' as if she's a prize specimen of womanhood and with all the cockiness he can muster,

"We're going to take a train to Spain - get off the train - find a campsite - pitch the tent - and start lovin' babe"

I thought Chapman was going to faint, we were in stitches and Steven is standing there like 'hey, look at me.' Brilliant, just brilliant; this guy actually made it through puberty, where do they come from? I sometimes wonder to myself what's he doing now? Probably working as a middle manager at some insurance company in Swindon - or maybe Stockholm, you never know. One thing's for sure, Steven the arsehole will always have a special place in my memory.

My friends in the café noticed my expression;

"Hey Phil, what are you smiling about?" I shook my head,

"Oh nothing."

The girls unfortunately were leaving for Spain, one of them had to meet her boyfriend, "He's not called Steven is he? Hey listen thanks for last night, I *really* appreciated it." As they walked off, I could see one of the girls with a somewhat confused look on her face.

I met Eric the Yank whilst sketching by the ocean, he was really pissed off with the French and how rude they were to him. I observed this over lunch and he was right, they treated him like shit. The French are a bizarre nation; a friend of mine once described them as 'un-happy Italians.' Having observed this nation close up and studying a fair bit of their history, they're still quite difficult to comprehend. It's not that they dislike Americans specifically; they dislike everyone, including each other. They are undeniably rude, in fact most surveys put the French at the top of the world's rudest nations; but why is this? It all seems to stem from their ego.

In schools they are taught to have an opinion, even if its wrong, it's as if the expression 'I don't know' is admitting to having a lazy mind. Teachers shout at the kids, parents shout at their kids and everyone shouts at each other should an altercation arise. This is a normal way of expression; it's their default setting, along with being rude, opinionated, obnoxious and belligerent. Ask them any question such as; do you have any tables free? - 'No,' is there a petrol station near here? – 'No,' does this bus go to Paris? – 'No.' What is even more strange is if you ask them the same question about three times, invariably you'll get what you want. Now couple all this with an almost pathological hatred of Americans and their way of life *and* the fact that the Yanks liberated them in WW2 and you end up with a nice guy like Eric being abused for asking for a cup of coffee, in a bar, in the south of France – Simple really.

"So what do I do?" asked a clearly upset Eric.

"Well I am no expert but for what it's worth, try some basic French, don't be loud, most Americans speak about three times louder than anybody else, and if asked, tell them your Canadian. When entering any establishment say 'Bonjour' to everyone, say 'sil vous plait' and never, ever, sit down at a table that is set for lunch when you are in for breakfast, even if it's full and those are the only tables left."

"But why not?"

"Because they are not serving you, you are entering *their* establishment, you do what they tell you to do, you have to be polite to them, good service is beneath them."

"But that's ridiculous it's a restaurant!" I smiled at his frustration.

"I know, I know, look, all this is very *foreign* to you but this is France, they are not interested in serving you or making money out of you, they don't care if you ever come back or not. Smile and if all else fails leave, you can never win so don't try, you lost when you walked through the door."

"This is ridiculous, how do you put up with it?"

"Well, firstly I expect it and secondly I don't care but, if I want to survive I follow the rules when I need to – also I'm British so I practice diplomacy whenever necessary." Poor Eric still looks lost, "You know the French are just as patriotic as Americans and fiercely proud of their way of life, they just don't value the American way. This is the most visited country in the world and the French are the least likely to go on holiday anywhere else, generally speaking if you're friendly and respectful to them they will be the same back to you, minus ten percent, I mean after all the French are just, well, you know ... French."

Eric shakes his head and ponders for a while.

"I don't know, it all seems very odd to me but I appreciate the advice."

"Well, look at it this way, this is a country with a strong social tradition, history and culture and they are extremely protective of it and so they should be. I believe it's a fabulous place to live. I don't know why the French seem so unhappy and angry all the time but my attitude is it's their problem; c'est la vie. We laughed and shook hands and both went on our merry way, I liked Eric, I really hope he found some Frenchies who behaved a little nicer to him in the future.

The great charm of travelling is in encountering so many different people in abnormal and various situations; the humdrum of a settled daily routine is what many people desire and possibly need - but not me. A fine example of this was just about to unfold. It was later in the day, by the harbour, a little girl and her father were patiently watching me as I pencilled a small fishing boat, "Papa il est tres bien," from an 8 year old this was praise indeed, if she thought I was good, well, that was it. I began to get flighty ideas of drawing and selling my pictures all along the coast - there is nothing like a healthy inflated opinion of oneself. I now had a Disque Bleu cigarette in one hand, a pencil in the other, Leo Ferre's 'Avec le temps' on the stereo and looked all the world like the tortured French artist, the blue sky, the sun, the sea, this was it, I was in the zone. Unfortunately all this was about to change when I heard a loud voice behind me shout,

"Hello ... you English?"

My first thought was to ignore this guy in the hope he would go away as he was seriously disturbing my street cred. What I didn't know was that I had just met the most unusual, unique and frankly craziest person I have ever met.

John was 6ft-3ins with short cropped fair hair and a gap in his teeth when he laughed or smiled. He had a lazy eye or 'dodgy wok' as he called it; at first I thought he was Australian – with due apologies to my Aussie mates. He moved in a lolloping ungainly fashion dressed in a totally non cool, non PC way, in fact John was non PC all over. When he did laugh he would throw his head back and guffaw, it was so loud everyone on the promenade looked over. He either didn't know this, didn't care or both. He had a strange vocal affliction; actually, he had many vocal afflictions, twang sounds, elongated words, sentences that would go on forever, that would appear to have no meaning or ending and actual words that nobody understood. His accent was a kind of broad south London, Dartford, Cockney mix and he delivered this straight into your face invading well inside your personal space. Combined with this was a very quick, intelligent brain, acute hyperactivity and a warm and generous nature; this was the man who now stood before me.

"So, what you doing 'ere then?"

"Well I was trying to look cool and pick up some girls … until you came along"

"Shot!" this was followed by hysterical laughter.

"Excuse me"

"Shot!" He said this so much in the early days that everybody called him 'John Shot,' however very quickly that was to morph into the name 'Crazy John,' he became so infamous just about everyone knew who you meant. I never did find out why he said 'Shot'.

"'Ad any luck?"

"Well" I said tentatively, "last night I …."

"Shot, I've topped up." What on earth was he talking about? "You're a good looking fella you must score big time"

"Well one tries" I didn't know whether to try and get rid of this weirdo or embrace his crazy energy.

"Are you an artist then or is this drawing malarkey a load of old bullshit"

"It's a load of old bullshit - sorry; I didn't catch your name?"

"Captain John"

"Are you a real captain then or is that a load of old bullshit"

"Nah mate, straight as a heart attack, and what do they call you?"

"Usually they call me Phil, although today I've been trying to give the impression of a Philippe." Uncontrollable laughter ensues once more from the nutcase as he proceeds to sit down on the wall next to me.

"Listen Phiwl, where are you styin?" I presume he meant 'Phil' and 'staying'. His pronunciation of 'Phil' was extraordinary, it sounded like 'fei-wul' but shorter. Somehow he'd taken a one syllable word and turned it into two.

"Here on the beach." I replied.

"I've topped up, what the fack are you doing on the beach?"

"Trying to get some sleep John"

"I tell you what, I'm camping near Biot, if you get stuck, give us a shout"

"I might take you up on that ... unless I get lucky of course."

"42 teeth in a horse's mouth!"

He was speaking a completely different language to me, it certainly wasn't English. Then, in the next breath, two girls walk by and he's off, "Hello lydies, do you want my mate Phiwl here to draw ya? Come on." To my surprise the girls walk over giggling to each other. "Right Phiwl, how do you want them, topless or what?" He then arches his eyebrows and does this strange aside in the mistaken belief that they can't hear him, "Phiwl, they are facking gorgeous."

"John take it easy you're embarrassing them." At

this, he breaks into his own version of old English 'chiv-alry' speak.

"Excuse me *lydies*, far be it from me to presume upon the nature of such beautiful angels descended from heaven." I sat them down, just did a quick sketch and after I had finished they giggled again and off they went.

"Thanks a lot John, I'm not that good!"

"But Phiwl," aghast and shouting at the top of his voice, "I *fort* you were supposed to be an art-ist."

"No, I told you it was bullshit"

"Well, you'll fit in down here in the South of France Phiwl. It's full of bullshit. Anyways what you do-ing here then?"

"I decided to set out and travel the world and work my way around, as in the old days."

"By old days, do you mean like when 'Knights were bold and maidens were fair'"

"Exactly John but without the jousting"

"Phiwl" he said laughing, "you really *are* full of shit."

Then suddenly he jumps up, looks around and says,

"'Ave you had any nose bag?"

"Any what?"

"Nose bag, you know, food. Come on let's grab a sarni instead of poncin' about here. I'm paying, I'll have to 'cos you'll have no money if you're a fackin' art-ist."

"Thanks for the offer and the compliment," I said laughing, "but its only 11:30, I think I will stick around here till lunchtime."

"Suit yerself." Then he promptly sits back down again. He was like a human yoyo; his mind and body were going the whole time, no breaks or pauses, just a walking talking stream of consciousness. He was potty, completely off his box and I pondered whether I should just cut loose right there and then; the problem was I couldn't stop laughing and although he sometimes sounded offensive, he would have been mortified to think anyone felt that way. It dawned on me early on that he was quite a clever guy despite the veneer of being as nutty as a fruit cake. There was no pretence, he was genuine and honest, he saw it, and he said it. His mind was going 100 miles an hour and consequently his conversation would drift off all over the place. If I mentioned the colour of the sea his attention would go there;

"You know the ocean at its warmest is 36 degree Celsius and the highest mountain is bigger than Everest," then inexplicably he would break into an impersonation of Jacques Cousteau - a famous French oceanographer on the TV at the time;

"Ze crustaceans zat I found beneath ze boat 'ad been zer for many years"

"John, John, slow down, what are you doing in France?"

"Well a few years ago after my Dad died, I thought, fack!"

"Sorry, how do you mean?"

"Fack, I've got two minutes to get my train" and

in mid conversation he's up and off but just as he crossed the road, talking to the traffic as he went, "Aw rite aw rite, take it easy you fackin' French fackers." He turns around arms outstretched and shouts, "Phiwl I will see you in Biot" and with a big, broad smile, "remember, God has brought us together" and with that he was gone.

Exhausted, I just sat there as all around became calm and still; the hurricane had passed. Slowly, life started back up again as if it had been frozen in time and the thaw had begun. Leo Ferre returned, the blue sky, the kids playing on the beach, the calm glistening ocean. I smiled to myself, 'what the fuck was that?' I made a mental note, John *was* crazy but at least he was different and if things became a little slow, a few days with him could be fascinating - to say the least. He had certainly made an impression and despite his odd nature he was quite intuitive and interesting, it's just that you had to fight your way through the jungle in his brain to get there.

It had been an eventful day and I felt contented just to be on my own. I climbed a collection of low rocks at the end of the bay, set up my little camping stove and had a mini feast of vegetable soup, baguette, ham, lettuce, cheese, tomatoes and a delicious tarte aux pommes for dessert. I went swimming as dusk fell and returned to a Zen state of calm and tranquillity.

This was to be my second night on the beach but as I am a quick learner I made a few adjustments to the night before. In the morning when the Police came they'd start at one end and take about an hour to work their way around to the other and, being French, I figured their routine would be exactly the same the next day. I rolled out the sleeping bag, brushed my teeth and had a shower – all possible, courtesy of the facilities provided on all public beaches in France. I loved the feeling of comradeship as all around my fellow natives settled down for the night.

Come the morning, my plan had worked perfectly, 'Les Flics', (the police) were still half way along the beach by the time I was already up and gone. 'I've cracked this' I thought to myself, 'I've got a free hotel for the whole summer'; it was a very comforting feeling. A glorious morning beckoned, I had been in St Raphael two days but tempus fugit and I was back on the road again. Things had been going well since my gay debacle of two days ago and I felt good about myself. Confidence is everything, I expected excitement, was determined to find it - and so I did.

Sylvie and Marie were two French girls, who picked me up outside the village of Boulouris in a classic yellow Deux cheveaux,

"Bonjour ca va"

"Oui, vous allez à Cannes"

"Oui"

"You are English?"

"Yep"

They giggled to each other as I jumped in. Marie was 18, had shoulder length hair with a nose that was just a tad too long, blue open necked shirt and jeans. It always amazes me that even the so so looking girls in France still have good figures and truly make the best of themselves. She was friendly and smoked the proverbial spliff. Sylvie was 19, about 5 foot 6 inches, shoulder length curly blonde hair, deep blue eyes, lovely tanned skin, red checked shirt with the sleeves rolled up, jeans and a dynamite slim figure that oozed a playful sex appeal. She was a total babe and my antenna – if you'll pardon the expression - was most definitely up.

My friend Bobby always used to joke that when "Phil had decided on getting a girl, nothing and no one would get in the way." Apparently I was quite ruthless being exclusively fixed on the target. I don't care who you are *focus* is everything, no matter what you are attempting to achieve, be it a job, an exam, a new car, a sport, or even a girl. It's not a guarantee of success but without it, I guarantee you will not be successful. Everyone in life develops their own personality and has strengths and weaknesses, the skill, in my opinion, is learning what they are and when it came to girls I knew instinctively what mine were and so, I went into action. (A bit of luck and a good haircut always helps too).

We drove all along the dramatic rocky coastline where the Esterel massif drops down into the sea. Being the first time I had travelled on this route I found it breathtaking. The girls were playing superb music which just added to the magic and when 'Hotel California' came on, Sylvie turned round from the front seat looked over her shoulder asked, "Phil I know *ze* words but what does *ze* song mean?"

"Well the song has always been ambiguous"

"What is ambiguous?" a lovely soft smile accompanied this question – I was hooked.

"It's when something is open to interpretation"

"What is interpretation?"

"Sylvie, are you taking the piss? and don't ask me what that means."

"Ha-ha no, please, I would like you too explain." Don Henley was not around so I gave it my best shot, next up was Steeley Dan and the Doobie brothers; I thought I've got my work cut out here. We were still jabbering away when we stopped for lunch at a café on the edge of the cliffs.

"So, where to next girls?" I asked expectantly.

"Cannes, of course."

"Of course."

I had never been to Cannes before and as we came around the final rocky headland above Theoule-sur-mer, the splendid beautiful bay swept majestically into view.

"What is that?" I asked motioning out the window.

"That is Cannes."

Dramatic and memorable describes my feelings the first time I ever saw this beautiful place. It is in my personal opinion the most sophisticated town on the planet and ironically, although I was a humble hitcher when I first arrived, with no money, or style and the last person Cannes would want to have stay in her town, I loved it and still do.

We passed a string of sandy beaches before swinging past the 'old' port into Cannes and onto the palm fringed Croissette – allegedly named after its croissant shape. It was a buzz of excitement and activity with a classic sophistication that has no equal. Cannes is probably most famous for its Film Festival - it is after all twinned with Beverley Hills - the sleek promenade is lined by a collection of famous hotels and beach restaurants; it is also very expensive as I discovered when the girls bought us all ice creams at £3 each! Relaxing there in the late afternoon sun with my two companions, they tasted delicious; the ice creams, not the girls.

"You know Phil some people don't like Cannes"

"You're kidding, how can you dislike this?" I said leaning back in my chair.

"Because they are afraid of it," said Marie. (I felt a French philosophical tete a tete coming on.) "People are threatened by the expense, by the sophistication, by *ze* expectation of style," she said drawing on a cigarette whilst eating ice cream at the same time – not an easy task.

"The expectation of style. Marie, what are you talking about?"

"Cannes is so elegant and chic. They don't like it because it makes them feel inadequate"

"I can see what you mean it's quite overwhelming and unique but I think it's cool and I haven't got a pot to piss in."

"A pot to piss in," she laughed, "please explain?"

"It's just a phrase, it means, I have no money"

"I like *zis* 'pot to piss in', anyway it makes very little difference, many people have style and no money." She now took a long drag on her cigarette and looked very chic indeed.

"Exactly," I said "look at us."

"Ha-ha but you forget, I 'ave a deux cheveaux."

"Yes and I have the company of two beautiful women."

"Yes," said Sylvie leaning forward "and we have ze 'andsome man." Crikey, this was all going a little too well but when the girls ordered two incredibly expensive cocktails I became ever so slightly worried. Quickly, I worked out that the bill totalled more than I had spent in France since I'd arrived! And when the waiter asked me what I wanted, I hesitated. Marie must have been quite perceptive because she just waved her hand and said,

"Phil, I hope you don't mind if *we* pay for the drinks, we are on our holidays and would like to treat you." Phew! What a relief.

"Merci, that's very kind of you, in that case I'll have a bottle of Bollinger." They thought this was hilarious and so did the waiter but being Cannes I figured I better change my order to a beer just in case he misunderstood the joke.

As the afternoon drew on, Marie announced that she had to go but Sylvie stayed. Marie kissed my cheek, "Phil you look after my friend, yes?" she then kissed Sylvie and whispered something into her ear, Sylvie just nodded. What was all that about I thought to myself? We strolled on the Croisette, rode the merry-go-round laughing with the kids and talked about silly things of meaningless inconsequence. The sunset burned crimson red across the horizon as the crowds began to melt away and finally, whilst sitting by the beach we kissed and I calmly asked,

"Where are you staying tonight?"

"Marie has a friend outside Cannes that I can stay with. What about you?" She tentatively enquired.

"I'm staying at the Three Palms Beach Hotel"

"That sounds lovely, where is it?" and pointing to the beach I said,

"Just there, by the water's edge." She held my arm,

"Will it not be lonely?"

"That depends," I said as my eyes focused on hers.

"I don't know," she whispered softly, "I'm not sure, how do I know I can trust you?"

"I understand. Listen, if it makes you feel any better, I can guarantee 100% that you can't." She gave a nervous giggle and then slapped my arm playfully. I took her hand, "come on let's go for a swim."

It was dark now but swimming together in the warm water was both exhilarating and fun and sometime later we found a private spot on the sand, away from the locals. We had a sleeping bag, a few blankets and a small bottle of rose wine. Her blonde hair fell across my face as her clear blue eyes fixed on mine. It was romance and excitement, passion and desire, all wrapped up together on a summers evening in the south of France.

In the morning a slightly embarrassed Sylvie explained that she had to go and meet her friend Marie.

"Why don't you stay awhile?"

"No, I can't, I feel very bad." She said looking down at the sand.

"Why, what's the matter, is it something I've done?"

"No and yes. It's, it's because I have been unfaithful to my boyfriend in Lyons."

"I understand, but what about your other boyfriends in Paris and Bordeaux?" I asked with a smile.

"No," looking confused "I only have one boyfriend."

I guess this humour was a bit too 'English' for her, still it made me laugh.

"Sorry," I said touching her hand "I was just trying to make you feel better, listen why don't we at least have a coffee?"

"No, I have to go, I'm sorry" She was on the verge of tears when she gave me one of the softest most sensual kisses I have ever had in my life; and then she was gone. What a babe and what a shame.

I stayed on the beach for a while pondering; obviously this was all connected to Marie's little whisper to her the night before. She had gone too far and now felt terribly guilty; I had gone too far and felt fantastic. Still, I am a guy and we're wired up differently, I did not feel guilty because I was in another world away from England, maybe it was wrong but it was how I felt. This was me doing my own thing, I had no excuses, I just thought it was all harmless fun and part of my adventure and so out went the thumb and off I went.

CHAPTER 3

CRAZY JOHN

"Monotony is the awful reward of the careful"

A.G. Buckham

By now I had a deep tan, my hair had been bleached aggressively by the sun and my eyes had appeared to turn a deeper shade of blue than normal. It seemed to be the fashion to turn your jeans up, so not wanting to appear uncool, I rolled mine up too. I gave the fags in the turn ups a miss though, with all due deference to Steven the arsehole. I was now so relaxed about everything I even lay down on a low wall by the sea with my thumb out expecting a lift. Clearly I was becoming over-confident as nobody stopped. I took it easy all day and just hung out on the way to Juan les Pins spending another night on the rocks just near the beach there.

Walking through Antibes the following day, my rucksack began to chafe the suntan on my shoulders, this is an occupational hazard of hitchhiking and you just have to get on with it. I realized I was nearing Crazy John country, should I try to find him or should I just pass him by? Things had got a little quiet so I figured what the hell, what have I got to lose, apart from my sanity, so off I went. Five miles later and in the boiling hot sun I am already questioning the wisdom of my decision but I see a sign to Biot and head up the road in search of the crazy man's lair. Another mile and finally, exhausted and desperately thirsty, I reach a campsite. The place looked deserted until the owner appeared.

"Is there someone called John or a tall English guy staying here?"

"No" came the laconic reply as he sat down on a chair outside a small office that appeared to be the reception. I walked around and asked a few more people in the campsite, "Do you know a slightly crazy guy called John?"

"No," followed by shrugs and shaking of heads. It wasn't a big camp so I guess it had to be the wrong place. I felt quite disappointed but that was that, he clearly wasn't here so I headed back to the coast. Then suddenly, as I was looking down at the white lines on the roadside on the brow of the hill, a voice boomed out.

"I've topped up, there he is. There's the *mayn*."

Yes, who can forget those dulcet tones and inexplicable tautology? Crazy John was standing in the middle of the road. I just burst out laughing. "He's nuts," I thought to myself. Then he launched into a conversation so fast it was scary, subjects were thrown around and dispensed with at breakneck speed as we began walking side by side back down the road

"So what happened to you then, I bet you met a girl."

"Well actually I did, a gorgeous French girl called Sylvie." He stops and instantly lets out a huge bellowing laugh.

"Ha-ha! I fackin knew it but the thing is Phiwl, did you score?"

"John, please, my French might be crap and communication a little difficult but in the end - of course I did."

"That" says John laughing, "is because the intanational language of love is 'orizontal." We made our way back to the same campsite I had just left. Incredibly the owner and all the others came out to greet us.

"Ah Jean," they shouted. "Bonjour Jean,"

"Hey John, where have you been?"

He strides through the camp waving to all and sundry.

"Bonjour Pierre. Alors Marie! Allez France ... long live De Gaulle.''

I could not stop laughing. The French really are unbelievable, they had stated categorically that they did not know any crazy English guy called John and here they were, best mates. He was more popular than Napoleon. Three days ago I am advising Eric the Yank about the French and now I am getting the same treatment. They were charming and friendly and yet 10 minutes earlier, belligerent and unhelpful. Even more bizarre was that John had the largest tent on the campsite with a plastic sign stuck to the tent door saying, **'Maison de Jean!'**

We chatted away and John told me his convoluted life story, he certainly was an intriguing person. He had built factories in the UK and rented them out at a considerable profit, he had a Yachtmasters sailing licence, a private pilots licence and had been a diver on the construction of the Thames Barrier.

"Shit John, I'm the same age as you and all I've got is a Classics Degree"

"Phiwl, quite obviously you are a lazy facker"

"Ha-ha, you're probably right. Anyway, what first got you into sailing?"

John fixed me with a bizarre rather scary stare and began talking in, what can only be described as, a strange Cornish pirate's vocal twang.

"It is an ancient Mariner,

And he stoppeth one of three,

By thy long beard and glittering eye,

Now wherefore stopp'st thou me"

"John, what the hell are you on about now?"

"Phiwl, you are an educated man, do you know what that is?"

"What, an educated man?"

"Oh fuck off"

"Yes, it's The Rime of the Ancient Mariner by Coleridge, 'water water everywhere' and his ten thousand verses, what's your point? You mean that poem inspired you to take up sailing?"

"Nah, I just like boats."

John was not on some weird drug trip he was just genuinely different. Four guys from Birmingham were camped nearby and John offered to cook dinner for all of us on two camping Gaz stoves and a DIY barbeque set. It was sensational, he was a chef as well.

That night he's chatting away about his girlfriend Sheila.

"So are you two going to get back together when you get home?"

"Nah I doubt it"

"Why not?"

"It's busted," and that was his explanation for the end of a long romantic relationship. Succinct I thought but then in the next breath he was off on another tangent and half way through he stops in mid sentence and is fast asleep. Christ, at last he's stopped talking and I can finally put my head down.

The next morning another of John's idiosyncrasies manifests itself. I awoke at about 7:00 am and was lying there and without warning he opens his eyes and completes the sentence he started the night before, without punctuation or breaks of any kind. I am sure a psychiatrist would have had a bloody field day. And it was during these first few days of knowing him that I coined the moniker, 'Crazy John,' it just seemed to sum him up in a simple and effective way. John was your 'typical' genius type, smart and crazy all wrapped up in some kind of enigma.

The Birmingham crew, including John and I, decided to head off to the beach. This *beach* consisted of millions of smooth pebbles stretching for a mile in each direction and was about 100 yards wide. It was flanked by the sea on one side and road and railway on the other. Every half a mile there were small kiosks selling food and drinks very close to where everyone hung out. It was hot and probably too much alcohol was being consumed than was sensible but, as the majority of the beach consisted of young girls and guys on holiday, nobody cared.

Everyone was in the mood to take the piss and Dave, one of the 'Brummies' with the strange nasal accent, was at it from the start,

"Hey Phil that *goy* over there is the image of Barry Gibb."

"Yeh, without the voice."

"Or the money."

John was busy trying to chat up any girl in sight but not having much luck; this was one particular skill that John had not yet mastered, still you couldn't fault his enthusiasm.

"Hey John try her over there, she looks fair game."

"Fuck off Dave, she must be over fifty."

"Yes, that's what I meant."

Next up was a guy from Persia (or so he said), called Yasser, who seemed to unwittingly be impersonating a Swede or at least their vocabulary.

"Hey guys, how is it with you? I am having bad time right now. Last night I was in local casino, you know and I lost 10,000 Francs in one hour - bloody fucking wanker yes?"

"Dead *royte* mate"

He bursts into hysterical laughter and then suddenly this bald, short, fat Persian with bright orange shorts and gold chains dangling down to his midriff does the classic John Travolta pose from Saturday Night Fever, right there in the middle of the beach. Fantastic.

"You should be dancing," I sing out to him.

"Phil don't encourage him."

Too late, he spots a group of girls near by and he's off disco dancing around them singing,

"Night fever, night fever." They are consumed with embarrassment but there's no stopping him, "Hello girls, I'm bloody fucking good, yes?" A bald Persian, imitating Travolta, imitating a Swede. Unreal. All I want to do is have a chill out on the beach and I'm surrounded by nutters and the chief nutter hasn't even started yet but, he was just about to. Out of the blue John jumps up and starts shouting his head off, I turned to Dave. "What's going on now?"

"It's the Crazy man, he's going off on one." John was incandescent.

"Oh, very clever, very fucking clever, you arsehole."

"John, John, what's the matter?"

"Look at that idiot. Arsehole!" He was shouting and pointing at a guy a full 50 yards away who was posing in his speedboat and going far too fast and very close to the shore where people were swimming.

"John take it easy."

"Phiwl, *that*, is bloody dangerous." John's eyes were glaring with rage I thought he was going to hit someone. Then the guy in the boat makes it worse.

"Pees off Ingleesh." John now storms down to the water waving his arms, he is utterly fearless. What am I doing in this mayhem?

"Allez, allez. If you don't piss off I'm calling the *sauvetage* beach police." Then, half the beach decides to join in and start yelling at John for disturbing their karma or maybe because the French just like shouting, I wasn't quite sure.

"Tais-toi. Monsieur, be quiet."

"Ca c'est dangereuse et illegal." Says John, who will not back down and now, whilst they're all screaming at each other, the 'bloody fucking' Yasser decides to give his eloquent opinion. I thought that's all we need right now, the disco dancing Persian,

"You tell them John, he is wanker, go and bloody fuck off." Dave the Brummie is sitting with all his mates in tears of laughter,

"Hey Phil, you can't pay for this entertainment, it's bloody priceless."

I was starting to get a little concerned about how all this was going to end up when thankfully the Police arrived. Everyone calmed down. John is now fully vindicated as the Police warn the French guy that they will impound his boat if he comes this close to the shore again in such a dangerous way. The French are now totally in agreement with John – what can you say?

When the afternoon's festivities are finally over and we're heading back to base, I turn to our heroic leader.

"John, do you realise that's the first time in history, that the Irish Republic and the Persian Empire, have joined forces to defeat the French on home soil." John shakes his head, smiles and now gives what has become his customary response to me.

"Phiwl, you really are *full* of shit."

We hung out the following day with the Brummies but the next day I suggested to John, that we go to Cannes as it looked as if there was plenty going on. I had once heard a saying that 'Cannes is a place where it's always raining somewhere else,' probably because it receives in excess of 300 days of sunshine per year. This is due to its geography and the onshore breeze which blows the clouds a mile or two inland. I mentioned this to John, who immediately adopted the saying by bringing it up at every opportunity and *always* getting it wrong.

"Cannes is a place where the rain never arrives."

"England is a place that's always sunny somewhere else."

"Bolton in the rain has less sun than Cannes in the sun," and on and on he would go recounting this saying to anyone who would listen.

John had decided to look for a job on the yachts that are moored in the two harbours in Cannes. They hold one of the world's most prestigious collections so it seemed a good idea especially with his qualifications. I decided to work on the tan. Whilst John was off I hung out on the rocks on the breakwater outside Port Pierre Canto and every hour or so he would return, sit for 30 seconds and shoot off again.

"Look John, if you're bored sunbathing here's a challenge for you. Go away and don't come back till you've got us both an invite to a really cool party in Cannes." I figured this would keep him occupied for the rest of the day and give me a bit of peace and then we'd all be happy.

Two hours later.

"Phiwl, Phiwl!"

"What John, keep your voice down, what?" John stands there in his classic stance with arms wide open and shouts.

"We have been invited to a film producer's party in the hills above Cannes. Tonight!"

"You have got to be kidding?"

"42 teeth in a horses mouth, (he wasn't), straight as a heart attack." It transpired that he had found a bar in Cannes called Le Saint Antoine and had met a girl called Nikki and her friend Mark and somehow had got us this invite.

"That's great but how are we going to get there?"

"Phiwl, 'ave a little faith. I thought about that. They've got a mini and will give us a lift. I told them my mate Phiwl is a laugh and a good looking dude - but a lazy facka." This he delivered with a big smile and a very loud voice. I suggested that tonight we sleep on the beach or the rocks where we are now.

"You mean 'Rock 'Otel,' alright, yer on."

So this latter day odd couple set off down the Croisette towards the old town of Cannes called Le

Suquet. Le Saint Antoine was a lively bar just at the base of an amazing old cobbled street called la rue du Suquet. It climbed up from the old port and bus station along a winding narrow route to the old town, arriving eventually at the top of the hill at an 11th century castle built by the local monks. It was becoming a major tourist attraction with bars and restaurants perched on the edge of the road as it snaked its way to the top. I wandered off up the street, which is the exact opposite to glitzy Cannes in that it has its own old worldly charm. By the time I return to the bar, music and people are spilling out onto the pavement and as it also doubled as a *Tabac* it was a hive of activity. I ventured inside to find John chatting away to two English girls. He really was unstoppable.

"Phiwl, Phiwl, here he is - The man of the rocks. I told you girls. Is he an han'some facka or what?" John stands there grinning away, "Phiwl, may I introduce Carol and Fay." They both look slightly bemused, to say the least, so I give it my best Sean Connery.

"I must excuse my friend, he's a bit over the top but he's harmless and a very nice guy." Fay replies. "No, it's fine, John has been a perfect gentleman." He stands there beaming away,

"Well I wouldn't go that far."

Fay is a gorgeous blonde, very sweet and good natured and Carol's not bad either; my satellite dish is fully operational. The girls are sitting in a little raised booth on one side of the bar so we all squeeze in around the table.

"May we join you? I think you might need protection from a couple of crazy English guys who have been seen lurking in the area." John lets out a huge cackle.

"John says you sleep on the beach."

"Yep that's true."

"Isn't that uncomfortable and a bit dangerous."

"No it's fun, you should try it."

"Oh no, I could never do that." I instantly thought to myself honey, you have no idea, I've just launched a missile five miles out at sea and it's heading in your direction.

"It's beautiful listening to the waves, lying on the soft sand and looking up at the stars."

"You make it sound very romantic."

"Well it can be, it all depends who you are with, not John obviously." I figured this line worked well a few days ago so stay with a winning formula. Fay now seems to be relaxing and getting a little flirty,

"I thought you were Scandinavian when you first came in."

"Well actually I'm from Yorkshire but I believe my great, great, great grandmother was raped by a Viking whilst he was on a quick pillage through the countryside."

"Phiwl, what are you on about now?"

"John you weren't aware of this but back home my car has a row of huge bronze shields running all along each side of it." We all laugh as John just shakes his head.

"Did I forget to tell you, he's full of shit as well?"

I turn my attention back to Fay, "So are you both on holiday?"

"Yes, we're staying near Villeneuve-Loubet, unfortunately we only have a few days left." This was accompanied with a rather beguiling smile; now there's a buying signal I thought to myself.

"How long are you here for?" asks Carol.

"Well hopefully … (and with a big smile) … until John gets us some drinks."

"Phil you are a bloody *noytmare*."

"And John said you were a gentleman."

"I am, I always try and use my elbows."

"And a bit tricky." said Carol

"John whose side are you on?"

"Phiwl, ha-ha, Phiwl," answers John with a guilty laugh.

I'm starting to think as this is all going so well let's forget the party and stay here but two minutes later John's off chatting to another table, he just can't stay on target. We are going to have to work on his focus – meanwhile, I'm still on it.

"So, listen were going to a party tonight, why don't you come?"

"I'm afraid we can't were meeting some friends later."

"That's a shame, maybe we can get together tomorrow?

"Yes," replies Fay "how about lunchtime at the

port."

"Perfect."

We arrange to meet and just as they walk out the door Fay turns and smiles.

"So Phiwl, what's going on?"- The crazy man's back.

"We are meeting them for lunch tomorrow."

"What?"

"Remember John, you must take every ball on the rise."

"Ha ha Phiwl, you're the man."

John has found Nikki and Mark, what perfect timing. They are friends but not a couple. Nikki is shortish and smiles a lot and Mark is tall and I guess good looking but unfortunately he has had his personality removed at birth.

"Hi Nikki, thanks for the invite."

"No problem, John seemed quite crazy but fun and we don't really know whose party it is but my friend Martin does."

"So let me get this straight, I'm invited to a party by my friend John, who I have only known for two days. He has got the invite from Nikki and Mark, who he's only just met and they were invited by their friend Martin, who knows a guy who's having a party." Martin arrives.

"Hi Martin, I'm Phil, so whose this guy with the party?"

"Don't know, he's a friend of Sarah's." At this

we all burst out laughing simultaneously and so naturally I ask, "Who the fuck is Sarah?" Martin points across the bar and as Sarah approaches he shouts.

"Sarah, whose party is it?"

"Well ..." Before she can answer I jump in,

"Sarah, I know we have never met and I don't want to appear rude but if you don't mind, please don't answer that question."

We all pile into the mini as Martin and Sarah lead the way on her scooter. None of us really know each other but it's an exciting feeling driving off to a party in the hills above Cannes, hosted by somebody nobody knows.

We arrive at a magnificent house with imposing steel gates and an array of security cameras dotted the length of a 12 foot high perimeter fence. Sarah, who is also a babe, though a little on the skinny side, nods to the guard and in we go. I turn to Nikki ... "Cool."

The gravel driveway sweeps up to the house of epic proportions and our motley crew are shown through the hallway and out onto the stunning Provencal gardens. Apparently the owner has a string of massage parlours which open only for the summer and in the winter he makes movies that he 'shows' at the Cannes Film Festival in May. I don't believe a word of it; it appears to Martin and me to be more like a scene out of the Godfather. Who cares? A barbecue and bar are set up in a sort of faux Provencal pastoral scene around a grand log fire. It is just packed with the beautiful people of Cannes, terribly avant garde and sophisticated. We overhear some of the French doing that philosophy of life shit that they do so well.

"Pierre have you seen Davide's film?"

"Yes, I thought it was life and art joined with a self expression that made my soul weep."

"Ah, I understand, you were touched by the essence of the man, who was himself but not himself."

"Exactly, he is not a film director, he is a poet of abstract expression on a visual moving canvas."

It really is the most fabulous bollocks.

The music is incredibly loud as they dance the night away - occasionally interrupted by the odd person throwing themselves naked into the pool, in a show of terribly exaggerated decadence. I truly believe our little troupe *are* the coolest people there because we *really* don't give a shit. We settle down by the log fire that is set in a large outdoor stone hearth as more English and Americans join us. The champagne keeps on coming, courtesy of Davide, who I don't believe exists because nobody has seen him all night. Martin, who is known as Leo, I guess because of his long mane of hair like a lion - but who knows, is quick witted, smart and constantly takes the piss out of Nikki. She gives as good as she gets, she's quite prickly when pushed but I like her. Leo thinks John is hilarious and is at him relentlessly. "Hey John, good party yeh?" said Leo raising his glass.

"I've topped up Leo."

"John, what the fuck are you talking about? Is that the champagne?"

"No, it's a *doyvin* expression."

"Do you mean a 'diving' expression?"

"Awrite, awrite, listen, years ago when I was

working on the Thames Barrier, you had to wear a diving suit, right." John demonstrates how to stand up in a diving suit with a pretend helmet and weights and walks around in big strides like 'Iron Man' - it was very funny. "You would then get lowered into the *wota*,"

"John, you mean 'water?'"

"Fack off Leo. You always have to make sure that you don't snag your suit, 'cos if you get a tear, it lets water in and if it lets too much in, you have to come back up because."

"You've topped up."

"Phiwl, you got it in one, fack me, that university education was not totally wasted then." Nikki, noticing that John's on a bit of a roll turns to Leo,

"Did you know John is a qualified pilot as well?"

"Bloody hell John, you mean they let you fly planes too."

"Well I don't fly facking boats."

"John tell them the story of when you flew to Dijon."

"Bladdy hell Phiwl, they won't want to hear that." I am laughing already as I look around the group fixing them with my eyes.

"Believe me guys, you do, you really do."

"Go on John, go on." Some people who have never met him before are just looking on, incredulous at a guy they think is drunk but who is in fact 100% sober.

"Alright, alright ... "

"So there was John flying a light aircraft to Dijon

with three passengers."

"Phiwl who rattled your cage, I'm telling the fackin' story."

"Sorry John but get on with it."

"Right. So there I am flying a Piper Cherokee down to the South of France and I look at my fuel gauge and it's a bit low but I figured I'd be awrite. Anyways we gets a bit of clag,"

"A bit of what?" asks Leo.

"Clag, you know shitty weather and that means I am using up more fuel than I thought I would do, so I thought I'll land at Dijon, get some jungle juice and be off again." I can see some of John's expressions are just way over the audience's heads but Leo, Nikki and a few others are already laughing and taking the piss.

"So John, you get some jungle juice."

"Leo, shut up, are you listening to the story or what?"

"Sorry John" says Leo sniggering away like a chastised schoolboy.

"So there we are flying over Dijon and I radio the air traffic controllers in the tower for permission to land – 'Hello Dijon, this is Papa, Romeo, Charlie, Bravo.'"

"John what are you on about now?"

"That Leo, is my call sign, PRCB. Fackin' hell, I bet you've got a university education an' all?" He is now getting frustrated at everyone's apparent stupidity but continues on anyway, with an impersonation of a Frenchman speaking bad English in his own cockney accent. Just hilarious.

"Hellow, Papar, Romeoo … Sharly, Bravoo … ze runaway iz fool … parmishione denied."

"Ha, ha, love the accent John."

"Phiwl this was serious, they wouldn't let me land and I had no fackin' fuel left, so I tried again. Dijon tower I need permission to land."

"Sorry, Papar, Romeoo, Sharly, Bravoo, no parmishione."

"Of course by now I was starting to get really anxious."

"Why didn't you tell them about the fuel?" asks Nikki

"Because it's illegal to fly that low on fuel, I could have lost my licence."

"Yes John but you could also have lost your life you dickhead."

"Phiwl, I know that, so then I said, Dijon tower I have a sick passenger on board, need permission to land - only problem was I hadn't told the passengers that I was low on fuel and now they're all looking at each other thinking what's he going on about?"

"Did they catch on?"

"Yeh, pretty sharpish and now they're all crapping themselves as well." We were all in hysterics at this point,

"Hellow, Papar, Romeoo, Sharl, Bravoo, please divert to Troyes."

"Ello Dijon tower, not possible … 'ave very, very sick passenger on board, need immediate, I repeat, need *immediate* permission to land." We are all spell-bound.

"Then, there's just silence for nearly a whole minute and I can hear the wind - *woossh*, *woossh* - and the ground is getting closer and closer outside, and I'm thinking, fack me, this is it. And it was just then I heard a crackle in me ear piece."

" ... (Crackle) ... *Hellow, Papar, Romeoo ... Sharly, Bravoo, (crackle, crackle) ... parmishione granted, cleared to land, runway deux."*

"John, I said laughing. "That's brilliant."

"Phiwl it gets worse, when we finally stopped, I put the dipstick in and there was no fuel left at all." He then lets out a huge cackling laugh.

"We had been flying on thin fackin' air!"

I think we laughed as much at the way he told it, as we did the actual story itself.

Leo, jumps up, points at John and shouts. "If you ever see me get on a plane with this guy - Fucking shoot me!"

As the evening went on, a few more people wandered over, probably due to all the howls of laughter coming from our little corner or maybe they were getting a bit cold, who knows. Quite a lot of the 'disappearing Davide's' champagne had been consumed by now but as the flow didn't stop, neither did we. The lovely Sarah then gets involved and asks Nikki if she could come back to life as any animal, what would it be?

"A Tiger."

"That figures." I said.

"Oh yes Phil and what would you be?"

"I'll tell yer what he'd be … a Lion."

"Well you might be right John, 'King of the Jungle' and all that."

"Yeh, Phiwl's got it all figured out. He would have three lionesses for his wives and they would all run around getting the food and looking after the cubs; whilst he would sit on is arse in the sun getting a tan."

"Hey John, that sounds pretty good."

"I know, that's because you're a lazy facka."

"You're probably right, what about you Sarah?"

I had chatted to Sarah a little bit that night but although she was very nice and lovely looking, she lacked a bit of sparkle; either that or she just didn't fancy me and thought I was boring. Or maybe she was just shy and found me overbearing, whatever.

"A Burmese cat." She mused. "Yes, that's what I would like to be - all warm and cuddly."

"A fluffy pussy. Excellent." I said.

"Phiwl!" cried John shrieking with laughter.

Leo turned to John.

"So tell us John, what would you be?"

"Well that's obvious in it."

"Is it?"

"Yes" and then after a very long pause he blurts out, "an American Bald Headed Eagle!" - I can honestly say that Leo and I nearly choked we laughed so hard and it was even funnier because John was totally serious. Added to this John has a large forehead with protruding eyes and a long nose that could be compared to those of an Eagle; so now his answer appeared even more bizarre. It took a good minute before anyone could get the words out to ask why and when he did reply, I actually couldn't breathe.

"Because you can spot a ham roll from 500 yards!"

The place erupted in laughter and all the while John looked on as if we were all idiots; it was wonderful.

"John, John, what are you going on about now? What the fuck has a ham roll got to do with it?"

"Fackin' hell Phiwl – because if you come back to life as anything at all, the most important thing is survival, and that means eatin.' And the Bald Eagle as got the best eyesight in the world and so can spot its prey easily ... or a 'am roll!" Even John smiled as he said this and general laughter ensued once more.

I think it's fair to say we didn't want the night to end but eventually we decided to make our way back to Cannes. We were all pretty hyped up and Mark was driving especially fast down the hill and back to the sea. The music was pumping, whilst Nikki and I were getting very friendly in the back seat. I must admit I didn't really notice how erratic Mark was driving and needless to say, disaster was being tempted at every corner. John, no stranger to scary moments, could see it coming a mile away. "Take it easy Mark; you're driving like a bloody lunatic."

No sooner had he spoken, the car lost its grip right on the corner of a hairpin bend. These things seem to happen in slow motion when you're actually in them. I remember Nikki gripping me very tightly and despite my ever ready enthusiasm I thought, baby, this is *definitely* not the right time. What followed was a collection of screeching noises, screams, and burning rubber as the car began to skid and roll over whilst heading straight for a brick wall. All I remember was a voice, which was obviously John's, calmly stating. "Here we go," and, at the precise moment we were about to go over, the wheels hit the kerb and I guess either the shock or the momentum or both, made the car do a little shimmy and spin. Thankfully this made the car miss the wall and slide into a dense hedge. We came to a stop with acrid smoke surrounding the car. Instantly we all jumped out, a bit shook up but otherwise okay.

Leo and Sarah pulled up on her scooter obviously petrified as they had seen the drama unfolding in front of them. Luckily there were no other cars on the road or we would - as John succinctly put it - "'Ave 'ad it."

Incredibly the only real damage was the wheel arch and the tyre which had burst in about three different places. I always marvel at how different people handle situations like this, in ways very different to what you might expect. Crazy John was first out of the blocks. "Right Phiwl let's get this wheel off and Mark, you get the fack out of the way." On a practical level he was correct but on a personal level Mr Personality now felt even worse but John's forte was never diplomacy. I looked at Nikki, who leapt to Marks defence,

"Piss off John he didn't do it on purpose."

"I know that but he was driving like a fackin' idiot."

"John let's fix the problem if we can. What do you think?"

"I don't know Phiwl, this wheel's facked. Get the jack out and let's see if we can get it off."

Leo then suddenly swings into action. He's jacking up the car before anyone's even moved. Luckily it was a mini so it was pretty easy to put a new wheel on and the axle didn't appear to be damaged. I was just relieved that we didn't have to walk back to Cannes at three in the morning. I turned to John and slightly tongue in cheek said, "John I am impressed, you handled that crisis very well."

Leo replied, "I'm not surprised, he's had enough fucking practice."

Nervous relief laughter followed. We were all okay and pretty grateful for that. I had sobered up and the moment with Nikki had obviously passed and so we all piled back into the car and off we went. Mark was now driving so slowly I think I could have walked there quicker but nevertheless, it was probably a good idea.

For some reason when we finally arrived into Cannes, we all hit the beach and went for naked swim in the moonlight. It was 4 am and I suppose the adrenalin was still flowing from all the evening's entertainment; it was quite surreal. We crashed out on the rocks and the beach just as the first light of dawn approached over the horizon. For some reason, as I lay there, I smiled to myself at the thought of a line out of 'Sgt Bilko,' the 60's TV show, that my friend Bobby always quoted in situations such as this; "Hey fellas, what a night!"

CHAPTER 4

FOOTBALL, FAY AND FIREWORKS

"This! This! I want this! ... This is what I want!"

Steve Martin - from Dirty Rotten Scoundrels.

I had not spoken to Jane since leaving England, I had called on a few occasions but we'd always missed each other. Finding a call box that worked was the primary goal before obtaining lots of small change as it was expensive phoning home. Although odd in today's world, phoning from a call box was my only method of communication. I could only steal a few minutes of conversation for the price of a meal that day and I finally reached her on my third attempt. It was wonderful to hear her voice. Jane was gentle and smart with an understanding nature that soothed my soul but she was also nobody's fool. I only had time to give her a quick ten second version of my trip and besides it was irrelevant, she just wanted to hear my voice just as I only wanted to hear hers. Some things are too simple to express and too complicated to explain.

We had a connection that had existed from the very first day she spoke to me whilst having breakfast at in the university restaurant. I never used to get up for breakfast and then one day, I did. When I went to sit down with some friends it was then that I noticed her at the end of the table. I had seen Jane around and had fancied her for ages but had never had the opportunity to talk to her. She had a sort of calm aura about her, very comfortable in her own skin, confident and yet understated. She laughed easily and had a killer smile which only further enhanced her underlying sensuality. I could tell she had a beautiful nature and was therefore a little taken aback at the first words she ever said to me.

"Hi … its Jane isn't it? Would you mind passing me the *sel*. That's French for salt."

She smiled, ran her fingers through her hair, then slowly picked up her knife and fork and gazed straight back at me. "*Non* … that's French for no." I think I was hooked right there and then, helpless, defeated and thoroughly enjoying every second of our first encounter. It was also the most delicious bacon and eggs, without salt, I'd ever had.

So there we were nearly four years later, attempting to have a conversation and a relationship from a phone booth 1000 miles away from each other.

"Are you okay?" she asked with a breathless excitement.

"Yes, I am fine, a bit burnt but looking terribly Californian."

"Mmm, that sounds lovely."

Christ, I was hooked again.

"You would love it here, why don't you come?"

"You know I can't, we are not all as reckless as you and besides I'd only cramp your style."

"I wouldn't care."

"Yes you would. Listen, if you find a place where I can stay, I'll think about it but you enjoy yourself for now. I'll come when I'm ready to."

All I could think about were her piercing green eyes and long auburn hair, this call was making me miss her terribly whereas she seemed relaxed and chilled. Despite all my infidelities, Jane was always extremely confident about our relationship and never doubted what we had together, she seemed to understand it better than I did.

"My money is about to run out ... I hate this."

"Don't worry," she said calmly, "call me when you can ... I love you" - *'Beep, Beep, Beep.'*

Tears filled my eyes, I was lost, my doubts returned, what was I doing? This was ridiculous. I was so blessed to have someone like her in my life and here I was selfishly fucking it up. I tried to pull myself together. I had a choice, go home or do something different with your life; who ever said this was going to be easy? Luckily John appeared; I figured he'd cheer me up.

"Who was that then?"

"Jane."

"Ah, the *bootiful* girlfriend you left at home."

"Yep. The one and only."

"Well, it's all your fault yer selfish facker. The way I see it is you makes you own bed."

"Thanks John," I said smiling, "for the kind understanding and gentle support."

"Phiwl, Phiwl. Listen, if you want, I'll tell you what a great guy you are or I'll tell you you're a twat … basically you're a selfish facker, live with it."

Why do people need to spend fortunes visiting therapists and psychiatrists? What they really need are mates. He was right of course but it was still a difficult dilemma when your emotions are pulling you all over the place. I was at odds with the situation and myself but I was here now and I resigned myself to get on with it.

We headed back to the town of Villeneuve-Loubet and lunch with the lovely Fay, Carol and some of their friends; it wasn't a bad way to suffer and we had a laugh and later agreed to meet up with the previous night's party crew in Cannes. It slowly dawned on me that all this fun was going to be drastically cut short if I didn't start earning some money fairly soon. John had got some interest from one of the boats he'd visited the other day and I found out later that Leo too had got a job on a boat in Port Canto. I had not even started look-ing, I guess I was still in hitchhiker mode and feeling cool, no doubt reality would bite - eventually it always does. Back in the St Antoine that night, Leo told me his Cannes theory.

"If you 'get' Cannes or if Cannes 'gets' to you, I believe it always draws you back, it's a magical place and totally unique."

"I agree maybe that's what Scott Fitzgerald tapped into in the twenties."

"Yes, well that and the drink, drugs and sex."

"What about all the European royalty in the late

19th century, they were all bang at it as well." This was obvious to anyone who visits Cannes today as most of the fabulous villas that are scattered on the hill, Le Californie, were built at this time. "Can you imagine the parties those guys must have had."

"I think you'll find they're probably still having them," replied Leo.

The bar was really jumping and our group seemed to continually expand as we occupied several tables outside on the street where the whole world passed by. We appeared to attract all sorts of travellers, probably on account of all the noise we were making, what I did not expect was what happened next. I went strolling up the street with Fay, lost in animated small talk, and on my return I noticed John sitting at the table with a rather odd expression on his face. Nothing unusual there, as John was a conglomeration of weird expressions, however this was new. There was a slightly strange dishevelled looking guy stood in front of him and I could tell from his body language that he appeared menacing and dangerous. I didn't know if there had been an argument or what, instinctively it just felt wrong. Suddenly, out of the corner of my eye I caught a glimpse of something in his hand. I froze. This nutter was threatening John with a gun, right in the middle of the street. He was obviously drunk but that only made the situation even more dangerous.

"Fuck off, vous tourist!" shouted the non descript guy who had got everyone's attention. At first he was waving the gun around but then he just locked in on John and put it straight to his head. John said nothing, didn't flinch and remained motionless. There was a silent impasse as all around nobody spoke and nobody moved.

"Fils de pute" - "Son of a bitch!" he screamed. I was petrified. I told Fay to quickly march back up the hill along with everybody else who was doing a rapid about face. In the bar not a soul stirred, they just either tried to ignore what was going on, which was impossible or sat there speechless. John saw me and didn't react at all and I had no idea what to do. I presumed someone had called the Police although that would hardly have made a difference because the situation was *now*, in real time. He kept threatening with genuine aggression whilst John just continued to stare into space. I was witnessing a glorious impasse between a madman with a gun and a crazy man without any apparent emotion. If it hadn't had been so serious, it could have been described as fascinating. The music inside the bar was playing but eerily no one uttered a sound; I guess they didn't want the gun pointed at them. Then, without warning, he withdrew, carefully placed the gun in his pocket and sauntered off mouthing some obscenity. I am convinced to this day that when a nutter is faced with the stony silence of another nutter, it freaks him out. It was as if he had nowhere to go because there was no reaction, so he left. It was utterly bizarre. Needless to say everyone was most impressed with John's calm under fire.

"Fucking hell John, you were cool," said Mark.

"Brilliant John, you're my hero," whispered Carol.

"Get that guy a drink," demanded Leo.

"That was pretty impressive. How come you kept so cool John? I think you actually freaked *him* out."

"Phiwl, I don't know what everyone's going on about, he was pissed and it probably wasn't loaded anyway."

"John you really are a fucking nutcase. It could have been loaded and just gone off!"

"Ha-ha, well if it 'ad, I wouldn't know anything about it anyways would I?"

I laughed and shook my head the whole episode was a perfect cameo of John's personality; if that's not crazy I don't know what is.

That night Carol, Faye, John, Nikki, Mark and I all slept on the rocks, Leo was on the boat in the harbour just over the wall, the 'Audrey Elsa.' The next day Leo rigged up a shower off the edge of the boat for us all to use and whilst this was going on, a guy on the next boat started laughing and joking with us. He was about 68 years old, tall, with long white silvery hair, very distinguished, and very flirty with the girls. I guess your typical bon viveur. His name was Hans. I have always admired people like him, they love life and it's infectious. His boat was called the 'Sirila.' I think he was Austrian or German, I couldn't quite work out which. He invited us all to dinner on board his yacht that coming weekend.

During the day we all drifted our separate ways but Fay and I stayed together. She had decided to sleep on the beach with me that night. I could tell she was a little nervous and inexperienced so I assured her not to worry.

"Believe it or not I can be trusted you know, even though you probably don't believe me."

"I do trust you, I just need a bit more time."

"I understand. Listen, I'm not going to rush you, let's do it tomorrow instead."

"John's right, you are a nightmare." she said with a cheeky smile.

"Can we please leave the crazy one out of our intimate relations; it does nothing for my libido."

"Nor mine," replied Fay.

She may have been shy and unsure but her cheekiness was very sexy. It was very windy that night on the beach so we just had a laugh. I found a corner of the beach by a wall and some steps to give us shelter. As we lay there in our sleeping bags, the sand started blowing all over the place.

"Fun isn't it?"

"Yes," she laughed, "I wish I'd done this years ago."

"But look at the stars. Aren't they amazing?"

"I don't know. I can't see anything with all this sand in my eyes."

"Well ... use your imagination."

"I could do that sleeping in a hotel or a tent."

She took it all with great humour and we actually had a nice time together despite the elements trying to ruin our night. In a way it drew us a little closer. I tried to shield her from the wind and protect her and I think that made her feel more comfortable and gave her more time to get to know me, without feeling under any pressure. I guess it's a woman thing. Later in the night the wind dropped, so I shagged her senseless – only joking.

It was a beautiful morning and the sand had got literally everywhere. Fay's lovely, long blonde hair was all tangled up into a bundle of knots.

"God, I must look a right mess?"

"I actually think you look gorgeous, sort of a freshly fucked look but without the fuck."

"Ssh, someone might hear you."

"Who's going to hear me, there's not another living soul within half a mile. What sort of idiot would sleep on a beach in *that* wind."

We packed up our stuff and did a quick hitch-hike back to Villeneuve-Loubet, just down the coast to where the girls were staying. It is so much easier with a girl and we got a lift in about five minutes. Later on we joined up with her friends on the beach.

"Do you realise that's two things you've never done before, sleep on a beach and hitchhike … and you've done both in 24 hours."

"Phil. I'm not daft, I think I know where you're going with this," she said with a *very* cheeky smile.

"I don't know what you're talking about. I told you, I am perfect gentleman." She shook her head with resignation, "I'm not going to last very long am I?"

"Nope." I said.

We chilled out for the rest of the day and Fay gave me a really soft, relaxing massage; it was great. I think we both knew how we felt as we headed back to the campsite. I have long disagreed with the notion that sex is best when it's spontaneous. I personally take the view that it doesn't make any difference. I think it's just as exciting *knowing* when you're going to sleep with your partner. It's a kind of tantric foreplay and the expectation is part of the romance and the fun. And besides, is sex ever truly spontaneous in the literal sense? Surely both partners 'know.' I believe once the pheromones start kicking in it has an obvious inevitability. Anyway, that's my view and no one has changed my opinion to date.

Fay shared her tent with Carol so this presented me with a slight logistics problem but I figured we'd work something out. Nearby were a group of German guys who, apparently, had been trying to score with the girls all week but having no success. I actually got on really well with them, they were nice guys just out for a good time and they were very polite and courteous with the girls - which is probably where they were going wrong.

We all took off to the bar with Carol and some other friends whilst Fay stayed behind. There were about five German guys that I christened 'The Krauts,' obviously, plus a concoction of other nationalities. It was all very cosmopolitan. I stayed with this group for about 10 minutes and then headed back. Carol stayed with the guys, she had got the message and so had I.

Fay was lovely if a little nervous but in the half light coming through the canvas roof it was all very romantic. What with the summer heat and moving shadows combining with the soft voices in the distance, it conjured up images of being on safari on the plains of Africa. My vivid and colourful imagination just added to the moment and prolonged the mood beautifully.

Later on, after Fay had fallen asleep, I joined Carol and the guys next door.

"Is Fay alright," whispered Carol softly.

"Yes ... she's fine." I thought it was lovely that she was genuinely concerned for her friend. It was a very hot night so she slept outside their tent to give us some privacy and I slept sort of half in and half out, in a strange sort of dance between the two.

Fay and I returned to Cannes the following day as she was meeting up with some old friends; I left for Villeneuve-Loubet in the afternoon as I had arranged to play football with the Krauts from the day before. They really were a stereotypical lot, tall, blonde, loud and built like tanks. There was quite a crowd by the time I arrived so I hooked up with the Panzer division, a couple of Swedes and two Dutch guys from the Total Football academy – well that's what I liked to believe. Our goal keeper was an extremely energetic Norwegian mountain climber, so he complemented our full squad of northern Europeans and of course they all spoke English too. Interestingly our opponents were a mixture of French, Spanish, Italian and South American. Some bright spark declared that it was the Latino's verses the Vikings. I turned to the 6ft-4ins head Kraut, Franz, "I like the sound of that."

"*Ya vohl* Phil, *vee* shall be victorious." Who can argue with that? I knew instantly I was on the right side.

The pitch was full size on really dusty dry ground. It was quite hard but flat and perfectly playable. There was a wall down one side with trees at either end. Along the other side was an area where anyone could sit and watch. We played in skins, firstly so that we were easily recognizable, secondly because it was hot and thirdly because we were all big heads and wanted to show off.

The World Cup in Argentina was on at the time so we were all up for it. We must have played for about two hours. It was frenetic and fast and every nationality performed true to type. Every time the Argentinean got touched, he went down with the accompanying histrionics and this was swiftly followed by the Italian going berserk in support of his colleague. Franz and his mates were disgusted with this show,

"*Zey* don't play in the spirit of the game."

"Your right Franz, *zey* need to be shot at dawn."

"Ya vohl, Phil. Attack!" I went charging up field and received a perfectly weighted pass from Rudi our Dutch midfielder. I didn't even think as I smashed it into the far right corner. Congratulations and respect flowed from my teammates. I was flying. A few minutes later a skilful move from the frogs resulted in our Panzer defence taking one of them out at about waist height and just inside the penalty area. It was a stonewall penalty which was fortunate because if there had been a dispute it would have been WW3. The French guy took it with ease as the mountain climber went the wrong way.

I must admit there were quite a few silky skills on display and then there were the guys who thought they were good but who in the midst of some trick, would have the ball snatched of them by a stoic Swede. The passion on both sides was intense. I ran non stop like a man possessed and again, true to the seventies English stereotype of a footballer, what I lacked in skill I made up for with fitness and heart. Just before half time the Latinos went ahead with a quite brilliant free kick from Pedro the Argentinean. (I have no idea what his real name was but I instantly hated him).

We regrouped and had a brief discussion about what to do. It was obvious that they were a skilful lot but I felt strongly that as a unit they would collapse if we put them under pressure. All agreed, then the two Dutch guys, Rudi Kroll and Johan Cruyf, laid out our tactics. (It was clearly obvious that at this point I was on another planet but they referred to me as Bobby Charlton, so who cared). The Krauts were impressed with the plan, not an easy thing to achieve but we were all on board and totally committed. The two Spanish guys were good but lazy and they never tracked back, so we pressed this weakness when attacking down the flanks. Rudi flighted another great cross into the box and Gunter headed home just on the hour. Fantastic.

The frenetic pace continued but nobody could get the breakthrough and then late on in the game the Italian had a sitter just in front of goal and sliced it. He was so distraught I thought he was going to kill himself. "Mama Mia, mama mia!" he screamed as he collapsed in a heap on the floor with tears welling in his eyes. The two French guys then started shouting and chastising him for his blunder, which of course just made him feel even worse. I glanced across at Franz.

"No wonder your lot swept through this country twice, come on Rommel lets get at 'em." I don't think anyone had ever spoken to him in that way in his entire life but all I know is that it had the required effect. He charged down the field like a human bulldozer but was fouled just outside the box. An animated discussion then ensued about who should take the free kick. In the end we thought we'd let Johan have a crack as there were only minutes left.

Both teams had earlier agreed to stop when the church clock struck 6:00, whatever the score. The tension was unbearable. I was exhausted but Rudi pointed out that they were in a much worse state than us and to keep going. He hit the ball hard but straight into the wall, it then ricochet out at an angle and dropped two yards in front of me. I was on it in a flash and as Pedro tried to close me down I hit it hard, low and on target. Somehow it squirmed through a crowd of bodies and hit the net just to the side of the wrong footed keeper.

Delirium ensued. A famous footballer once said that to score a goal in an important football match is better than sex and at this precise moment I was inclined to agree with him. The proverbial clock rang out and we were victorious. It was a great moment and one that I shall never forget. We all shook hands, it had been an enthralling contest. We slowly made our way back to the campsite, tired but exhilarated. The shared emotion and camaraderie of the game continued with laughter and banter along the whole route. I went off to have a shower and change whereas most of the players headed straight for the bar.

"Phil, you drink something yah?"

"Yes of course, I'll join you in five minutes." As I came out of the shower Carol had kindly left some towels ready for me.

"I hear you won," she said with a soft smile.

"Yeh, it was brilliant, we are all meeting up for a drink, are you going to join us?"

"No, it's nice and quiet here. I think I'll just, you

know, stay behind."

I was all pumped up and ready to have a good time with the guys at the bar who were now in full flow singing what sounded like German drinking songs. It was clear that a long night of partying was in store for us all. I turned to her and smiled.

"Maybe I'll only have a quick drink, my legs are a bit stiff and anyway I probably wont last long with that lot, they look like professional drinkers to me,"

"I could always give you a massage later ... if you'd like?"

"That would be perfect. I don't think I've got the stamina to go all night."

"Really? I doubt that." She just looked at me with hardly any expression at all. She was very cool. I returned to join the throng.

"Ah Phil, Kommen zie here!" comanded Franz, who slapped me on the back so hard I nearly keeled over.

"I feel we have won ze World Cup ... *again!*"

"Ha-ha, dead right Franz, me too. Where's that drink?"

More people gathered around and started to debrief the match in minute detail to any one who would listen. The day's exploits becoming more and more spectacular depending on the level of alcohol consumed. It was a lot of fun and though I hate to leave a party, I was acutely aware of another agenda developing and I had no intention of missing that one either. After about half an hour I noticed Carol some distance away, she looked over and smiled. It was like déjà vu from the night before but with different personnel. Within a few seconds I had quietly slipped away from the bar and was by her side. I took her hand. "How about that massage?"

As our eyes met she replied softly, "forget the massage."

The next morning just as I came out of the tent I was spotted by *zey* Germans, who of course were up before anybody else. Franz called me over. "Phil, would you like a coffee?"

"Thanks guys. Quite a party last night."

"Yes but I noticed that you left the party early."

"Fucking hell Franz, the Gestapo isn't dead yet is it?"

"Ha-ha Phil, you are a terrible man. I thought you were tired after scoring those two great goals, I suppose you went back to be with Fay, ya?" At the precise moment he said this Carol appeared through the tent door in a somewhat dishevelled state and headed for the showers. I couldn't let the moment pass by without saying something,

"Actually Franz, I think you'll find I scored *three* times yesterday." Gunter, Franz and the rest of the guys instantly burst into loud boisterous laughter.

"We have been trying to score all week with *zees* girls and you have both of them in 24 hours!" I didn't know if he was going to hit me or kiss me. "Phil, you are my hero." More laughter ensued. I am afraid this is a guy thing and to mid-twenties males, whatever their nationality, this was just about as good as it gets.

Luckily by the time Carol returned, they had all composed themselves and resumed their polite and courteous personas. She was completely unfazed by the situation and joined us all for breakfast; nobody mentioned the night before.

As Carol and I returned to Cannes I guessed it might get a little awkward as we were meeting up with Fay and the others but although she was a lovely girl, she didn't appear to be daunted by the prospect at all.

"How do you want to play this?" I asked.

"Well, Fay is not stupid and I'm not going to lie to her. I will probably tell her later when you're not around."

"What ... tell her I got you drunk and took advantage of you?"

She smiled and replied. "Yeh, something like that."

"Thanks a lot." I said laughing,

"Well, she'll assume you're a bastard and don't really care."

"Thanks again, and is that what you think?"

"Yes, pretty much" and with a big wide smile she continued, "but if it makes you feel any better, I had a really nice time."

"Well, just for the record, so did I." Besides, who was kidding who, we were all away from home, over twenty one and knew the score. She seemed pretty cool about it and so I went with the flow.

It was a boiling hot day and I felt pretty stiff from the day before (no pun intended), so Carol went off to find everyone whilst I met up with John in the San Antoine.

"Hey Phiwl, come and 'ave a look at this."

We wandered up le rue du Suquet to a restaurant that we both liked that was run by two cool French guys, Pierre and Henri. It was nearly 1:00 pm and quite a large crowd had gathered outside the Café obviously waiting for lunch, except no one was going in. They all seemed quite agitated and annoyed about something. John just starts laughing "Look at this." On the door of this normally very busy restaurant was a sign scrawled in pen and stuck to the window.

'RESTAURANT CLOSED, TOO HOT, GONE TO BEACH.'

John lets out a wild guffaw, "Now they really are cool guys." It was brilliantly French, for despite the fact that all these people had reservations they didn't give a dam. I thought to myself, I hope Eric the Yank isn't one of them as he'd have taken it personally and got the first flight home.

"So what 'ave you been up to then."

"If I tell you, you probably won't believe me."

"Phiwl let me guess, does it involve a woman?"

"Well not quite, it's two women actually." This was followed by the usual mad laughter,

"Fackin' hell, well you seem to have gotten over that phone call to Jane then."

"Christ John, you hit that ball back a bit quick."

"I told you Phiwl, selfish facker, anyway, never mind that. Who are they and did you shag 'em?"

"John, you really have no class whatsoever. I wouldn't dream of casting doubt on their honour ... Fay and Carol and yes, I did."

"Ha ha, you're the man!"

That night there was to be a huge firework display; it's a tradition in Cannes that during the summer a different country sponsors these displays each week. I had no idea what to expect, the girls had arranged a picnic on the beach and when we finally arrived it was packed and our lot had somehow grown exponentially. There was Carol, Fay, Sarah, Mark, Leo, Nikki, Martin (not Leo), John, another Sarah and myself. I just couldn't believe how many people were on the beach, there were thousands.

"Hey Nikki, this must be some firework display."

"It is."

At about 10:00 pm all the lights on the Croisette went out, including all of the lights in the hotels and bars as well; this was impressive in itself, I thought, 'Shit.' The next minute music began booming from speakers all around the bay and the sky was filled with what the French aptly name a 'Spectacle' of truly awe inspiring fire, light and explosions. The noise was so loud that it reverberated against the hotels and bounced back to the beach; it was actually quite scary but amazing nonetheless. We had yet another great night that went on very late and ended with us all finally crashing out on the beach.

I felt reality getting closer and closer; surely this couldn't last. I had lost track of the days, too many late nights, too many laughs, too much fun and today was our lunch date with Hans, I guess it was Saturday. He welcomed our motley crew on board with a glass of champagne and a large bowl of chilled grapes. Wow! I suppose reality had been postponed for another day. The large craft slipped its moorings and headed out into the bay towards the Ile de Lerins, two small islands adjacent to Cannes about a half a mile out to sea.

Hans stood on the bridge holding the wheel in an immaculate display of a man who was master of all he surveyed. He adored having all these young people on board and not in a creepy way, he just loved to be around people having fun. As we slowly came out to sea I looked back at Cannes, it really was majestic and being out on the ocean just added to the moment. The spray dusted us all with a fine mist as we lounged around on deck and after a short voyage we had arrived between the two islands. This was a protected spot that formed a natural barrier to the wind and swell of the ocean. We glided serenely into a small inlet and dropped anchor, it was so peaceful in contrast to the buzz of Cannes. Hans explained the history of the islands; his English was perfect, with no accent whatsoever.

"The small island is the Iles de Saint-Honorat, it has a monastery," he announced, with his arm outstretched to the left, indicating its position, "which was founded in 410 AD and is still inhabited to this day. And on your right," other arm now extended, "are the Iles Sainte-Marguerite, which has a fortress where The Man in the Iron Mask was held captive for a time." It was like having our own personal travel guide.

Anyway, history lesson over, we all settled down for a fine lunch of *penne gambas*, with the most succulent prawns I have ever tasted and accompanied by the local Cote de Provence Rose wine. Meanwhile Hans would regale us further with his stories and anecdotes.

More fabulous yachts and boats anchored nearby as we chilled out, diving off the boat and swimming in the clear cool water whilst chatting and laughing the afternoon away. I thought to myself this is not bad for a lone hitchhiker with no money. The cold and damp of Victoria railway station at midnight seemed a long, long time ago.

Later, Fay and I started talking. She had definitely been giving me the cold shoulder since yesterday and I thought it was time to bury the proverbial hatchet.

"How do you fancy swimming to the island and trying a bit of intrepid exploration amongst the pine trees." (Which I thought wasn't a bad opener.)

"Why don't you ask Carol as well?" (Ouch!)

"If I had wanted Carol to come, I would have but I don't, unless you do?"

"Of course not, don't be ridiculous." She snapped.

"Come on, let's go." I took her hand and jumped in, we swam quickly to the rocky shore and I helped her out. It was a stunningly beautiful and serenely peaceful place. "No wonder the monks have lived here for thousands of years."

"You really are a total shit aren't you?"

"Well, I wouldn't say *total*, partial shit possibly.

"Oh fuck off. How could you sleep with my friend the day after you slept with me?"

"Well, it wasn't easy, what with all the noise coming from the bar that night."

Thwack! Was the sound of her hand slapping my arm as she blurted out in frustration.

"You know what I mean."

I smiled. "Look Fay you have a perfect right to be angry with me and you can slap me again if it makes you feel any better," - and so she did. *Thwack*! Right on the other arm. I'm afraid at this point I just started laughing as I pretended to dodge the next blow like a prize fighter.

"You are impossible. I'm upset and you're taking the piss."

"Sorry, you're right, listen, you need to know something and I'll be honest, I did fuck Carol but … "

"Go on."

"But …" and with a broad smile and incredible sincerity, "… I made love to you."

"God, I think I'm going to be sick. Crazy John is right, you are a nightmare and totally full of shit."

"I thought it was quite a good line actually."

Fay just stood there and burst out crying. "It's a terrible line." I felt really sorry for her, she was a very sweet girl and if I'm honest she reminded me a little of you know you. I gently wrapped my arms around her and with tears rolling down her cheeks she said, "I am not stupid, it's fifty per cent Carol's fault too. I just thought … oh I don't know what I thought." I kissed her, wiped a tear away and kissed her again.

"Come on … let's go. Don't blame Carol too much, she'll be your friend along time after you've forgotten me. I'll just be some tosser you met in the South of France one summer."

"You know perfectly well that's not what I think and it's not what I **feel** either." God she looked gorgeous, her long blonde hair bleached nearly white by the sun. "I am going home in two days and it would have been lovely to spend it with you without this … this Carol thing."

"I know I feel the same way. Listen, it was just bravado. I know it meant nothing to Carol either it was just a bit of fun and … "

"Oh stop talking about it," she said as she kissed me again. We both decided to let it be as we made our way back to the boat to join the others.

Over the next two days we had a lovely time together messing about near Leo's boat, swimming and sleeping under the stars and when we finally said our farewells at Cannes station, it was all quite emotional. She was returning to her life in England and I was continuing on with mine; our ships had passed in the night.

July in the South of France is hot, it's as if after Bastille Day the country closes down, the temperature goes up another notch and the Mediterranean becomes just one big frenetic playground for the whole world. Although I was in it, I felt surprisingly detached; money being the obvious reason. I had the grand total of £20 left and that was it, no credit card, nothing; clearly I had overdone it in the first few weeks. It was still great fun hanging out on the rocks because most of us were in the same boat, so to speak. We all helped each other, some of the girls would work on the boats as waitresses on daily temporary charters and the guys would look to join a crew on board a yacht for the summer. Leo of course, had already got a job on the Audrey Elsa; he was a very capable guy so I was not surprised.

The boats in Port Canto ranged from small craft to ocean going ships, though by far the most popular were the floating gin palaces. The name derives from elaborate pubs in early 19th century London but the nickname today applies to the huge and sometimes quite gaudy yachts, bobbing about in the chic resorts of the world. What never ceases to amaze me is the amount of time the owners spend away from them. Sometimes they would not visit these boats for years on end and so they would just float about all day absorbing money. I have never understood why people, who work so hard to earn so much money, would choose to waste it in such a spectacular fashion; I can guarantee none of them are from Yorkshire. There was of course one colossal advantage to their stupidity and that was for the people who lived and worked on them all year round. There were the local French as well as a myriad of other nationalities, including Italians, Germans and English. Some yachts had just one guy and some had 30 or more crew. It was quite a cosmopolitan little village nestling in the port and it had its own rhythm and life, somewhat separate to Cannes itself. I was living on the periphery of this and yet it was my home for the time being. John returned one afternoon with a major announcement.

"Right you lazy fackers. I, 'ave got a job."

"You're kidding."

"42 teeth in a horse's mouth."

"Don't start all that again. Where?"

"Here, in the port, it's on a boat called the 'Willie."

"That's brilliant John, when do you start?"

"Tomorrow!"

I was pleased for him because he was going nuts just lazing around all day. It was also a wake up call to me, as if I needed one. I had had a great time so far but if I didn't get an income soon I would be on my way back to Blighty and my adventure would have been just a long holiday and more importantly, a failure.

As the days went on I became more and more conscious of this, I tried the local papers job section in 'Le Nice Matin' and got a possible offer as a gardener but eventually it came to nothing. There were many people who broke their promises down here; it was something I would have to get used to. Also, to be honest, I wasn't truly focused on getting a job, I was having to good a time sunbathing in the day and visiting the local bars at night.

A friend of Leo's from England had just arrived called Rob and we got on really well; he was just a very funny guy and would take the piss remorselessly, and he too became another member of our merry band.

Both Leo and John would come and go depending on whether the owners were in town and wanted to take the boats out whereas the rest of us would just lark about and have a laugh. The only problem was I kept thinking I was on borrowed time and this slowly began to affect how I felt even when we were having fun. I started to think of the future and where I was headed and Jane. These thoughts filled my head as I wandered along the quay and it was then I heard a shout from the wall above me.

"Fuck me! Phil, Phil! *Hee hee hee*." I knew instantly who it was,

"Graham, you wanker, what the fuck are you doing here?" He jumped off the wall and bounded over.

"I had a feeling we'd meet again," he said, "I just figured if I kept hanging around the coast long enough then our paths would cross, I mean you're hardly going to keep a low profile are you."

"Thanks a lot, who needs friends like you?" We laughed and then recounted our war stories of what had transpired since we last met. We walked around the port to John's boat, I tried to describe the person he was about to meet but it's a fruitless task because the average person doesn't have a reference point for someone like John.

"John! John!"

"What?" He shouted arriving up the steps from the engine room covered in grease, oil and general shit.

"John, this is the guy I told you about when I hitched down here, Graham. And this … this, is Crazy John." I said with a grand gesture.

"Bloody hell, not another lazy facker," shouts John, high up on the bridge fiddling with some piece of engine part.

"You'll get used to him Graham, he's all charm and diplomacy - honest."

"Phiwl, I thought you were lookin' for *wuurk* today."

"What did he say?" enquired a baffled Graham.

"Listen *Gryam*. I wouldn't go lookin' for work with him. He can't even say the word *wuurk* let alone do any." Yelled John.

"Work, Graham, he means work."

"You see *Gryam*; the most important thing in life is to have that leg muscle contraction at 7:00 am."

"What leg muscle contraction?" asked an even more bemused Graham.

"The one that makes one leg go over the other one, that makes you get out of bed. Phiwl doesn't have that muscle, so he can't get up and so he can't go to *wuurk*." John now shrieks with laughter and Graham looks at me the way everybody does when they first meet the crazy one.

"Told you he was nuts."

I then took Graham to our little sort of area that we called home. "You're like super squatters aren't you?"

"Mmm, I never thought about it that way but yes, I suppose we are, though I like to think highly sophisticated ones."

"Well you would."

"Quite."

He put his stuff down and we had another addition to our merry band on Rock Hotel.

Graham too had to find work, so later we set off together full of confidence and youthful expectancy. There are several yacht brokers in Cannes so that was the obvious place to start if we were serious. They buy and sell boats so they must know who required crew — university education, you can't beat it! Only problem was, we were told, was that you had to have a special stamp in your passport in order to get a work permit and without a work permit nobody would hire you because it was illegal. French bureaucracy is well known and we were stuck right in the middle of it. You couldn't get the stamp unless you had a sponsor and you couldn't obtain a sponsor unless you had a special skill. The sponsor would then have to write a letter to ... blah, blah, blah. After an hour or two of this it was clear that we were going bloody nowhere slowly. We passed by Leo's boat.

"What do you think Leo?"

"Waste of time. Look guys the only way you're going to get a job here is by word of mouth, that's how I got this, someone I knew put me in touch with the owner. I mean even Crazy John got his job that way and the only reason he got it, is because my boss new his boss."

"But isn't he nuts?" asked Graham.

"Of course he is but he has unbelievable qualifications and the owner is French and didn't realise he was nuts. Also the Brit workers are cheaper than the French and we'll do anything. We also have a reputation for hard work."

"Well he hasn't!" John had suddenly reappeared and stood there pointing at me with a big grin on his face. Graham just didn't get John at all.

"Well, what do you suggest John?"

"Leo's right, ask around a bit, try Le Circle bar and the Saint Antoine."

"What's 'Le Circle'?"

"It's where all the crews can get subsidized lunches. That's a good idea John, I am sure we can get them in. Come on, let's go," said Leo.

I had probably walked round Port Canto fifty times and had never seen or heard of this place. It was tucked underneath and to the side of the Capitainerie, which was the port authority centre of administration. We tagged on to Leo and John and the people who ran it just assumed we were crew like everyone else. They made out we were in between jobs and looking for work and what followed was the usual gaelic shrug - and we were in. It was very small and full of mostly French and Italians and a fug of cigarette smoke. Along one side was a large mirror that magnified the amount of people in the room and made it appear even more frenetic. They did a set lunch every day for £1, yes £1 and it was delicious. What a find! All I could think was that we now had free accommodation and virtually free food as well; in my mind my trip had just been extended, ever so slightly. This just took the pressure of a tiny bit which was exactly what I needed. I had felt for a while now that when I chatted to anyone about work it had all felt a little desperate and that's *never* a good thing.

The days passed and I kept trying but to no avail. I needed to make a decision and so I announced to myself one sunny morning that if no job materialised in the next 3 days, I would return to England. This thought filled me with dread but I was virtually skint and had no choice, I couldn't keep relying on the kindness of others and just lately I'd started to feel like a bum. The glamour of the rocks was starting to wane a little and I wasn't moving forward, I'd got stuck. I was in a rut, a very beautiful rut, but a rut nevertheless.

I told everyone I knew so that they could see I was serious and determined, as I hoped that by sharing this decision it might somehow galvanise the situation. In this state I have always succeeded, it's as if you are laying down a marker to the Universe and then and only then, do things come together. I believed something would happen and I was going to make it happen, even John recognised it, "Fackin' 'ell Phiwl, I think I can see that 7 am muscle startin' to twitch."

I remembered a saying I had once heard 'if you keep doing the same things the same things will happen.' With this in mind I thought I'd try something different. I took off that day to the old port at the opposite end of the Croisette and started asking around, no joy, so I continued walking along the old pier to the small lighthouse at the end. I got to the very last boat that was moored there and noticed a man with his back to me with silvery hair; it was Hans. I shouted out to him, "Hans! Hans!" he turned around and smiled, "I thought you had left Cannes?"

"I did but as you can see, I came back but I couldn't get a birth in Port Canto and this is all they had. Come and have a drink, where are all the girls that I always see you with?"

"Oh they're around," I said with a feigned nonchalance.

"So Phil, what are you up to, still partying no doubt."

"Well you know how it is, what about you?" I said as I walked on board and shook his hand.

"Oh, I am chartering the boat out for the next month or so, this boat is expensive to run and I am not as rich as most people are around here."

"What, you're going to do it all on your own. What about the two crewmen you had?"

"They got a better offer on a larger boat so I will have to do it myself, I have no choice." If ever I was staring at an open goal this was it. My father had only ever given me two pieces of advice in his life; 'always tell a woman you love her and if you want some thing, ask for it'.

"That's ridiculous Hans, why don't I help?" his body language reacted instantly.

"You ... but you don't need a job."

"I know but I am getting bored and it could be fun. Some of the girls I know could help us out occasionally. I could live on board and you provide the meals and maybe I could earn a little from tips from the charters as part of the arrangement. What do you think?" I had got his attention.

"Are you sure, I mean it's long days and hard work."

"I am not afraid of hard work." I hoped and prayed that Crazy John would not suddenly appear and blow it. "When is the first charter starting?"

"This weekend."

I held my hand out. "Then it's a deal."

He smiled, nodded and shook my hand. Fantastic, all I could think was thank God I hadn't lost my touch; I just knew this would be great. It was much better than a formal crew job and right up my street. It was more rock and roll and cool. I ran so fast back to Port Canto to tell all my friends I nearly fell over I was so excited. The camaraderie between us all was wonderful, they knew, as I did, that I was going to be around a lot longer. My plan and personal ultimatum to myself had worked yet again, that, plus a little bit of luck. I instantly felt different about my situation. My whole view of being here had been transformed.

Before meeting Hans I was starting to drift, one moment it was cool sleeping on the rocks and the next I was a bum. By changing my state I had changed my circumstances, it was remarkable. I now walked into Le Circle and felt very different. I was now on the inside looking out, rather than the other way around. My excitement was infectious and it made Graham determined to get a job, which he did, a few days later in the port of La Napoule further down the road. This was a great feeling, we were all getting it together and becoming part of the community living and working in the South of France.

The next day I packed my things and headed off for my new home on the Sirila. The sun shone as I skipped along the quayside, crisis had been averted and my adventure sustained.

CHAPTER 5

THE BARON

"You should wake up every morning as if it's on purpose."

Will Smith from 'Hitch'

Hans's boat was situated in the part of the old port called 'the graveyard,' I guess because that's where they put all the older boats whose owners were not exactly loaded. Interestingly we looked across the harbour to the other quay and this was full of the larger and more expensive crafts and had the name 'millionaire's row.' I was blissfully happy where I was because this side just felt more hip. The old port is not that big compared to Canto but fortunately it is situated right on the edge of the old town enabling me access to any of our regular haunts in seconds; a major advantage. The name old port is very apt, as a port of some kind has been situated at the base of Le Suquet for over 2000 years and now I took my place as the latest member of the Ligurian hordes. In those days they were desperately looking out for the Romans whereas these days I could spot the Armani brigade a mile away.

My first job was to wash down the boat; this involved positioning myself on the roof of the bridge with a hosepipe in hand. Whenever we returned from a trip I would stand there adopting a magnificent pose as if in total command of my vessel, so to speak. I have to admit I copied this attitude from a friend of John's who we noticed one day in the port. German, Italian, French, Spanish and all manner of international crew were gathered on the quayside chatting away when 'Russian Dave' appeared on the deck of a rather cool 110 foot cruiser. The strange thing about Russian Dave was that he was not Russian; he was in fact a Brit and a very proud one at that. One of the Italians calls out,

"Hey Davey, we go to the bar for dinner yeh?"

"I will join you scoundrels later."

"Come on," says another guy waving for him to join them. Dave begins to unravel the hose and climb high up onto the bridge. The guys all stop and look back,

"Davey the boat is clean, what are you doing?"

"I'm going to hose down the boat of course."

"But why you do that, it's clean and besides ze boat has not been out today." This was very odd behaviour, very few crew would ever clean a boat on a clear warm sunny day if it had not been out of the harbour and the owners not in town. Dave had no intention of listening to the minions below him as he stood, there legs apart and standing tall.

"You lot carry on I shall join you when this boat is spotless." They all stared incredulous at his thoroughness especially when he uttered the immortal line.

"*This!* he said with arms outstretched, "is a British boat … and that's why we won the war!"

John and I burst into laughter as the others just looked on in an even more bemused state than before.

What a great moment and with due deference to Russian Dave this was the stance I was now perfecting.

Hans recommended covering the boat thoroughly with a fine spray to begin with and then leaving it for a few minutes to let the salt crystals dissolve. Next, spray the whole boat with the high pressure hose. Salt is extremely corrosive on a boat and as Hans explained and no doubt Russian Dave would agree a boat that is washed down regularly and looked after properly with still look fantastic in years to come. I discovered very early on that there were two more advantages, one it kept me nice and cool at the end of a long hot day and two, it was a fantastic pose. Some people thought it was hard work; try commuting to work on a train for an hour in the pissing rain and then sitting in an office feeling all damp and wet whilst being bored out of your brains - that's work.

The Sirila was a 100 foot cruiser with a large aft deck and a partially covered area for dining. Several cabins and inner lounge area led to my quarters at the pointy end, they were quite small but I didn't share with anyone so I loved it. The forward deck outside was raised and flat and on this were placed an array of soft and luxurious deep blue custom made mattresses. It was very compact and easily maintained and though it was quite a few years old, it looked great. I was basically the only full time crew but from time to time Hans would have several old friends come on board to help out. One of these was a guy called Barry, a failed Captain, due to the fact that he was an alcoholic and two girls, American and French, Liz and Marie. Marie would cook if it was a large charter and Liz would assist and also translate. Why he needed a linguist I don't know because he spoke about five languages himself but they were all really nice and good fun so who cared.

I learned some time later that the boat was named after the three ex wives of the previous owner Gustav; they were, Siegfried, Rita and Lara and that the boat was left to Hans in Gustav's will. He must have been some friend because the boat was probably worth about half a million pounds. I also learnt that my friend Hans was in fact a Baron; he had never mentioned it as I think he was kind of embarrassed. I, of course, was not.

"Hey Hans, someone has told me that you are a Baron."

"Who told you that?" he snapped back in a very Germanic way.

"Oh, one of your many hangers on." I said with a smile.

"Yes, it's hereditary so it's really nothing to do with me."

"In that case you won't mind me addressing you as the Baron …. If it is nothing to do with you."

"Well I would prefer it if you didn't mention it all actually." And laughing I continued,

"The thing is Hans, where I come from, if a good friend asks you not to mention something - then you do it non-stop."

"Phil, what are you talking about?"

"It's an English thing Hans, it's called taking the piss. From now on I shall refer to you only as, the 'Baron.'

"If you do that, I will fire you," said Hans with a broad smile.

"Fair enough," I said apologetically, "I understand, in that case I will respect your privacy."

He could not believe it when on our very first charter as I welcomed the guest's on board the yacht I turned, held out my outstretched hand and announced,

"And **this,** ladies and gentleman is ... **the Baron**!" Hans just shook his head and told them that I was a fantasist and to ignore me. I loved it and I suspect he did too.

Most of the charters were day trips and on the free days I just hung out on board. On hot sunny mornings we would have breakfast on the stern of the boat and I would do bits of work during the day. Breakfast was the highlight of my day. I would awake in my little berth to hear the Baron pottering about at first light. I'd don a pair of swimming shorts and was instantly dressed, then I would clamber up a little ladder and come out through a hatch in the roof and end up on the floor of the upper deck. As I showered off with the hose on deck I would stare at all the state of the art yachts and sailing boats bobbing up and down in the harbour, set against the backdrop of the old crumbling town of Le Suquet. Every single morning it took my breath away and I was filled with gratitude just for this daily experience alone. Next I would make my way to the table and then prepare coffee, whilst the Baron would be off in search of croissants.

The fishing boats would return with their morning catch, their engines making a soft put put sound in the crisp morning air, accompanied by a lazy wave from the crew as they passed me by. I would holler out,

"Bonjour, vous avez bien fait?" – (You have done well?)

"Bonjour Monsieur, oui, pas mal." – (yes, not bad.)

I was acutely aware that this type of conversation had probably been going on for thousands of years, it was a humbling experience and sent tingles down my spine. I would close my eyes and lose myself in the moment before the Baron returned.

"Ah, I think the English sailor is lost in another world." He was back.

"Ah Baron, you are right and why not?" I said with a broad grin.

"True true, why not indeed." Hans was one chilled dude, he got it completely; I think that's why I liked the guy so much.

"Today we have to practice for tomorrow we have a charter."

"Sure, what do you have in mind?"

"You Phil, shall pilot the boat."

"Isn't that illegal, don't you need a licence?" I said thrilled with the prospect.

"Well I won't tell if you don't tell." He may have been pushing seventy years of age but he was still cool.

So life on board the Sirila was all very leisurely one minute then hectic and hard work the next, I loved the variety. Piloting the boat was a great buzz; we cast off and were out of the harbour in no time and just as we had with Fay and the gang, made for the islands. Hans explained about the various controls and the different buoys and flags and what they meant as regards navigation. In the clear blue ocean it all appeared relatively straightforward, apart from the odd idiot shooting past in a speedboat, some of whom clearly were not in control. I enjoyed every minute, mind you Hans made sure he was right next to me the whole time, just in case of problems.

On approaching the Islands he took over because there must have been about fifty boats converging on the small inlet between the two and therefore potentially hazardous. We had about fourteen people on board, including ourselves, as we dropped anchor adjacent to the Ile de St Honorat. A fabulous lunch was being prepared, so whilst waiting I swam to the island with a few of the girls. It was cool and clear and as peaceful as the last time; save for my argument with Fay of course. We sunbathed on the shore and yet despite a plethora of boats there still seemed to be nobody around. The island appeared to swallow them up, so after awhile I suggested we all go for a wander and a bit of intrepid exploration into the forest to find out what was going on.

"Phil where are you going?" hollered the boat Baron.

"Just going to have a look around, why, when is lunch ready?"

"About 5 minutes ago. I'll send the tender out to get you."

The tender was a small speedboat that we pulled behind the Sirila for occasions such as this. We all piled in and nearly sunk the thing.

"Hey Hans I'll swim back with Liz as there's too many of us." Hans clearly thought I was making a play for her but I wasn't, she just wasn't my type. I think she liked me but I found her too obvious and in no way sexy and I never, ever, went with a girl I didn't find sexy. I have always had certain standards and rules that mean something to me; not sexy, was one of them and a big arse, another. Later on she took the huff but, whatever.

As we were sitting down for lunch an enormous powerboat growled majestically into view, with a strikingly older woman piloting it all on her own. The Baron instantly went into action, I was impressed.

"Bonjour Madam, you have a beautiful craft. Would you like to tie up alongside?"

"Yeh, say, that's real friendly, thanks a lot." She was a yank, a very wealthy yank.

"Perhaps you would care to join us for lunch?" He was very good and very smooth, she didn't stand a chance.

"Sure, where y'all from?"

"I'm from England, I'm Phil and this is Liz, she's one of your lot from across the pond." I introduced everyone except Hans and then asked her name, I could see Hans thinking what's he up to?

"I am Julie."

"Pleased to meet you Julie, oh, I nearly forgot to introduce our host. This is 'Hans the Baron.'" Hans looked suitably embarrassed and Julie nearly wet herself and consequently came over all giddy,

"Oh, do I call you Sir or Baron or ..."

"Hans is fine, please take a seat next to me Julie, I don't want you sitting anywhere near Phil, my young friend is a complete embarrassment." He laughed, we both knew exactly what I was doing,

"Sorry Baron." I said in a pseudo apologetic manner. Instantly Hans picked up a bread roll and through it at me,

"Is he your son?" asked Julie in her now obvious Texan accent.

"God forbid," said Hans.

"Oh don't be like that Dad." Julie just didn't have a clue as Hans just shook his head in complete resignation. This entertaining banter continued on all through lunch but I always made sure that Hans looked good the whole time; she was hooked and so was he.

After lunch a few of us went out in the power-boat which had a deep blue hull and pristine white seats, when she hit the throttle it was both terrifying and exhilarating in equal measure. The beast flew out of the water and then smacked down hard in a continuous cycle of punishing thuds, I thought it was going to break apart as we raced across the bay. Julie assured me we were only going at half its capability; she was quite a lady, all I could say was *Shiiit!* - as my words took off behind me and disappeared into the spray. This was like a mad fairground ride but much worse, the sea became a blur as we took of even faster. Suddenly the boat did a quick shimmy as we hit the side of a wave and the engines growled in anger, instantly she pressed the throttle again and we were off. I really believed we were going to go over or rupture the hull or worse, I was hanging on for dear life, my belt dug into my chest as the G - forces pressed me back into the seat. I became even more concerned that my seafood lunch was about to make a dramatic return to the ocean at any moment. The day was boiling hot but we were now going so fast I felt freezing cold as the wind whipped into us, Hans shouted over.

"What do you think of her, Phil?"

"Bloody petrifying but the boat's quite nice."

"Ha ha" cried Hans, "faster Julie, faster." These oldies were nuts and for once I felt like the sensible one, what was going on?

"Guys, take it easy." I screamed. Thankfully after a few minutes more of this exhilarating madness she steered us back to the islands and the beast sank slowly into the water and glided back to the stately Sirila like a prowling tiger. What a relief.

"I must be getting old, that was scary." Hans and Julie laughed.

"Phil, we are going out again later, do you want to come?"

"No way. Listen, you guys deserve each other, you're both crazy - go break a leg."

My heart was still pounding five minutes later, it had been fun and an experience but I wouldn't be rushing back for the return trip. Actually what pleased me the most was to see Hans and Julie getting on so well, they both had the look of two people who really enjoyed each others company; I had a suspicion that we would be seeing a lot more of Julie over the coming weeks. In the early evening after she had left Hans invited me for a walk to show me the island. The serenity of the place was captivating; I never tired of it.

"Are you going to stay here after the summer?" I asked Hans.

"No, I will probably sell the boat, I adore it and I feel bad about it because Gustav was a good friend but I know he would have understood."

"So why sell?"

"The upkeep, boats just drain money away and there's always something going wrong or needs fixing, it never ends and as I told you I don't have the money of your average yacht owner."

"How long have you had it?"

"About three years. I have had a lot of fun but you know, things change." He seemed quite resigned to it but sad at the same time.

"And what about you Phil, how long are you going to travel?"

"Oh, I don't know, I am torn between doing this and being with Jane, my girlfriend, it's a real dilemma. I can't seem to square the circle between the two. Jane likes living in England but I find it too claustrophobic, it's hard to describe as there are a lot of good things about the place, my family and friends, the humour, it's just …"

"The weather?"

"Well yeh, obviously but its more than that. I find it lacks grace."

"What on earth do you mean by that?"

"I'm probably talking shit but to me it is very dour, you know, a bit grim."

"Maybe you just love the sunshine, that's why I left Germany." So he is a kraut after all, I thought to myself.

"Where were you born in Germany?"

"Oh I wasn't, I just lived there for a while, I am actually Austrian." (I know, I know, I'm a dickhead.)

"Do you have any family there?"

"No, unfortunately they have all died but you must have family in England?"

I could see it was quite painful for him to talk about it and as he was quite a proud man I thought it best to let it go. We continued on in our stroll through the glorious pines,

"Yes, I have always had a pretty close family and so that's why I could never leave England for good, not for the moment anyway. There's Jane and well, there you go. I thought maybe coming out here might straighten my head out but I think it's made me even more confused."

"Well if it makes you feel any better it doesn't necessarily get any easier as you get older. I mean you don't solve everything."

"Great, so I will probably always be a fuck up then?"

"Yes probably," he said with a smile "but the good news is that you just learn to accept things more, you will have had more of life's experiences and so you become a little more philosophical."

"Yes, you're right, maybe I just ask too many questions."

"That's youth. As you get older I think you just stop asking and become more contented with who you are and what you have."

"Do you mean instead of racing about, you sit and relax more and take it easy?"

"Yes, that's right"

"Like on the powerboat today?" I smiled.

"Ah, you have a point. Maybe I haven't quite grown up yet."

"Eureka!" I announced, "I have it. As you get older you must act a little younger and in your youth you must behave with more maturity. That's it, all life's problems solved on the Ile de St Honorat."

"Be careful Phil, a local monk might be hiding behind a tree and claim it was his idea based on years of meditation."

"Bastard!" I yelled.

We both laughed and continued on our walk along the various paths that criss-crossed the island. Passing by an old World War 2 battery that seemed to grow out of the foliage I asked Hans if he remembered much about the war. His demeanour shifted noticeably,

"No, I was living in America during the war so I had a very different perspective compared to most people."

"How do you mean?"

"Well, when Hitler annexed Austria in 1938

many of my countrymen appeared to support it but most just had no choice. I mean the rest of Europe just let it happen, probably thinking that it wasn't worth going to war over."

"Was that Mr Chamberlain and the other dick-heads?"

"An interesting turn of phrase Phil but yes, quite accurate."

Talking about the war and surveying this concrete mass at the same time was a little surreal. Hans continued, "My parents had suggested I go to America a few years before that as they could see which way the wind was blowing - even if nobody else could."

"It must have been a difficult time for them?"

"It was. The economy was in a terrible mess too but fortunately they were part of the lesser known European nobility so they had an opportunity to go to England, which they did just before the war broke out."

"So what was it like being in the USA in war-time?" I said as I climbed over the top of the bunker.

"Oh, I had a wonderful time, most of my countrymen were in New York but I took off for California within the first few weeks of arriving."

"God I would love to go to California, that must have been great?"

"It was and Phil I can categorically state that one day you will" he smiled warmly, "your wanderlust will take you there."

These words were more prophetic than I ever could have imagined but I still detected a hint of sadness. I pushed a bit more.

"So did you feel any guilt about what was happening in your homeland?"

Hans looked down at the hard rough ground beneath his feet "It is difficult to describe, my parents were safe and I felt largely impotent towards the whole thing going on in Austria. I was still a young man and I knew that one day I would return so I focused on my own life," he shrugged, "selfish perhaps but that was how I felt. It was only later that I learnt that I had lost some friends and that is when the guilt set in." He seemed to sink into himself,

"I can't say I understand because I would be lying. I have never lost anyone close to me."

"And Phil, I hope you never will." He looked up and smiled softly but he had tears in his eyes as he said, "Sometimes people are terribly cruel, it really is impossible to comprehend …" He gazed out to sea recalling memories from the past. I said nothing and let him have a moment. After a short while he straightened his posture and turned to me.

"Come, I think we should get back to the boat, we still have work to do."

A remarkable sunset was developing as we approached the harbour, the vivid red and burnt ochre combined to form shapes reminiscent of deep luxurious curtains, hanging in the sky, we all just stood there; it was truly breathtaking. As we approached our berth a small crowd had gathered to watch. I don't know why but they always did this, of course I didn't care because I loved having an audience. I carefully moved the tender to the front of the boat as Hans turned the vessel around. He dropped the anchor and reversed in and as we approached the quay. I threw out the guide ropes to the guys there and they secured them onto the dock. Captains and owners the world over always want this job done in a very smooth manner; it is a sort of ego thing. Pride in the crew and the professional way it's done is all part of the unwritten etiquette. I lowered the gang plank, checked it was secure and helped our guests off, I thought the day had been quite a success and happily so did Hans. I had received a small tip for all the hard endeavours of the day. All that eating, swimming, chatting and sunbathing really takes it out of you - so I strolled off to the bar to chill out for the evening.

On some days when it was quiet I would take off to visit friends; one day I met up with Graham in La Napoule. He mentioned that they had a large charter at the weekend and could I help out. I checked with Hans and he was cool as there was nothing going on. I earned £20 for my hard work and it was great to have a bit of cash for a change. On the way back I got a lift from a German guy in an immaculate Mercedes, which was a bit odd as you never got lifts in cars like this from middle aged businessmen. He was not gay, he just didn't fit the normal profile.

"Good afternoon. You are going to Cannes?" he commanded in a strong German accent.

"Yes, Colonel." I replied. Luckily he found this very amusing.

"Ha ha, you are a confident young man I see."

I shrugged. "I guess so. This is the most beautiful car I have ever been in in my life."

"Danke shoen."

"Bitte shoen."

"Ah you speak German?"

"Unfortunately not, you just got my entire vocabulary in one hit. I have to say it's a little unusual getting a lift in a car like this."

"Ah, I understand, normally the cars that stop are more scheisse, ya?"

"You said it. I'm Phil by the way."

He shook my hand and replied, "I am Walter, I always give lifts to hitchers when I can. When I was much younger I too used to do *ze* hitchhiking myself."

"Really?"

"Ya, so I know it can be very hard, so I decided when I was older I would give lifts to as many persons as I can." He was a funny bloke, very smart with specs and quite straight and cerebral.

"How long have you been doing this?"

"Oh, I only waited 15 minutes."

"Ha ha ha, no no, I meant how long have you been doing *ze* travelling?"

"Oh I see, about two months."

"Ah that is good but you have to be careful you know because if you do this for more than three years it is difficult to stop." He was quite serious. "It can be like a drug. I know many friends who still travel today and cannot stop."

"But, why?"

"They find it too hard to get back into the normal routine of life."

"What are you, a psychiatrist?" I said half joking.

"Yes."

"Oh I see, excuse me. I thought you were a nutter." He smiled,

"Well, we could debate that for hours but unfortunately we are nearly in Cannes."

We arrived near the old port, I thanked him for the ride and as I jumped out he shouted.

"Remember Phil … three years!"

It's a funny old world and although I had only met the guy for a few minutes I took on board what he had said. It was not so much what he said, more the way he said it, direct and completely serious. I made a mental note never to forget the advice.

One evening Hans asked if I was staying for dinner as he was having some friends over. This was a bit unusual because he had people for dinner all the time; he just loved playing the host, so I thought he was being polite and maybe he wanted me to disappear for the night.

"No no, I want you to join us."

"Oh I see, yep love to, who's coming?"

"Siegfried."

"What the Siegfried of the 'Si,' in Sirila?"

"Correct."

I could tell from his preparation that he had a lot of respect for this lady who, he explained, was from quite an old aristocratic family and it was important that I behaved accordingly. Luckily I had been brought up by my parents to treat everyone with the same courtesy - so consequently she had no chance. Hans really did push the proverbial boat out; candles were placed not only on the table but along the actual quayside and harbour wall. Crikey! I thought to myself, I had better put some pants on.

Siegfried arrived in a stunning, chauffeur driven Rolls Royce and as the car swept along the quayside you could just smell the money, I recalled the famous F. Scott Fitzgerald quote. "The very rich are different from you and me." It was all terribly grand and high society as the Baron welcomed her on board and led her onto the aft deck, she was about 65 years old but looked about 50. He introduced all the various guests to each other, Maurice and his wife, who were involved in the Film Festival and Bernard and his wife, who were antique specialist. There were other assorted luminaries of the Cannes scene, including two high society ladies aged about 60, who were both quite obviously gay. Hans had organised a top chef and waiters for the evening so I was there as a guest, which I thought was rather decent of him. Siegfried wafts straight over to me, "And you must be Philippe, one of our English cousins?"

"Enchante." I said as I kissed her outstretched hand - my mother would have been so proud. I could just make out the Baron out of the corner of my eye thinking, nice touch but what's he going to do next?

"I believe you are working with the Baron this

summer." What a lovely way of saying you work *for* someone without saying it, this lady was pure class. I beamed a smile back and said,

"That's correct; he of course was aware of the naval prowess of the British fleet and sent for my expertise." She smiled.

"Ah yes, the Baron also told me that you were full of *shit*!" I nearly choked on my hors d'oeuvres I laughed so hard, she was a scream.

"Baron, your young friend Philippe will sit here next to me so I can keep an eye on him, I wouldn't want him misbehaving in such distinguished company."

The ice had been very definitely broken and so I proceeded to misbehave all night. Maurice was quite an interesting guy but somehow I just didn't quite believe that he was as important as he made out. He had a plan to extend the Film Festival so that it would bring in more tourism and join up more to the other festivals during the year. I sort of got the impression that Siegfried and I were on the same page as regards Maurice; she said nothing because she was far too polite, it was just a hunch. Hans too was very entertaining, he had certainly seen it and done it in his life and I could tell that Siegfried adored him.

"You know Phil, Gunter and Hans were very close, like brothers really. My husband was the serious one who worked hard and Hans just made him laugh."

"I see, but if Gunter had three wives he couldn't have been working *all* the time?"

She smiled. "That's a good point but you see he was never at home and that's why the marriages didn't work. I was the last and the longest and we were very happy until he died."

"Still it was quite decent of him to put the names of all his wives on the boat."

"Not all Phil," she said shaking her head, "two of his wives were excluded!"

"Crikey, he was married five times!"

"Yes,"

"Well bravo Gunter. I think I shall propose a toast." I stood up raised a glass and said.

"To Gunter, his wives and all who have sailed in them."

Hans and Siegfried found this very amusing whilst the other guests looked on somewhat incredulous. Siegfried lent over to me and whispered softly, "I think Gunter would be very happy that you are helping the Baron, I know I am."

This was all going rather well and though I was not quite sure what I was doing with all this lot, it was good fun and on a warm summers evening in Cannes, a welcome change to my normal nightly pursuits. Hans came over to join us.

"Phil have I told you about the book I am writing."

"No."

"Ah yes Hans tell him," said Siegfried,

"It is about my grand theory of women and their place in the world."

"How do you mean?"

"I am developing a theory that women are stronger, emotionally and intellectually and therefore their approach to problems has more balance and strength than men."

"You could be right but I guess we have to see more women in power first before we know in practical terms whether that's true."

The conversation meandered along and to be fair to Hans, what appeared to be a novel idea at the time, has since, in many respects, been proven to be true. In those days there were very few women who held positions of power whereas today it is more commonplace.

Later on I chatted to the old lesbian lovers, which was a bit odd because one was pretty and terribly sweet whereas the other one quite simply resembled an East German shot put thrower. They were looking for a chauffeur and though I thought it might be a fun job for a while, I later rejected the idea. Of course if they had been 22 years old I would have done the job for nothing.

All in all it had been an interesting evening and as the guests were leaving Siggy, as I had now christened her, invited Hans, myself and some other guests to her house for a barbecue a few days later.

"Phil, I promise you there will be other young people there so you won't have to hang around with just ancient relics the whole time." I smiled and thanked her and then she added. "My daughter, by the way is 24 years old and very, very pretty,"

"Oh, great," I said enthusiastically.

"So I will make sure that she is at least thousand miles away that day."

I looked hurt, "Siggy why would you do such a cruel thing?"

She replied with a warm smile. "Because Phil, I have many faults but being stupid is not one of them." I kissed her goodbye and gave a little wave as her chariot glided away into the still night air.

The varied days on the boat rolled into each other and sometimes I had no idea what day it was, John would frequently come over and chat to Hans. He quite liked John because he often helped him when he had a problem with the engines or some other mechanical glitch. Hans was particularly impressed with his nautical knowledge. I remember a Captain on another boat telling me a story about John's staggering retention of maritime statistics.

"You know Phil everyone thinks he's crazy?"

"Yes."

"Well one day I was flicking through the list of International Maritime Signal Flags."

"Like you do." I said sarcastically. "What on earth is that?"

"It's a book which basically lists all the flags and their combinations; each flag represents a letter and has its own individual meaning. A combination of flags then carries another meaning for example, I require a tug or diver working underwater or medical assistance required."

"I get the picture; it's an international maritime

language."

"Exactly. Anyway, John and I were sitting there one afternoon and I asked him what a few of the combinations meant. I mean there are a myriad of different meanings and permutations and most Captains know the main ones and then look the rest up, that are more obscure or hardly ever used."

"Okay, so what are you getting at? I know. I bet John knew the most."

"No Phil your wrong."

"In what way?"

"He knew all of them!"

"All of them?"

"Yep,"

"Is that possible?"

"Well I have been in this profession for 25 years and I have never met anyone who knows *all* of them. I mean you don't need to but he didn't get a single one wrong, he knew them all. If that guy is crazy then I don't know what the rest of us are." It was just another example of the crazy man and his endearing enigma.

The next day we had a another charter to the islands, I loved it, although I was always surprised that nobody ever seemed to go anywhere else, I mean there was all the Mediterranean to choose from. This time when we stopped for lunch, John was there on the Willie (waving his flags around), together with another huge sailing yacht called the 'Tonga', which was fully computerised with every gadget under the sun. An American couple owned it and it was immaculate and though I know very little about these things I thought it was beautiful. Shortly after arriving Julie came powering around the headland in 'the beast', accompanied by a younger blonde American girl. I hollered over to John, "Is it me or is it raining Yanks today?"

"Phiwl, I think its 1945 all over again."

We spent the whole day ferrying different people between the various yachts for lunch and drinks and general messing about. Barry was the acting Captain on the Sirila that day as it was quite a big charter. My job, if you could call it that, was even easier, as I was more entertainments manager than anything else. There were yachts everywhere, I suppose this could only be described as the high life in the South of France and I was living it. The lines between who owned the boats and who didn't were so blurred that nobody cared; if you were there, then you were part of the scene. Maybe it's always been this way, I mean everyone brings something to the party. A yacht, a beautiful girl, money, entertainment, fine cuisine, power, fame, it doesn't really matter; even scintillating conversation as essentially all these things contribute to the occasion.

In my brief experience, in this supposedly rarefied atmosphere, I found there were probably two common denominators, one was money and the other was a desperate need to avoid boredom. With money it was possible to obtain most of the other ingredients but avoiding boredom and by default, having fun, was a slightly more esoteric need and therefore much more difficult to acquire. Maybe this is where people like Crazy John and I fitted in, who knows? All I do know is that if you didn't provide anything then you would soon be ruthlessly dispensed with. Luckily I was part of the scene for the time being and we all had a great day and though I experienced many, many days similar to this throughout the summer, I never took it for granted and was always grateful as I knew it wouldn't last forever.

I became quite friendly with Julie's young blonde friend, Sandy. She was slightly older than me and was just on holiday visiting her wealthy Aunt Julie. We hung out together quite a lot and although on one occasion we had a little dabble, we just sort of drifted into a friendship which I think we both preferred. She would talk of Sam, her boyfriend in the States and I would talk about Jane, it was actually quite comforting. Whenever I would have one of my 30 second snatched telephone calls, she would listen to me drone on and on about what an angel she was and I too, would be there for her.

One night we went to an incredibly expensive nightclub in Cannes, she paid £25 for both of us to get in. All I could see was a crowd of very sad old people desperately trying to be young again.

"Sandy, do you think we can ask for your money back? She laughed, "Phil you are terribly cruel, accurate but cruel."

"I know but why would you go to a nightclub when you're 60 years old, it's just sad."

"Maybe they're having fun."

"Nah, some old guy trying to pick up a young girl and failing 'cos he's old, well ... that's just sad."

"You will be that age one day."

"That's true but I would like to think that I could gracefully surrender the things of youth when the time comes."

"Ah, Desiderata. 'Go placidly amidst the noise and haste'"

"Exactly, come on let's split, I'd rather go for a walk on the beach than watch grandpa disco dance."

Another night, after a very long hot two day charter, we went to a party in an apartment in a large house in Cannes. It was pretty wild, so much so that half way through the evening someone fired a shotgun off at the house on account of the noise levels. This caused a bit of excitement for five minutes and then everyone carried on regardless. John, Sandy, Leo, Rob, Sarah, Nikki and all the usual suspects were there including two brothers who I had heard of but never met. No one ever told me their real names, they were just known to everyone as Pinky and Perky. They were gangsters or criminals of some description and were very relaxed about it, probably because they had never been caught. They openly declared that if there was anything anyone wanted, they could get it for them, they were sort of bespoke made to measure crooks. They actually would receive orders off people and then go and acquire it in their own inimitable fashion. I said to Leo, who didn't bullshit, "Are these guys for real?"

"Apparently. There's a famous story of some wealthy yacht owner in Cannes who wanted a specific speedboat as a tender for his yacht. He'd heard of Pinky and Perky and asked them to get him one as they were practically gold dust. I don't think the guy took them that seriously though. These boats were like £50,000 each and the brothers said they would acquire one for £25,000."

"Did he know they were crooks?"

"Well I would have thought it was obvious because they said they would get it, no questions asked."

"Anyway about a week later, one sunny morning, Pinky and Perky arrive into Port Canto with this magnificent brand new speedboat."

"What, you mean they had it hidden on a trailer?"

"No, they sailed it directly into the harbour, they had stolen it in Italy and sailed it all along the coast back to France."

"So what did the guy do?"

"Well he started getting cold feet and tried to renege on the deal."

"And?"

"Well put it this way, the guys got their £25000."

I decided at this point that although Pinky and Perky had fun names and were cool guys it might be best to not get over friendly. Sandy agreed and we called it a night.

The underside of the Cote d'Azur is almost never spoken about; crime here seems to take on a more sophisticated approach, much like the place itself. Apparently the mafia is rife but you never see anything, apart from the odd Mayor being done for fraud as a result of some building permit irregularities. Hand bags and the like do get stolen but it's all fairly low key and petty although there was one occasion which John told me about that was a little different. The story goes that a few years ago a guy was sitting on the back of his mega yacht having breakfast with his family and two guys appeared on a motorbike, stopped, walked up the gangplank, took out a pistol and shot him dead. I checked with a few other people and this frightening tale, bizarre as it sounds, was completely true. As I knew from my own little experience in St Raphael and John's gun experience outside the St Antoine, there is always a flip side to life, we all just find it easier to ignore it. On one occasion in Le Suquet I came across a tramp being beaten very badly by another bum down a side alley of the main road.

It was dark and very late at night and my gut instinct was to do what everyone else was doing and walk on by but as another kick was slammed into this guy's head I knew I had to act. I am a born coward and did not want to get involved in a fracas between two down and outs who could have had knives or anything but I just couldn't walk by. I thought he would stop as the guy was nearly unconscious and there was blood everywhere but he didn't. Some local women nearby were getting very upset and agitated and looked to me to do something. I thought what can I do? I am not exactly the heroic type. I pondered for a while and then decided the only thing I could do was to copy what I saw tough guys do in the movies. I had no other term of reference so that was that. I took a deep breath and as my adrenalin began pumping I attempted to take on the persona of a movie stereotype. I strode purposefully over and just at that moment the assailant spotted me in the corner of his eye, I instantly slammed my hand down on his shoulder hard, turned him around and then barked directly into his face, "Arret!" - "Stop!" He was so shocked and frightened by this aggressive nutter before him, he instantly shrugged his shoulders and began to move away. I yelled at him again "Fuck off!"- "Foutre le camp!" and waved him off in a manner that suggested that if he didn't go he would have had to deal with me. Luckily he was so surprised and drunk he just muttered something and slowly slinked off.

I have to say I was extremely relieved that he did, I shudder to think what would have happened if he'd called my bluff. The women then moved over and began to attend to the poor tramp's injuries, I had done my bit so I just wanted to leave but as I did so one of the older ladies just nodded and softly said "merci." And that was my little cameo performance in the seedy underworld of the Riviera and as far as I was concerned it would hopefully be my last.

Another scorching hot August weekend was fast approaching and Hans reminded me that we would be going to Siegfried's barbeque on Sunday.

"Phil, I have promised to take Sandy to Nice to get a new passport but I am too busy, could you take her in my car?"

"Of course. I didn't know you had a car here."

"Oh yes, I just keep it garaged most of the time. Here are the keys," he then gave me a very serious look, "and be careful."

"Okay okay, take it easy Hans, what is it a Bentley or something?"

"Yes"

"Oh," I said laughing, "right, will do."

A little later I picked Sandy up in the gleaming

Bentley and she just giggled,

"It suits you."

"Fits like a glove," I replied in feigned nonchalance and a regal wave of the hand.

I hadn't driven a car since I'd left England so it felt quite strange and I was understandably nervous at first. We glided along the Croisette in this amazing car past the Carlton Hotel and all the other chic Hotels, bars and restaurants, the palm trees canopying above our heads. It was the ultimate pose and I soon got into it and felt utterly relaxed.

Arriving in Nice we had to make our way to the consulate through the busy streets. The city of Nice is different to Cannes; it is a city on the sea and not a resort like Cannes. It has a definite working vibe, much more commercial and frenetic and is the official capital of the French Riviera. The sea has a startling azure colour, encompassing a majestic sweep around the bay; the whole place feels a bit more Italian and full of character, probably because it was part of Italy until the middle of the 19th century.

"Do you know Nice was believed to have been founded by the Greeks around 350 BC after a victory against the Ligurians, hence the name Nice," said Sandy surprisingly,

"Ah, don't tell me, it's derived from Nike as in Nikaia which is Greek for Victory."

"Very good Phil, I am impressed."

"Well I have just graduated in Classics," I shrugged, "hopefully I learnt something."

"It seems you did. I studied ancient history in

America."

"Ha ha, well you couldn't exactly study the ancient history *of* America could you."

"Don't be facetious." she laughed.

"I thought that was rather good. Anyway what is this? A game of what the fuck do you know?"

"Oh shut up, anyway where's the Consulate?"

"I believe it's over there," I said pointing, "adjacent to the ancient burial site."

"Just drive the car before I hit you."

Sandy was good fun and I was going to miss her when she went back. We had a lovely lunch and then later returned to the car and disaster.

"Oh shit!"

"What's the matter?"

"Look at the car."

"Oh fuck." Someone had reversed into the front of the car and damaged the bumper, this was an occupational hazard in France, their method of parking being to reverse until they hit the car behind. This is the reason why most cars in France are all bashed up one way or another. I was angry but actually I was really worried about Han's reaction.

"Listen don't worry," said Sandy, "maybe we can fix it. Let's ask Barry when we get back."

I hardly spoke during the drive home, I had really enjoyed the day and now I just felt shit. Barry, the alcoholic Captain was working on the boat when we got back to the Sirila, fortunately Hans had gone out.

"Barry look at this, look what I've done." By now I was getting a bit panicky. He sauntered down the gangplank as Barry never did anything quickly.

"Oh shit, you've had it now."

"I know, I know."

Barry took a long slow drag on his cigarette and then burst out laughing. I thought that's all we need,

"Have you been drinking?" said Sandy.

"That's a stupid question, I've always been drinking. You didn't check the car before you left did you?"

"What do you mean?"

"I mean you idiots, that bump has always been there."

"You're kidding?"

"Nope. I did it years ago and Hans never got it fixed, he reasoned that it was his token prang and if he left it he wouldn't get another and so far he hasn't ... I suppose he forgot to tell you." I was relieved, a bit annoyed that he hadn't mentioned it but mostly relieved.

I had been looking forward to going to Siegfried's barbecue for some time and finally Sunday arrived and a big group of us took off on the Sirila and headed west past Theoule. Then along the rugged seashore where the red rocks of the Esterel Massif dive dramatically into the sea. The waves lapped gently against the hull as the boat glided through the water as if somehow conscious of its illustrious destination. We dropped anchor a few miles past le Pointe de la Galere and then took the tender to the shore where stairs had been cut into the rock all the way up to her magnificent house and gardens. It really was beyond description; like a scene from a movie, stunning gardens, outstanding stone built villa, waiters in white coats and maids in black skirts and white crisp aprons. Music filled the air as a band played under the mimosa trees, a wild boar was being roasted on the spit and all manner delicious cuisine was laid out on the meticulous lawns. Siegfried approached.

"Ah Philippe come with me, I hope you like wild boar."

"Actually I am a vegetarian Siggy."

"No Phil you are a very naughty Englishman. Come."

I looked back over my shoulder to see the beautiful Mediterranean, arranged as if on purpose to compliment the day. It really was another world and I recalled Scott Fitzgerald (again), from 'This side of Paradise', describing an existence similar to Siegfried's.

'You will admit that if it was not life it was magnificent.'

Hans had introduced me to this remarkable reality and I was grateful to him for giving me a glimpse of a way of life that few people ever see or experience

Siegfried was a great lady and we all had a truly wonderful and unforgettable day. My life with Hans was far removed from what may be classed as normal and as we left I had a feeling that my time in this other universe was sadly drawing to a close.

It was the end of August and over the next few days

Barry and the others left. There was just the odd charter but it was generally quieter and I could see Hans was working up to giving me the bad news. I had been living the life of multi-millionaire all summer long but the reality was I had no real job and no money. Psychologically it became a little disturbing. The practical part of my day was fun but I felt a sense of disillusionment approaching as I suspected things may go downhill from here, if it meant leaving the Sirila.

I fully understood my arrangement with Hans, I had bed and board in exchange for the work I did but now it just didn't feel right as I realised Hans was keeping me on just because he was a nice guy. He had to consider what he would do for the winter as all the charters were now ending and I didn't want to overstay my welcome or abuse his hospitality. If I left it would mean literally living in squalor compared to the Sirila and a sense of desperation began to creep in.

At the end of another long day, whilst docking, John appeared and a few of us had dinner on board. It was a lovely evening but I felt the time had come to pack my bags.

"Hans, it's pretty quiet now so I was thinking of moving on; that's if you don't need me any more." I said half hoping he would ask me to stay.

"Well Phil I was going to mention it. I have had an offer for the boat and so I think I will take it and maybe go back to Austria."

Whether this was true or not it didn't matter, it was time to leave and we both knew it. The important thing was that we had great memories to take away with us and the next morning we said our goodbyes.

"Hans, thank you for this experience and your friendship."

"*Thank you Phil*. Good luck and say hello to California when you get there."

We both laughed. What a great guy. I walked down the quay as I'd done hundreds of times before, feeling a strange mixture of happiness and sadness. Unfortunately I never saw the Baron again.

CHAPTER 6

SLIP SLIDING AWAY

"If we don't change the direction we are going, we are likely to end up where we are headed."

Chinese Proverb.

La Rentree had begun, it was the end of August and the whole of France went home. It seems inconceivable to most people that an entire nation should return to work, all at the same time but they do. I had heard of it but never seen it; the cafes empty, the beaches lose at least two thirds of their sun worshippers and the traffic disappears from the town. Red days are declared on the roads to warn every one of the mass traffic jams they will encounter on the journey home. Ridiculous queues develop at the peages and service stations and the motorways are choc-o-block. Why do they do this? Bizarre, is the only word I can think of but if you speak to a Frenchman they think you're strange for not understanding it; to them it is just the normal way of things.

For a short while I felt pretty down after leaving Hans and the Sirila but soon after I became enthused with a new vigour. It was back to living on my wits again, I would survive. My time on the boat had been wonderful and those were the memories I clung too and would always cherish. Looking forward I would continue my journey in a positive state of mind. I had made some great friends and they were a tremendous source of encouragement and support. My number one problem was *money* or more importantly, the lack of it. I had the grand total of £12 left, which I suppose in some respects was not bad considering I had been away for over three months.

It was back to the rocks which, after my life of luxury, took a bit of adjusting to; it still felt cool and chilled out but only just. I had a limited time available to me and I knew it. Crazy John, Leo, Rob, Nikki, Mark, Graham, Sarah and all the rest helped out as much as they could. If the owners of the Willie were not around John would cook and we would have lunch or dinner on the back of the boat, Leo too would do his best. The rest of the time I lived on Pan Bagnats and meals in Le Circle. I was hardly slumming it as the sun shone everyday and there were always opportunities for fun and general silliness.

John really was an excellent chef and could concoct the most delicious dishes from next to nothing.

"What's on the menu tonight John?"

"Steak of the sea."

"What's that then?"

"Phiwl, do you know anything?" he chortled, "it's tuna."

"Never heard it called that before."

"Well tonight you have had an education." And so it was yet another revelation from John's galley kitchen. The only problem with his cooking was the mess; the kitchen resembled a battlefield of pots and pans, bowls and all manner of crap that I had to wash up. Don't get me wrong, that was the deal and fair enough but shit, it took me longer to clear up than it did for him to cook the meal.

"Phiwl, when an artist is at work, he is not interested in the state of his studio."

"Yes. But I am."

"Oh Fack off."

It was strange how one minute John would be producing Thai pasta or a delicate sea bass accompanied by a delicious sauce and the next, he would be found surfacing from under the boat with full diving gear on, goggles and a brush in his hand.

"John, what *are* you doing?"

"What does it look like I'm doing?"

"I have no idea; scraping off barnacles perhaps?"

"Got it in one Phiwl."

Now John in full diving gear is not a pretty sight, especially when he is covered in crap and smells of chemicals. It all looked a bit dangerous to me but he wouldn't hear of it.

"What's the matter with ya. I am only cleaning the boat's arse."

"Rather you than me and I hope you wash your hands before dinner."

Sometimes if the weather turned nasty, I would sleep in the crew cabin where it was lovely and warm but we had to be careful because if the owner found out John would have been fired. We had some good times and when the owner had to go back to Paris we could afford to be a bit more relaxed. I spent a great deal of time walking up and down the Croisette so at least I was fit and healthy and I was grateful for that.

We had plans to go to Greece as there was, allegedly, a whole scene going on in the winter but it was impossible for me to go anywhere without money. Things began to get more difficult and Jane and I would talk more frequently.

"Why don't you come home? What are you trying to prove, you've had a good time, what's the point in staying there?"

"I know, I know, you're right, I just feel I need to keep going, I don't know why."

"I miss you so much."

These words cut into me like a knife; Jane was an angel and I desperately wanted to see her but for some reason I pulled back. Practically it would have been so easy to stick out my thumb and head back but the thought of retracing my steps back to England and the depression I would feel on the journey home, just overwhelmed me completely - *I just could not do it.* When I called my mother it was the same thing, it felt like the easy option when in fact it was the opposite. The only person who said 'stay' was Bobby.

"It's crap here, wet and cold and the same old same old."

"But I miss Jane."

"I know you do you wanker but what the fuck

are you going to do here? If I could choose I would rather struggle where you are; who wants to struggle here, nothing's changed and the moment you get back it will feel like you've never been away."

"You're probably right." I said in a rather meek tone.

"Listen you tosser, everyone here wants to be there."

"I know. It is beautiful and fun here, it's just sometimes I feel, you know … second class."

"All your friends here think that what you're doing is romantic and exciting and it is, so don't let them down and don't let me down. You are living a dream that they would love to live but they haven't got the guts to do it. They won't give up their jobs and their cosy lives and take a chance; you did, so you must keep going and besides, I want to join you at some point so you've got to stay there."

"I know it's just sometimes I feel I should come back."

"Well come back then."

"And then other times I feel I should stay."

"Well stay then."

I could feel Bobby smiling down the phone at me, he knew me better than I knew myself, everything he said came from a good place. Anybody who has ever met him knows that Bobby is just a beautiful person and a gentle soul. I was very fortunate to have people who cared about me so much and I knew it.

Bobby was kindly putting me in my place, it was

great that he was giving me the flip side and it put into perspective what my life here represented compared to back home. I knew it couldn't all be fun and games. When I first arrived I never knew about the fantastic life I would live here but I suppose we all normalise even the amazing after a while. I decided to retrench and seek the positive and not allow myself to drift. I had to try to find work to sustain my time here and if not, then I would have to move on. To be honest I felt comfortable in Cannes, I had friends and I knew how to survive and how it all worked. To leave would be leaving all that was now familiar. These thoughts and mixed messages were crammed into my head it was driving me nuts and I desperately needed clarity.

The following day the sun shone brilliantly in the sky and this was my true nourishment, this is what kept me going; it was a drug like any other and I was hooked. I could not get off it and it was then the realisation hit me - I didn't want to get off it. I was an addict in the truest sense of the word and so too were a few of my friends who lived here. A sun junky, now there's a thought. At the bar that night I developed my theme with Leo. He pondered for awhile.

"Problem is Phil it sounds cool."

"Yeh, but isn't that what all junkies think." Rob came over to join us.

"Hey Rob,"

"What?"

"Phil thinks we're all junkies."

"Don't be ridiculous, none of us have that sort of weak mentality and lack of self control."

"Yes that's true."

"Anyway you haven't got a spliff have you, I am dying for a drink and Leo don't forget we're off to the Casino later." Rob then waddled off as if he was out of his head and we all just fell about laughing.

That night I met a girl who was married to a friend of the brother of an ex girlfriend of mine called Julie from England. It took several drinks and about an hour's conversation to work that one out and then she told me she had left him. This was all rather confusing to me but John and her seemed to hit it off instantly, which was great. They began a sort of relationship and they hung out together quite a bit, although John told me much later that the affair, "never got fully consummated." Whatever that means - C'est la vie.

I continued in my quest for work, people heard of jobs and then it all came to nothing in an ever depressing cycle. It was September 1st and the mood had changed. From one perspective it was more chilled out and relaxed but from another there were fewer opportunities as the tourists had left and jobs were now even harder to come by. Then disaster, the Saint Antoine closed temporarily, our watering hole, the centre of our social scene. What were we to do? This sounds quite trivial but it threw us completely. We dispersed to different bars, Le Vol au Vent and Le Cintra but they seemed to attract a slightly different element, bums basically. This association did not sit well with our motley crew and we became even more separated.

John and I began to notice a different type of person surfacing in and around town; the underbelly of society. When the sun shone, vibrant fun people were travelling through and it was great but now we were left with the residue as the tide had gone out and now the bums, buskers and alcoholics were all that remained. John got really pissed off with what he saw, he didn't like it and neither did I.

This was not what I had signed up for, it's not that I wasn't still having fun, it was just this creeping sense of impending doom. It's as if we were all putting off the inevitable and maybe we were, maybe we all do. The thoughts on life and where I was going filled my head. I knew nothing then of the unbelievable joy that was attainable and the unspeakable horrors that life had in store. I have always disagreed with the notion that 'youth is wasted on the young'; I believe it would be utterly wasted on the old, they wouldn't know what to do with it. They *would* know too much and *would* have all the answers, that's not being young it's the abject opposite. Youth *thinks* it knows and *thinks* it has the answers and that is its celebration.

Many times I would retreat back to the simple fun things of living here. Rob, Leo and I took out the tender on his yacht and attempted to water ski. The only problem was that it was underpowered and not fast enough and so consequently we all kept sinking. Water, spray and bodies were left flapping about in the middle of the ocean, accompanied by us laughing and yelping in imprudent idiocy. Our attempts were pathetic.

"Phil you're supposed to look cool." yelled Rob.

I am trying."

"Lift your arse up you look like a duck."

"That's because I am going about as fast as a fucking duck. Speed up a bit."

"We can't, we need to jettison some ballast." Said Leo.

"Then throw the fattest one over the side." I shouted. Leo and Rob looked at each other and both jumped out at exactly the same time, I laughed so hard I nearly drowned. All three of us were now in the water and the crappy dinghy was sailing on alone … and finally going fast enough.

"Okay guys, so what's the plan?" asked Rob.

Our situation was slightly awkward but as the dinghy slowed down we all began to swim back to it, giggling pathetically as we went.

And then suddenly!

"Ahoy. I am looking for three fackin' idiots who 'ave lost their boat."

It was of course the crazy man in a small sailing yacht coming to our rescue.

"Ha ha John, where have you been? We've been waiting here all day." I said as I jumped in with John. Slowly we pulled the dinghy back to the others.

"Hey John, let me try this."

"What, you're going to sail a yacht now are ya?"

"Well it can't be that hard it's only small with one sail."

"Yeh well, correct me if I'm wrong but didn't you just lose a fackin' dingy. Since when did you become Captain Ahab?"

You have to admit, he his hilarious. I took the sail boom line, held the tiller and off we went,

"Fuck me John, I'm a natural."

John shook his head and laughed. "I am not going to say it Phiwl but you are fackin' full of it."

That night a big crowd of us had dinner on Leo's boat the Audrey Elsa. Rob and Leo would constantly take the piss in crisp upper class English accents as they posed on the back of the yacht.

"I'm off to the Casino tonight."

"Really? Gonna work the tables' ya?"

"Of course, high roller suite."

"Biensur. Taking the Ferrari?"

"No,too gauche and you?"

"Monte Carlo darling."

"Really?"

"Yar."

"Fabulous."

"Yar."

And on and on they would go. It was on days like this that any thoughts of returning to England were a million miles away and yet the underclass still lurked. We had noticed that whilst we were all laughing and joking on the yacht the weirdos were watching from the rocks; which were of course where we slept. They quite obviously viewed us as the young, wealthy elite of Cannes and fair game. On the boat and on the quay all was fine but later when we went back to sleep they would probably presume we were being crazy and pretending to slum it with the poor people, not realising that we actually *were* the poor people. It was all too confusing and definitely too dangerous. Leo could tell that the girls were quite worried, so that night the whole lot of us took the coward's way out and slept on the boat – Fantastic.

Harold Robbins was a famous inhabitant of Cannes at the time and one night I met his secretary. She was blonde, sophisticated, had the ubiquitous little dog accessory and much more importantly, a fantastic arse. Her name, unfortunately, was Sharon and we hit it off instantly, so much so that when Leo and Sarah came over they didn't get a word in edgeways. As they walked off I heard Sarah say something like.

"Well Leo, we all know where that's going."

"Do you think she does?"

"Oh absolutely," replied Sarah.

Needless to say we had a real laugh together, she was punchy and confident and I loved the way she dressed. It very sexy and ... who am I kidding the simple truth was that it was just pure lust. We arranged to meet the following day and we bombed around Cannes in her little Mini. She had a friendly enthusiasm that I found beguiling and terribly sexy. She had many many stories about Harold and his lifestyle which quite simply were a pastiche of his books; drugs, women, gambling etc etc. I met him once and all I remember was this big hat that he wore and the fact that he was a bighead but Sharon liked him so fair enough. Besides, I was not interested in him; I just wanted the blonde with the great arse. The big night arrived.

"Listen, let's go back to John's boat, he's made himself scarce for the night."

"How romantic. Are you going to wine and dine me?" she said looking terribly coy.

"Nope."

"So what are you going do?"

"I am going to sing you a love song and then dance with you in the moonlight."

"Really," she said looking straight into me eyes, "I doubt that."

We both laughed and hit the bedroom in a swirl of pure naked lust and unadulterated passion. We both had a great time and I had certainly had no complaints … apart from one tiny little detail. On one occasion during the night, at a point of fevered excitement she suddenly started moaning, "explode baby explode" and then "shoot, shoot." The first time she said it, it was very sexy and a real turn on but then she said it again, "explode, explode." I felt like I was in a fucking war zone. I didn't know whether to keep going or dive for cover. After a while she calmed down a bit but as soon as her enthusiasm returned she was off again "shoot baby shoot." It slowly began to have the opposite effect on me as I suddenly had visions of Clint Eastwood walking through the door any second and it put me totally of my stride. However, I am happy to report that in the end I got it together, took aim and succeeded in wasting all the bad guys with just one single burst of fire. What a night and by sunrise I was tired, exhausted and completely out of ammunition.

I looked forward to seeing a lot more of her but unfortunately a few days later she had to go off with her boss in the big hat for a few weeks and by the time she returned my world had changed completely. Things were now changing for everyone as the reality of life after the summer began to set in. As Rob so succinctly put it,

"No job, no money, no stay in South of France."

And that was basically it in a nutshell. Rob himself took off to Draguinan to find work picking grapes. It was quite sad to see everyone leaving and it brought the reality home even more. Two days later he returned with no job and even less money.

"What happened?"

"Draguinan was a total fucking drag and completely lives up to its name. What a shit hole."

"Hey, maybe Leo's theory that no one is able to leave Cannes might be true."

"Yeh, yeh, you can check out anytime but ..."

The problem was he was happy to be back and we were glad he *was* back. No one wanted the status quo to change as we were all having too much fun.

Then, Leo's job finished and some of the girls who had been working as au pairs had to return to Paris or wherever their respective families lived. The feeling of it all ending was not only sad it was scary. Leo and Rob now moved into a van with no engine that had been left on the quay in the port. Apparently it had been attached in some way to Robert Stigwood's yacht and his entourage. It had its own history having been to Greece and all manner of places. It had bullet holes all along one side and stickers from Yugoslavia, Turkey, Spain; this van had been around. Later we were to discover that 'The Van', as it was now titled, was wanted in several countries by Interpol.

A friend of Harold Robbins, called Leslie Conn, had been put in touch with me by Sharon before she left, he said he had great job offer in Antibes. I set off with my ever present enthusiasm only to have my hopes dashed once again. Just a complete waste of time – he certainly lived up to his name. The slow slide to the exit door of my life here continued unabated, we were all hanging on.

Rob and Leo decide to head off to Italy and John, having finished his season on the Willie, was off to Greece with the non consummating girlfriend. My sadness was personified and then, out of the blue, salvation! "Phiwl, Phiwl, I have topped up."

"What John?"

"The owner of the Willie wants me to stay as guardian on his boat through the winter and I told him I can't 'cos I'm off to Greece and I suggested you and he said ... Alright!"

"Fucking hell John, that's fantastic, unbelievable, *incroyable!*"

"Mais vrais," said John.

True enough and it got better as the job paid £150 a month and I would live on the yacht, keep it clean and guard it through the whole winter. My ship had most definitely come in and just in the nick of time. As John, his chick, Rob and Leo were all leaving the following day and I had got this superb job, it was a great excuse for one big celebration. A huge crowd of us took

172

off to 'La Pizza', a well known Italian restaurant on the port. I was so excited and happy it was ridiculous, I just couldn't stop laughing. The wine and general bonhomie flowed all night and kicked off with the obvious Willie references.

"So Phil," Rob began, "the girls have told me you have an 80 foot Willie?"

"No its only 70 foot but it has a long pointy end."

"How often do you wash it?" asked Mark

"Once a day."

"I like a man who keeps a clean Willie" purred Sarah.

"Listen Sarah, whenever you would like a ride on it, just let me know."

"Is it difficult getting your Willie into its docking bay, considering its size?"

"No, it's easy as long as you have someone ready who can give you a gentle guiding hand."

That was pretty much the *thrust* of the evening and as we all discussed our plans for the future I felt a warm glow around the table of a celebration of the great summer we had all spent together. Although many of us were going our separate ways I knew that none of us would ever forget the time we had experienced. The festivities continued on late into the night and ended up at the St Antoine, that had just recently re-opened. I probably spent a little too much, we all did,but I figured as I now had a job, this was one occasion when it was worth it.

John and I slept on board and the next morning I moved all my stuff in. We were both a little hung over but later I got up and washed the boat down, ready to be introduced to the owners. Unusually it was a very dark overcast day but I had no idea it was a portent for disaster.

The owner arrived and John became involved in animated conversation. Something was up. After about 5 minutes John approached me with a long face, I don't think I had ever seen him like this, he could hardly get the words out.

"Phiwl, they've binned it."

"What do you mean?"

"Sorry mate but they've canned the whole idea for the winter."

"You mean there's no job."

"No, they're taking the boat out of the water for the winter and so they don't need a guardian."

I was devastated and so was John, I had never seen him so upset. I think he felt worse than I did and that was saying something. All he could say was "sorry." I told him it wasn't his fault - after all it was their boat. I took my stuff that I had just unpacked and repacked it all up again. I felt terrible, I thought well, that's it, I guess it's over. As I trudged off the boat and down onto the quay I felt a big whole opening up before me and I was staring into the abyss. John's *girlfriend* arrived as they were getting the 11 am train to Milan and had to go. I had no idea what I was going to do. Rob and Leo had already left, Nikki and some of the others were leaving too and here I was about to say good bye to John. To say I was at a low ebb would be the under statement of the year, we both felt dreadful. John and I were never male touchy feely people but we hugged and said goodbye. To say farewell would have been hard enough but in my current predicament and John's sense of responsibility it just exemplified it more. He put on a brave face.

"Listen Phiwl, they won't keep you down for long, you'll bounce back. You talk so much shit some fackin' idiot will believe you."

I nearly burst into tears for the way I felt, for the great times we'd had and for the losing of a good friend. I watched him walk down the road in that lolloping fashion I knew so well and tears finally did run down my face, as I stood on the harbour wall of Port Canto that cold wet Sunday morning. I would not see or hear from Crazy John for many years and when we did finally meet up again, my life was to have changed in ways that I would have thought unimaginable.

My spiral downhill continued at an ever quickening pace as I moved into the now vacant van. It was very grubby so I tidied and cleaned it up as best I could as the rain came lashing down outside. Christ I felt shit. I curled up into a foetal position feeling damp and cold, the grey skies outside the tiny back window just added to the malaise. Negativity built on depression that then looped back into the loneliness and hopelessness of my situation. I must have lain there crying nearly all day. Every time I tried to venture outside, the fierce winds and horrendous rain just forced me back into my little box. I was pissed off, wet and miserable. How different it would have been living on a beautiful yacht for the winter instead of inside this shitty disgusting wreck. I had imagined Jane coming to stay with me and how brilliant it would have been but now what should I do? This was not living; this was a tramp's life. Maybe on a cool beach in Hawaii surrounded by surfboards and sunshine this might be cool but in a crappy car park in France, hemmed in by the constant drizzle, it was not even funny.

The day dragged on into night and I let this pathetic mood of sentimentality, of feeling sorry for myself, wash over and through me like the waves crashing on the rocks outside. I never bury bad feelings I exorcise them, I guess it was how I was brought up. I was taught and encouraged to get things out in the open and to get rid of them, for if you keep them locked up inside and bury them, then your storing up real shit for the future. I believed one hundred percent in that philosophy then and I still do. There are too many fuck ups in this world as a result of the grin and bare it persuasion. I cried it all out and in the morning I felt much better.

Hitching to La Napoule that morning I went to see Mutley who was working on a boat, the Blinder. Over the next few days we had a few meals together and although I felt down, his laugh and the beautiful view of Cannes as the sun went down kept my spirits up briefly. But, I couldn't afford to phone home and so I slipped again into a mood of resignation. I kept trying to lift myself and every time I did I would hit a speed bump and fall back further, this was getting ridiculous.

The only people left in Cannes now were Sarah, Graham and Mark - he of the zero personality. One night I met two guys in the bar and one of them told me how he had been working on Robert Stigwood's yacht in Greece all summer and the charter had just ended. The irony of this was not lost on me.

"That's how I got into this mess in the first place." I joked.

One guy told me how he had been having problems with his girlfriend back home and how Barry Gibb's wife had lent him some money. It felt so bizarre meeting these people who had been working on the boat that I had been offered the job on, all those months ago. It gave my trip a peculiar symmetry and strangely enough a sort of closure on all of my journey so far. The other guy Terry, told me that a good place to get work was in the vendange in Bandol.

"What is the vendange?"

"Grape picking and Bandol is a famous wine growing region between Toulon and Marseilles about 100 miles west of St Tropez." As my options were zero, I thought that's it, time to get the old thumb out again. "I know this country" he said. "You will be picking grapes in Bandol tomorrow." He was amusing, a bit of a wanker, but amusing.

The sun burst through the window of the van the next morning, this was it, make or break. I left my bag in the van and decided on a very risky but unique option. It was quite a long way to Bandol so I took only my sleeping bag and a sweater wrapped up inside it. I took a piece of cord threaded it through the bag and slung it over my shoulder. This would free me up and make it easier for me to get around rather than carting a heavy rucksack. The only problem with this plan was that I had no back up stuff if I got into difficulties. I was comparing myself in my mind to 'free climbers' who drop everything and go for the mountain summit in one hit; my vivid imagination was spurring me on, what the fuck, I literally had nothing to lose.

I had £3 left.

Out went the thumb of fortune and I was off. I felt fantastic. I had cleared up all the baggage in my head and all bad thoughts had been dispelled. I had no idea what the day would bring but I sensed something in the air and as I could not take my music it was down to singing to myself - always a superb option.

Taking off in the direction of Brignoles I got a lift in minutes, it seemed I hadn't lost my touch and I was brimming with confidence. I began to realise that I had probably become quite lazy in Cannes; it had been lots of fun but too easy. I knew it, but it's always hard to give up on a good thing. Anyway now I was striking out again and all those feelings I had when I first left England of hope and expectation came flooding back. I was back in the groove, the sense of freedom returned and I felt liberated once more. This was a new page and a new chapter and as I walked along the roads the songs burst out of me, Joni, Marvin, Stevie; I was in my own Hollywood musical.

Arriving in Brignoles I asked around but although it is regarded as the centre of the Cote de Provence wines it felt too big and impersonal and I really didn't know where to start and besides it was too early for the vendange so I just kept going. I took off south in the direction Rocbaron just because it sounded dramatic and anyway I was enjoying myself just being on the roads and pathways. The dappled sun filtering through the trees reminded me of those early days in

France and I was energized once more.

Singing at the top of my voice when a car stopped to offer me a lift, they could hardly believe it when I declined their generosity. I explained that I felt contented just walking along the road and was in no hurry. The young couple inside just nodded and smiled with approval at my utterly cool approach to hitchhiking and for that tiny little moment, I was free again.

This feeling of personal liberation continued and as I sauntered along I refused to let it go, it was intoxicating. Later, I stopped and just listened to the sounds of the birds and a distant tractor working the fields lying on the grass that was warm and soft to the touch. It is times like these that are precious beyond compare but, time always moves on and when the moment had passed, I accepted my next lift with grace. It was a Volvo and was driven by a guy called Claude who was a psychiatrist.

I smiled, "You're the second shrink I've met in the past two weeks."

"Maybe it's a sign," he replied in perfect English.

"What, that I am a potential nutter?"

"Well, let's look at the word 'potential' and the word 'nutter'."

"Ha ha, good point."

We talked of my trip, my plans for the future and more importantly my plan for today. It was all very loose as he was quite a relaxed dude. I stared out of the window as the car raced along through the forests and fields as we continued south to Bandol.

"What will you do if you don't find work?"

"Then I suppose my options will be somewhat limited."

"To say the least," he replied.

"I just feel something will turn up."

"That's interesting and does it normally?" he said with a tiny hint of scepticism.

"Yes, usually. I mean you never know but when I am positive, things happen."

"Your experience feeds the attitude that you already have and the cycle continues."

"Yes, I like that, it sounds cool and that reinforcement helps me grow I guess."

"Ah, the path to self knowledge."

"That's me, a Socrates man," I said with a smile … "never really into Plato and his stupid cave."

"I see, so you have just taken one of mankind's greatest thinkers and one of **the** great philosophical ideas of the last 2,500 years and wiped it out in two words."

"Yes, well there you go, as Socrates said, 'I know nothing'."

He laughed, amused at the hitcher with the limited self knowledge. He was a fascinating guy and talked a lot of sense rather than the usual French bollocks. Claude and I stopped at a little café and ate a *salade du chef*. He insisted on paying, which was just as well, otherwise the hitcher and the shrink would have been washing the dishes. When we arrived in Toulon he kindly drove me through it and dropped me off on the other side of town and put me on the road to Bandol.

"Good luck my young friend. I feel good fortune is coming your way." My God, I thought to myself, two hours with a Gaelic shrink and we're all thinking happy thoughts, with so many positive waves, how can I fail?

I walked all the way to Bandol as unfortunately no ride materialised and my first surprise was that it was on the coast and I was pretty sure you don't grow grape vines on the beach. I was confused as Bandol was apparently a well known wine region with a reputation for very high quality wine; I didn't get it, where were the vineyards?

I continued on through this rather shabby little coastal town until the road literally stopped. I was in a car park and could go no further save for a small hut and a guy selling hot dogs. Right, I mused, so this is it! I have travelled all day with a fantastic attitude to arrive at a crappy hot dog stall at the end of a road that goes to nowhere. I turned to the only source of information available – 'Mr Hot Dog.'

"Bonjour Monsieur, ou sont les vignobles?"

He shrugged (of course) and then proceeded to explain that the vineyards were a few miles inland and not actually in Bandol itself. Oh shit, it was getting late and to hitch inland to find work at this time was not exactly what the doctor ordered. A lady nearby explained that all the wines from all the seven surrounding villages are called Bandol because years ago its tiny port was used to ship the wine overseas hence, wine from Bandol. I was most grateful for this spectacular piece of information and at a loss about what to do. I resigned myself to my fate and ordered a hot dog, a basket of French fries and a bottle of Coca Cola. I gave him the last coins I had left in the world and he graciously gave me an extra hot dog and that, as they say, was that. It was one of the finest meals I have ever had, probably because I thought that I may ever eat again.

My life had come to this moment, no food, no money, no home, no job and family and friends a thousand miles away with no possible way of being able to contact them. This was one hell of a slippery slope. I remembered a Bruce Springsteen interview when discussing his songs and the fact that many of them had the recurring theme of taking off and driving to the edge of town and freedom. As he explained, the only problem with this ideal is some times there's nothing there and you have to turn around and go back, it isn't romantic, it's just life. The strangest thing was I didn't feel down or depressed, I was just pragmatic and rather amused. Maybe it was the first stages of delirium setting in but I just thought, oh well, fuck it. I considered my situation as I sat there casting my eyes over the ocean, the sun having already disappeared from view. I had a lot to be grateful for; my health, my family and friends, Jane, my charm, wit, intelligence and overall good looks – come to think of it maybe it was delirium after all.

Once again I resigned myself to my fate, I could sleep on the beach which would be a little chilly or I could have one last attempt of finding something. I had no idea where to go, they just said 'inland'. I retraced my steps about half a mile down the coast back through the town and passing by the bustling cafés as the light began to fade, a sign appeared directing me to La Cadiere. This was one of the villages mentioned by the lady and Mr Hot Dog and so I swung inland.

After a short while I crossed the entrance to the autoroute and another dilemma. Do I take the tiny country road to nowhere or the grand freeway to Marseilles? As I stood there a pristine Mercedes with a really friendly couple pulled over and offered me a ride to the city, I chatted to them explaining my predicament. Their car was a very comforting option, offering a pleasant leisurely two hour drive with lovely people in the fading evening light.

"I do not think you will find work here at this time of the day, why not come to Marseilles with us, it is a big city with many more opportunities?"

"I know, it's just that I made a commitment to myself that I would find work here and (I had decided) that's what I must do. Thank you for your help."

"Okay, bonne chance et bon courage." As the car sped off and all fell still around me I instantly thought, 'Come back!'

I trudged off down the road into the gathering gloom without a clue about where I was headed or what I was actually going to do. There was a cool dampness hanging in the air and it was all beginning to feel a bit unreal as the road vanished into a long tunnel of dark foreboding trees, with no light and not a soul around. What on earth was I thinking?

Life can often throw up the unexpected in the strangest ways and at the most unusual times. I walked for about half a mile and then just as darkness fell a small white car appeared out of the gloom and gradually slowed down along side me; a door tentatively opened. I had

no idea that another page of my life had just been
turned.

CHAPTER 7

DOMINIQUE

"You just picked up a hitcher a prisoner of the white lines on the freeway."

From 'Coyote' by Joni Mitchell.

The first thing I noticed as the door opened was a tiny auburn haired daschund that wagged his tail before jumping onto the lap of the driver. A beautifully tanned slim French girl with short fair hair and a gorgeous smile leaned over and asked, "Vous allez ou?" Wow, was my initial response but as this was a lousy answer to the question just posed I summoned up my best French,

"Bonsoir, je vais La Cadiere, pour le vendange."

She smiled again, "You are English?" Fantastic, I thought to myself, she speaks English and with a very cute and sexy accent.

"Yes, I am looking for work but I don't really know where to go or who to ask."

"I live in La Cadiere and I know many farmers who own vineyards, jump in and I will take you." I was in the car before she'd finished speaking,

"I am Phil and you are?"

"My name is Dominique."

She wore a long floral summer dress and was barefoot; she was your original bohemian chic before the term had ever been invented. I knew instantly that she was cool, as any young woman prepared to pick up a strange guy at night on a country road had to be, either that or she was a complete nutter. She had an easy confidence and was very sure of herself but was in no way conceited. I felt relaxed as we drove along and so did her dog who jumped on my lap and snuggled into my arms.

"Pillule likes you."

"I'm sorry, what did you call him?"

She laughed, "Pillule, that's his name, he's a *varry* good judge of character, he does not like everybody." I loved the way she spoke, her English was excellent but occasionally she would over pronounce the odd word and it just made me laugh.

"'Ave I said something funny."

"No no it's your accent, It's very, er ... cool."

"Oh, merci." She betrayed no hint of embarrassment. "So have you picked grapes before?"

"No, it will be my first time."

"It is *varry* hard work, you have to have lots of *energie* you know?" She threw her head back and laughed and as we sped through the vineyards that I could just make out at the side of the road, I thought shit, what a babe. Unusually for me I was very polite and not my normal cheeky self, I don't know why, I think I was so grateful for the lift I just didn't want to fuck it up. She told me that she had been on the beach as she always went at sundown and I asked her why?

"Because I *lurve* the quiet at that time of the day. It is magical."

"Yes it is very peaceful." Fucking hell, I sounded really boring, this was ridiculous, 'she's going to drop you off in a minute dickhead, get with the program or she'll be gone.' I spoke too soon as suddenly the car stopped on the brow of a tiny country lane,

"Try asking at this farm here, he has many fields," she said pointing to her left.

"Thank you for your help, do you know the guy's name?"

"Yes, they call him Monsieur Maurice." I got out and closed the door desperate not to lose this gorgeous gift but what could I do. I heard dogs barking and the house looked quite spooky in the half light,

"I hope his dogs don't bite." I said pathetically. She smiled,

"Don't worry about his dogs; he's more likely to shoot you at this time of night."

"Shit, maybe I should forget this entire vendange thing, it sounds a bit dodgy."

She laughed, "What is dodgy?"

"Well in this case; life threatening!"

She laughed again, "I think you should go and try and if you survive, come and see me and let me know what happened."

"Where do you live?"

"There," she now pointed to her right and I

could just make out a stone built farmhouse nestling below a vineyard on the slope of the hill.

"Okay, see you later."

Her wheels spun on the rough gravel as she drove off into the darkness.

Tentatively I began walking up to the drive to Mr Maurice's house and knocked on the imposing front door. I heard the clang of bolts slide as he shouted, "Qui est la?" Fuck me, I was crapping myself. A typical French farmer, the type I have seen in every French movie ever made opened the door. He wore an old vest, dirty pants was nearly bald and had a fag hanging out the corner of his mouth. It was obvious from the aroma wafting through the house that dinner was about to be served and if I know anything about the French, a strange guy knocking on the door after dark at supper time and asking for a job has got, as Crazy John would have put it "two chances, Bob hope and no hope." Three huge black dogs came to join him at the door. "Arretez!" He commanded as he held them back. The least I could do was to make an attempt,

"Bonsoir Monsieur, avez vous travail pour le vendange?"– Which I hoped meant do you have any work for the grape picking?

"Non. Deux semaines."

He was clearly a man of few words because he then promptly closed the door. Wandering back down the track in the pitch black was easier said than done but finally I reached the road and without hesitation made my way down to Dominique's. It was very dark as I picked my way along the rough cobbled driveway eventually reaching another imposing front door. I banged on it and Pillule started yapping but nobody answered. I banged again and then I heard a voice shout, "Allo. Qui est la?"

"Hi, it's me, the grape picker. Where are you?"

"I'm here, at the window." She was standing a few yards along inside the house and looking out through the bars of an open kitchen window. I walked along and began chatting to her through the thick iron bars. I smirked,

"Oh, that's where you're hiding." She didn't smile and I knew instantly why. It was obvious she was alone and although she had been all chilled in the car she had clearly had time for a rethink, after all, it was late and I was a total stranger, I understood her caution.

"How did it go?"

"He said to come back in two weeks … at least I think that's what he said." She smiled and I thought well, that's a start. It was clear that I had to kick into gear big time if I wanted this state of affairs to go any where.

"What are you going to do?"

"Well I don't know; maybe go back to Cannes where I have been working all summer and then perhaps come back."

"What were you doing in Cannes?" She was being polite so I just kept talking. I told her of my trip and some of the people I had met and as she listened I got the impression she was sort of weighing me up. As we talked she seemed to soften a bit and then suddenly a hairy something appeared by my feet.

"Shit what's that!" I said as I jumped back.

She burst out laughing. "It's Pillule he has gone through the flap cat."

"You mean the cat flap."

"Excuse me, my English is not very good but I think it is better than your French, no?"

I agreed, "Absolument." She smiled again.

I picked him up and stroked him, "come here you little sausage."

"Ha ha, why do you call him a sausage?"

"Because he looks like one."

"I see, so first you insult my English and now you insult my *darg*."

"Yes, well, English grape pickers are like that, it's how we roll."

She laughed again, "It is how you roll?"

"Yep." I had been standing outside now for about twenty minutes and we were just reaching that impasse of what happens next when Pillule started shivering. "I think your sausage wants to come inside."

"Mm … I wonder if he will come in without you," she said being ever so slightly coy,

"Nah, I doubt it, especially if I am holding him by his balls."

Dominique now screeched with laughter and the door slowly opened.

She was gorgeous.

"If I let you in will you be nice to me and my *darg*?"

"Well if you make me a cup of tea I'll even be nice to your cats."

"Why, what is wrong with my cats?"

"Nothing, I just hate cats."

She laughed again and as she closed the door I remembered what my friend J.C, used to say, "Take every ball on the rise Phil." Well this ball was starting to rise and I was definitely going to take it.

We sat down in the most idyllic kitchen imaginable with its solid stone walls and old fashioned cooking hearth. A large pine table dominated the room above thick stone slabs placed in patterns on the floor. In one corner a staircase wound its way upstairs, this too was stone but extraordinarily worn down and smooth, it must have been there for centuries. The thick walls were quite plain and in parts the faded plaster was peeling off but in a way that looked like it was meant too. There was a dresser and several chairs that were beautifully decorated with delicate patterns and pictures in soft pastel hues. I could hear the faint sounds of a Crosby, Stills and Nash harmony floating in from another room. What a place.

"I love your house and the way your furniture is decorated is fabulous."

"Do you like it?"

"Yes, very much."

"This is good because I painted it all myself, it is my work."

"You are an artist?"

"Yes"

This was beginning to sound a little unreal; a beautiful French artist picks me up and invites me in to her idyllic farmhouse set amongst the vineyards of Provence, in a minute she was going to tell me she was single.

"I hope you don't mind me asking this but is there a man of the house?"

"Yes of course," my heart sank, "Pillule." She smiled and ran her fingers through her hair, then she got up and walked barefoot across the kitchen floor and slowly poured me a cup of herbal tea as she shooed away the cat. Dominique was without exception the coolest chick I had ever met; it seemed inconceivable to me that she didn't have guys crawling all over the place.

"My lover and I parted a few months ago. I like my time alone for now I am free, I can be myself. I have my animals, my work, my 'ouse and my friends; for now I am happy. I always know that another lover will come, so I adore the space between love."

"I love the way you say that, only a French girl can say that she loves the space between love ... it's very beautiful."

She dipped her head towards me and said softly. "Merci Pheel."

I had never heard so much bollocks in my entire life but she was a babe so she could say whatever she wanted. At one point as she moved across the kitchen her dress brushed past me and I felt a frisson of excitement. "I hope you won't mind me saying this but you smell fabulous." It was a bit risky and a bit forward bearing in mind the delicate balance of the situation but it was the truth so I didn't care.

"Merci, it is a parfume that a friend of mine makes in Grasse it is not Chanel but it is from flowerrs that are similar and that have a comparable aroma." Dominique had a fabulous grace in that she combined sophistication with a sort of hippy style and confidence all wrapped up as one.

It was getting late, and then without warning she said, "If you would like to stay I have a spare *rooom* in the attic." Though somewhat surprised by the offer I replied calmly,

"Merci, that's very kind of you."

She invited me in a very matter of fact way with no edge to it at all and so I replied in exactly the same manner. Dominique seemed a few years older than me and she knew herself very well and she had obviously decided that although I was a complete stranger it was safe to let me stay in her house. I admired her coolness and her poise. The bedroom was plain with a low ceiling and two small windows with closed painted shutters along one side and the bed had soft clean sheets and delicate squashy pillows. There was a lamp and nothing else. She closed my door and said good night, I thanked her again and she replied, "de rien – it's nothing."

I lay there in complete darkness as my eyes closed on another remarkable day, if I had made this up no one would have believed me - come to think of it I could hardly believe it myself.

I only knew it was morning because of the knock at my

door; the room was still quite dark due to the heavy shutters. She just walked straight in and opened them up; the room was instantly bathed in sunlight. Pillule waddled in and jumped on my bed very excited to see me, I smothered him with affection; I may have many faults but (to copy Siggy's line) being stupid is not one of them. Without any hesitation at all Dominique then moseyed over and sat down on the end of my bed, this was some wake up call. She dipped her head to one side and then slowly ran her fingers through her hair.

"I am going out to get some croissants and will be back in 5 minutes, why don't you take a shower and I will join you outside on the terrasse. Please would you make me a coffee for when I return?"

"Sure, do you want to leave Pillule with me?"

She grinned, "I don't think I have a choice." As she walked out of the room in her pale pink blouse and tight blue jeans, two things popped into my head; she was even cooler than I thought and what an incredible arse.

After showering I ventured downstairs and poured her a coffee from one of those inexplicable machines that all French people possess – have they not heard of Nescafe? I then walked outside and sat down at a table that was just casually placed on a floor of uneven but smooth cobbled stones and then I turned to look back at the house. The first two words that came out of my mouth were, fuck me! And idyllic was the third. It was the most beautiful house I have ever seen in my life and remains so to this day. It was only two storeys high but elongated; some of the walls were covered in peeling plaster and some in stone. Jasmine climbed all over the walls and framed the windows and doors. Large white stone blocks ran along the base of the wall and these were covered with an array of pots bursting with geraniums and summer pansies. Only French houses in places like Provence can have old scruffy shutters that look just perfect and all the windows had them. At either end of the main living space were several barns. One of them I could tell, even from the outside, was her studio. More low barns stretched to the west of the house and they contained an old tractor and other assorted rustic objects that had been there for years. The rough courtyard was beautifully unkempt save for more flowers and pots, stone benches and low walls. I just loved the way the fields of vineyards grew nearly up to her door with no fencing or hedges at all. I surveyed the area around the house and all I could see were miles and miles of low rolling hills covered in vines.

I had no idea the night before of the scene that was to greet my eyes on that fabulous morning. If ever a house matched the person living in it, this was it. Dominique's house was spectacular and restrained in equal measure and I adored it, it was perfect. The aromas bursting from all the nature around me, the distant sounds of tractors in the fields and the skylarks overhead were just intoxicating. By the time she returned I was in a misty haze; she'd only been gone five minutes and I had already moved in. Her little white Mini tore its way up the driveway and swung round to stop right next to me. She smiled, "You seem to have made yourself comfortable."

"Well it's not difficult, I don't know which is more beautiful, your house, your garden or ..." I looked directly at her and paused, "your dog." I smiled as she looked straight back at me,

"I am very lucky, I have many beautiful things in my life."

This woman was unfazeable, she knew exactly who she was and what she wanted, this was a challenge. Passing her the coffee I said, "I 'm afraid your café, il est un peu froid."

She giggled and said, "I like your accent, did you know it is very sexy when an Englishman tries to speak French."

"I didn't, I wish I had known that years ago. It is also very sexy when a French girl speaks English you know."

"Then we must both be careful who we talk to in future."

"Oui, we would not want to give anyone the l' impression false."

"You mean *fausse*, a false impression" she said laughing.

As we sat there eating breakfast she told me about her life in Provence, her paintings, the local farmers, her friends and the village of La Cadiere that she adored.

"I have never been to La Cadiere."

"Then you will come shopping with me later."

"Well if you insist." I said.

"I do but you cannot wear those trousers."

"Excuse me, you want me to remove my pants?" she beamed a little smile at me,

"Yes you 'ave a big hole in the back."

"Where?" I stood up and as I did she lent over and gently touched my bum.

"There."

"What do you have in mind?"

"I have some, how do you say, dun-garrees that I think will fit you."

She walked off into the house and returned with a rather cool set of dungaree jeans. "Try these on." And so I did, right in front of her and she didn't bat an eyelid.

"Parfait" I said as I stood up and shoved my hands in the pockets.

"Yes you look very cool in those."

"That's amazing really, I mean you French girls … I've known you less than 24 hours and you have already had my pants off."

We both laughed, that's what I liked about her the most, she was cool and yet she could laugh easily. She then showed me her studio and her paintings and explained how a colleague of hers would acquire the furniture, then another friend would prep it and she would then paint it with her various designs. Many of her clients would provide her with their own pieces which she would decorate according to their requests. I think she made a decent living because she was obviously well known and well respected as clients came from all over Europe.

Later on we drove the short ride up to the beautiful medieval village of La Cadiere, one of the seven villages that is part of the Bandol wine region. The village is perched on the top of a hill with majestic views over the fields below and on the opposite hill sits the other village of Le Castellet. Truly stunning and completely unspoilt; we wandered through the tiny streets laden with the slow passage of time. I sensed a few of the locals wondering who this guy was with the fabulous Dominique; she sensed it too.

"I think some of my village friends are intrigued by this new stranger." she said as we passed a busy local café.

"I know, I wonder if I will pass the test."

"It doesn't matter what they think ...." she paused and smiled, "it only matters what I think."

I returned her gaze, "And what *do* you think?" She stopped at an open fruit stand and carefully placed some fresh tomatoes in a bag, paused and smiled,

"I think you are, how you say, dodji."

"Moi?" I feigned surprise and then laughed, "I thought you said last night you didn't know what dodgy meant."

"Maybe I am learning."

I shrugged, "Well at least your dog likes me. I think I'll run away with Pillule."

"It would never work with Pillule because he is a male and I think very much that you like the girls."

"I don't like any girls, I am very particular." I said as we sat down in the café under the shade of a leafy platane tree.

"So what type of girls do you like?" she said warming to the theme.

"Well it depends, I'm not keen on French girls with short blonde hair and I really don't like girls who are artistic and cool and beautiful."

She butted in, "who have dogs and cats."

"That's right; don't like them at all."

She giggled and then leaned forward, "And I don't like English guys who are dodji."

"Well it's a good thing there's none of them around then."

She sipped her coffee and gave me a lovely smile, "So, would you like to stay tonight for dinner?"

"Love to."

As we walked back to the car I gently put one arm around her waist as I opened the car door with the other. She turned. "Merci Philippe, I didn't know you were a gentleman."

"De rien Dominique, it is how you say … mon plaisir."

The warm breeze filtered through the car windows as we raced through fields and forests. September is a glorious month in Provence, the crowds have gone and it's warm but not stifling hot. We drove around the stunning vineyards and everywhere we went people would wave or shout "Bonjour Dominique, ca va," she would peep her horn and wave back. I was captivated by her life and the pastoral nature of her existence.

"You are very lucky to live in such an amazing place, I love the calm, I love the serenity, I love it all."

"Maybe this is how you should live."

"Was that an invitation?" I pondered.

"I would love to but reality tells me I need to find some work first."

"If you like I will ask Monsieur Maurice again and see if he definitely wants you to start in two weeks. If that's what you think he said."

"That would be brilliant, I would love to live and work here. Of course it would mean that you might be seeing me around a lot more."

"Pillule would like that," she smiled "... and so would I."

This was the very first time that despite all our joking around she had lowered her guard and said something more serious, 'and so would I' was a big statement. I felt a frisson of excitement as she stopped the car at a fabulous viewpoint point across the valley. The tranquility and silence were in stark contrast to the pheromones that were now firing of between us. The tension was quite unbearable as we both stepped out of the car to gaze at the panorama below us. Turning towards me she fixed her eyes on mine, "Do you like what you see?" I put my arms around her waist, drew her close to me and kissing her gently replied,

"Don't be ridiculous."

Slowly she looked up at me "I thought you didn't like French girls."

"Sorry, I lied."

I don't remember the drive back to her house as we just seemed to arrive there. I took her hand as we climbed the stone steps to her bedroom. The lacy curtains billowed in the breeze and the warm afternoon sun washed over us as we lay down on her bed of pure white silk sheets. I imagined I was appearing in some typically romantic French art house movie as she kissed me softly and whispered something beautiful in French. Dominique by her very nature was a romantic free spirit and I felt myself falling into a trance as I lost all awareness of time and place. It was quite an afternoon.

Later on, as we lay in each others arms, I surfaced from the fantasy. She kissed me gently her soft skin rubbing against my cheek,

"Wait here, mon coeur, I have to shower."

I thought to myself, "Honey, right now a herd of wild horses could not drag me out of this bed." I watched her walk slowly cross the room, she had such a delicate figure that belied her strong will and yet complemented her artistic nature. This was going to get complicated.

The beauty of youth is, amongst other things its complete lack of responsibility and no cares for the future; I thought only of the moment. There were no distractions, there were no mobile phones or internet; there was just the moment. The feelings I experienced were real and present and totally self-centered. Life had not delivered its flip side to me yet and if truth be told at twenty four years of age and in my present circumstances I never even knew a flip side existed. This was another world and right now I wanted to stay there. I listened to her singing happily in the bathroom some typical French melody. Her hair was wet when she returned and her beautiful soft suntan glistened as she smoothed almond oil all over body. I patiently waited until she had finished and then dragged her back onto the bed.

"Pheel, no, no, my hair is wet."

"Sorry, can't understand a word your saying."

Over the next two days we had a great time together, meeting some of her friends and visiting her favourite haunts on the beaches she loved. She taught me that the secret to having a fabulous tan was to sunbathe between six and eight in the afternoon as the rays didn't burn and as she looked fantastic I accepted her word for it completely. Together we went back to see Monsieur Maurice and firmed up my job for the vendange, the moment he knew I was with Dominique I was instantly accepted. It turned out that he was a really nice guy, a typical rustic rural French farmer, who dressed like a peasant, lived like a country yokel, talked like a man without any education and owned land and vineyards worth millions. He was great, he loved to laugh and I could tell that he and his wife were really hard workers. The vendange was due to start in two weeks and on the drive back home I said to Dominique, "This is going to be hard work but a lot of fun."

"Yes and by the time you have finished you will be very healthy and very strong and verry tired at night."

"I know, that's a good point. In that case we better get back to your place whilst I've still got some energy left."

After two days I now had a severe clothes problem and I had to return to Cannes to get my stuff. Dominique had been really helpful and her friends lent me shirts and stuff but I had to get organized. At dinner that night we discussed my trip,

"Why don't you take my car?"

No, that would be great but you need it for your work. I'll hitch."

"How long will you be gone?"

"Only two days, unless I get picked up by a beautiful French artist."

She smiled, "And how do I know that you will come back to me?"

I leaned over to her, poured her a glass of wine and whispered, "Because I am in love … with your dog."

"I am now jealous of Pillule," she said in mock anger.

"Well, he is beautiful."

Dominique suddenly came over all serious, "Do you know something?"

"What?"

"I have picked up one or two hitchhikers in the day before but never as late as that night I met you."

I smiled, "Really? I thought you were a regular hiker fucker."

"You know that's not funny. I have never done anything like that before." I could see she was on the verge of being offended.

"Listen I'm sorry. You saved my life that night and I am happy and grateful that you did … but then why did you pick me up?" I poured her a glass of wine and began stroking Pillule who just lay there in heaven.

"I don't know, it was just spur of moment thing but I noticed the hole in your pants and it made me laugh. It gave me the impression that you were a guy who didn't care and I think it was, how you say? … cool."

"Well let's drink to my pants," I said and she laughed.

"How come you let me into your house to stay the night; that's *really* unusual?

"Because I could tell you were a nice guy …" and interrupting her.

"And you already new I had a nice bum."

"Exactly."

And then, pausing for a moment I asked, "Are you okay with me living here with you during the vendange?"

She lent over and gently stroked my hand, "I want you to live wiz me," then she kissed me. When a gorgeous French girl says that, in a voice like that, then there's only one thing to do. Dinner was over.

The next morning Dominique took me to the peage only yards from where we had met.

"Will you call me?"

"You know I will, take care - and stop picking up strange men at the side of the road!"

She laughed and drove off and fortunately within minutes I had a lift. I looked out of the window as we drove east and reflected on the past few days, what a strange bizarre turn of events. I was actually quite exhausted and at one point nodded off in the car, luckily my companion didn't mind as he listened to the radio most of the way and later, after some good rides, I arrived back in Cannes. It was late afternoon as I made my way back to the mystery van. It felt so weird. In just over 48 hours my life had changed out of all recognition, the transformation in my circumstances had been quite incredible. As I walked into the St Antoine that evening the first person who noticed me was the lovely Sarah, "The prodigal returns. So where have you been?" she asked as if addressing a naughty schoolboy.

"Well you're not going to believe this but I met this girl and …"

"Don't say anything, Mark. What did I say? What did I say?"

Mark replied in a dead pan voice, "Well everyone was wondering what had happened to you, and Sarah said, 'he probably got picked up by a French chick knowing Phil.'

Sarah laughed; unfortunately Mark had not been successful in developing a personality whilst I was away and as my eyes darted around the bar a couple of familiar faces were smiling across at me and I just burst out laughing. One of them stands up and shouts; "You pommes are *awrite*, you got everything, you're educated, you drink piss, you're *awrite*." It was, of course, Rob and Leo,

"I thought you two had buggered off to Italy."

Rob minces over doing his gay Frenchman routine and we all just pissed ourselves laughing, "I take great exception to the word buggered." It was great to see them both,

"Hey Leo your Cannes theory is holding up ... everyone keeps coming back!"

"Told you."

Apparently they had arrived in Milan and after ogling the Italian babes all day, got bored and headed straight back. Graham joined us a little later as I was recounting my short but eventful trip and when I'd finished Rob asked,

"Phil, tell us about the almond oil thing again and this time can you add a little more graphic detail."

Sarah slapped his arm, "Rob don't be disgusting. Phil is a gentleman; he'll do no such thing."

"Thank you Sarah, you're quite right. So anyway guys I am lying there and ..." Laughter followed for the rest of the evening and when I returned to the van I packed my stuff ready for the morning. Rob and Leo came over first thing as I ceremoniously handed the keys back to them,

"Good luck, I hope you're both very happy together."

"Thank you, we love you too, now fuck off back to your French *loverrrrr*." said Rob.

It had been great fun seeing everyone again and it was such a positive way to leave Cannes compared to the last time. Just before departing I made a quick call to Dominique to let her know the score, she seemed really happy to hear from me. As I picked up my things by the harbour wall a guy who was quite clearly a yank, asked me for a light.

"Gotta light fella?

"Sorry no don't smoke. The fags are just for effect." - Now he was a confused yank.

"Excuse me did you just say you are a fag for effect."

"Ha ha, that's very good, no, 'fags' are cigarettes. I guess you thought I was talking about our gay friends."

"Your gay friends!" The poor guy was becoming more baffled by the minute.

"Look I'm sorry, let's start again. My name is Phil, I am not gay, but I do have friends who are gay, I do not smoke, I just carry cigarettes to look cool.

"Oh I get it, sorry man. I'm Barry," he said laughing.

The first thing I noticed was his moustache and long dark hair, he looked like your typical ex-hippy from circa 1967 and as it turned out, that's exactly what he was. He asked me about the van and what I was doing in Cannes and whilst chatting he found his lighter and lit his cigarette. "Light up and live, man." he said as he drew the smoke into his lungs in a long slow motion savouring every ounce of the nicotine. As he did this his head tilted back and his eyes closed, then carefully, as his head rocked forward smoke blew from his lips like steam from a kettle; he turned to me and smiled. I stood there utterly mesmerized by this simple devouring of a cigarette.

"Looks like you enjoyed that." I said stating the obvious.

"You got it man."

"So, what are you up to in France?"

"I am building an extension on a house for an old friend of mine near Entrecasteaux," he said with a laconic Californian drawl.

"Sounds pretty cool, how long have you been doing that?"

"Couple a months."

"How long will it take to finish."

"Couple a weeks"

"I see you're a man of few words" and laughing he replied,

"Yeh man I guess so, anyways, I thought I'd come down here and take a day off, visit the ocean. How about you, you gonna split from here?"

"Yeh, actually I'm just about to hitchhike my way back to Bandol."

"Well if you want I can give you a lift to Brignoles. I guess it's about half way."

"Cool 'preciate it." I said adopting his Californian speech with consummate ease. On approaching the car we passed a payphone. I stopped and called Jane, we spoke for seconds and I melted; she was so lovely. Driving out of Cannes I was disgusted with myself, I was disgusted with what I had done and with what I was about to do. It's as if I was covering both options but with one gigantic difference, I *knew* how I felt about Jane right down to the core of my being and yet for some inexplicable reason I was still on my way to Dominique's.

"You okay man?"

"Yeh, cool."

I didn't know Barry well enough to have this type of discussion; apart from Jane, the only person I could speak to was Bobby. Feeling distinctly uncomfortable with myself I did something I never do - I buried it. This would return and when it did the hole would be deeper and much harder to clamber out of. This was my sin.

Barry chatted away about his life and his project at a place called Les Bregieres near Entrecasteaux. An ex-hippy friend of his had asked him to finish some work that had been started but never completed. To say that he had lived an interesting life would be an understatement; he had some strange ideas and some compelling theories concerning subjects as diverse as world monetary control, Roswell and Kennedy.

"Ever heard of the twelve guys who control the world?"

"The what?"

"Sure. There's these guys who get together and determine the politics, power and wealth of nations."

"Really?"

"Yeh there's a lot of shit going on that we just don't get to hear about."

"What, do you mean things like the Bilderberg group and Prince Bernard and all that?"

"Hey Phil I'm impressed. You know about those guys then?"

"Well not really, I mean does anyone know

what they do?"

"Exactly that's my point." he said staring straight back at me, "They sit around behind close doors and determine the world's fate and we know nothing."

"But I thought there were more than twelve of them?"

"Sure there are … look I'm not saying it is them or a splinter part of a similar group, but it ain't right whoever they are."

I guess Barry was about 32 years old, deeply political and suspicious of many of the world's powers. Maybe it was a leftover from the sixties thing. He wasn't a nutcase, he was colourful. I liked him. As we drove along some pretty profound ideologies were being discussed, our conversations ranged all over the place, they were both stimulating and illuminating in equal measure and half way through our journey he suddenly said "fuck it" and decided on a rather large detour that took us all the way back to Dominique's. We arrived in mid afternoon with nobody home; he dropped me off.

"Hey Phil I don't know if your interested but I may have a week's work at Les Bregieres and I could use some help to finish it."

"That's a great idea, the vendange doesn't start for another two weeks so it could fit in really well."

"Fantastic, I'll call ya."

"You got it Barry." To be honest I didn't expect to hear from him again.

Outside the house I lay for about an hour in the long parched grass, the dry heat parched my throat as I waited nervously for the return of L'artiste Francaise.

Eventually the car arrived in the ubiquitous cloud of dust, opening the door she stepped out and sauntered over, Pillule charged ahead of her, leapt on top of me and tried to shag my brains out. I detected just a slight sense of hesitation in her eyes; after all we had only known each other two days. Somehow I felt we had to re-engage once more.

"I'm sorry Pillule, I just don't fancy guys, you're a dog and I'm an Englishman, it would never work. It's over between us, I'm sorry I have another lover."

"And who is this other *loverr*?"

"Some French chick." I said tilting my head up towards hers. She smiled, knelt down on the grass next to me, stroked my cheek, and kissing me softly said,

"Tu m'es revenu mon coeur" – "You've come back to me my love."

It really is the most beautifully romantic language and it hooked me again as her perfume drifted through the air. I followed it all the way up to her bedroom, to her white silken sheets, to her soft sensual touch and I was lost in the fantasy once more.

Sometime later when the mist had cleared, we lay there in the late afternoon sun that was now bathing the bedroom in a deep golden glow,

"Do all French girls welcome their men home this way?"

"Only the ones who are in lurve." I said nothing; this was becoming more complicated by the minute. "I have a gift for you." She leant over and gave me a striking necklace of vivid blue glass beads and stones. "It is Moroccan, they have a tradition; a woman gives this to her man as a symbol of her love for him."

"And what does he give her in return?"

She paused ..."His lurve."

The next few days were a carbon copy of our first but more so. If I loved her existence before, then this was another level, even the mundane became an adventure, a trip to the store or helping her deliver some paintings was for me a unique and exciting activity. I would sometimes go for a run along the dusty country lanes near her house and every now and then just stop and marvel at the beauty of the place. One lazy afternoon she called me, "Pheel, I have a surprise for you."

"Can't wait , shall we go upstairs now?"

"No, it is in the garden."

We walked through a small clump of trees and nestled in the shade was a large cream hammock scattered with soft cushions.

"You've bought a hammock?" I said with undisguised enthusiasm. She smiled and went inside to grab the stereo and a bottle of wine whilst I shooed away the cat that had taken up residence. We both lay there as she played some Crosby, Stills and Nash, the sound of 'Guinevere' and 'Déjà vu' swirled around as she made love to me in the dappled afternoon shade. The tranquility of yet another serene afternoon consumed me once more.

"I want to play you something else" she said softly.

"Well as long as I don't have to make love to that as well. I'm exhausted."

"No, I will leave you on your own."

I had absolutely no idea what she was talking about but Dominique did. I lay there looking up through the trees to the clear blue sky, and with Pillule sitting close by I could just hear the faint sounds of a chaffinch calling in the distance and the smell of Dominique's enduring fragrance. The scene was set for an epiphany that I did not know was coming and as I sank into the cushions I perceived the distant sound of people clapping and an American voice saying "Who? Who … Joni Mitchell, alright." A guitar began to play and Joni sang.

"No regrets coyote we just come from such different sets of circumstance."

To people who love Joni Mitchell it is inconceivable for them to understand anyone who doesn't. I knew most of her work but for whatever reason I had never heard this song before. It was a live version of the song 'Coyote' from the movie 'The Last Waltz.' The simple metaphor that ran through the song is of the Coyote as a ladies man who is addicted to the road and the life that brings.

"That Coyote's at my door, he pins me in a corner and he won't take, 'No!'"

The fluid base and Joni's heartfelt and soulful singing conjured up that feeling of the freedom of the road whilst the descriptive lyrics suggested an obsession that neither Joni nor the hitcher can escape from.

"I tried to run away myself to run away and wrestle with my ego."

The haunting melody and visceral words flowed over and through me; she was describing my very existence at that exact moment in my life.

"Now he's got a woman at home, he's got another woman down the hall and he seems to want me anyway."

I imagined myself drifting off across the fields whilst still lying in the hammock secretly observing the coyote's movement and listening to the enticing metaphor of the song.

"He went running through the whisker wheat, chasing some prize down."

Joni continued to weave her story and with increasing depth she captured a time and a feeling that seemed to relate only to myself. When she finally came to the chorus, tears were already running down my face.

"You just picked up a hitcher a prisoner of the white lines on the freeway."

Not wanting this sensation to end, I played it over and over. I became addicted to the song as well as its message but unlike a normal dependence it fed and nourished my soul leaving me in a state of complete harmony with myself and the environment. Music has always had the power to cross time and space; this song has lived with me ever since and each time I hear it, I am back in that hammock on that blissful day, reliving a singular moment of pure happiness.

That night to my surprise Barry called, he had six days work that paid £75 including food and lodgings for the week. He could pick me up tomorrow if I was up for it. Dominique and I discussed it and we both agreed it was a good idea. I needed the money, the vendange was still about 8 to 10 days away, and she had a lot of work to catch up on, "I do no work when you are here," she smiled.

"I know but I feel I have only arrived and now I am off again."

"No, it is good because I know you will come back and now I have some space to myself and I will be excited and look forward to when you return." Concise and to the point I thought.

The next day Barry arrived in his pick up truck, I kissed Dominique goodbye and the prisoner of the white line vanished once more down the freeway.

CHAPTER 8

RICHARD NIXON SAVED MY LIFE

"I had these Hare Krishna's staying at my house but I had to sack them, they were very nice gentle people but they kept going around saying 'peace' all the time, it was driving me mad. I couldn't get any fucking peace."

John Lennon.

After my experience of the day before I felt utterly complete and 'in the zone', this time may never come again I would embrace it and go for whatever emotion or experience came along ... *Carpe Diem*.

As we sped along the stunning countryside Barry and I picked up on the conversations from our last journey together. Although clearly a bit loopy he had an intellect not dissimilar to Crazy John's in that he was well read and incisive however there were two obvious differences, primarily he was a Yank and secondly he was an ex-hippy. This made him a rather unique individual, especially to me ... Mr Naïve.

"Do you know Barry I've never met an ex-hippy before ... aren't you supposed to be all strung out and fucked?"

"Hey Phil don't knock it till you've tried it."

"I mean how did you ever come to be building this house in France?"

"It's like I told ya, I got this wealthy friend from back in the Sixties and he asked me to come on over and help finish the job," said Barry with one hand on the wheel and the other looking for his cigarette pack in his shirt pocket, "I guess he fell out with the locals … I mean the house is wacky … too much LSD man," he said smiling.

"So are we staying at the house?"

"Shit no, they're all fucking weirdos. A guy I met when I first got here said I could live at his house and kind of look after it for him …" He lit up a cigarette and did his now customary full inhaling routine. "Apparently he's on British TV show."

"Really."

"Yeh … Monty Python."

I guffawed loudly, "Monty Python? What's his name?"

"Eric. Eric Idle, yeh that's the guy I think."

"Shit, he's like a comic God in England," I said with no hint of understatement.

"Well I ain't ever heard of him but he seemed a pretty regular guy, you know."

So now I was on my way to build a weird house, full of nutters, accompanied by a mad hippy who was living with a crazy comedian … having just waved fare-well to a love struck French artist amongst the grape vines of Provence - commuting to an office in the city, it was not. Barry blasted music from his radio and sang at the top of his voice whenever he heard a favourite song. Bob Dylan's 'Like a rolling stone' came on and the roof nearly flew off the car.

We were now in deepest rural France. Arriving at Eric's house was not quite what I expected. Firstly it was literally in the middle of nowhere and secondly there was no road.

"You know Barry this looks just like a dry river-bed." I said pondering the mini ravine located beneath the truck.

"That's because it is man."

"What happens when it rains?"

"Fuck knows," he said throwing his head back in wild laughter.

The truck then snarled at us somewhat annoyed at having to attempt this daily climb up a steep rocky and heavily rutted track. Barry's 'truck' was a work of art, filthy inside, filthy outside, bashed up with bits falling off, the perfect builder's wagon. It was so old it was like something from 'The Grapes of Wrath.' He wrestled with the gears as I got thrown from side to side resembling heavy turbulence at 30,000 feet *and* with Led Zepp's 'Black Dog' on the box at the same time - Jesus!

Finally Eric's *palatial* house hove into view.

"Is that it?" I said motioning to the half built Algerian ruin – (It's a Python thing).

"Yeh ... pretty cool, huh."

"Well no offence but it's a little basic."

"That's *nuttin*, it's got no electricity either."

"Fuck!"

"Yeh man, we got a gas cooker, a weird old gas light thing and a box of candles."

"Groovy." I said.

Actually it just appeared to be unlived in, I mean Eric wasn't there at the time, he was off shooting a movie but I got the impression that Eric wasn't there ever. It was quite small, old and scruffy with only one bedroom in the main house; at least I think it was a bedroom. Adjacent to it was a crappy outhouse, as Barry called it, with more rooms and a pool that resembled a swamp or maybe it was a swamp. The tiles on the patio were all smashed and broken with wild grass and weeds invading every orifice. "You can sleep in the outhouse or crash in the lounge on a mattress."

My idea of how the other half live was somewhat shattered, I guess Eric was a creative type and just went there to hang out, write and get away from it all – anyway it was still a dump but 'beggars' and all that. To be fair, it had a killer view that snaked down to a long valley of trees running away into the distance. I looked into the crumbling outhouse and thought; no thanks, I'll sleep in the lounge.

"Looks a bit grubby in there." I said pulling a face.

"It was good enough for Ronnie Wood and the Rolling Stones when they stayed," he said laughing.

"Yeh well they're Rock stars and all drugged out like you so they were probably tripping on LSD and imagined it was Indian ashram."

At this Barry burst into raucous laughter, stuck

a fag in his mouth and the top of his voice shouted his personal mantra.

"Light up and live man. Yeh! mind altering drugs, rock and roll man. Yeh!"

A few reservations about what exactly I was doing here began to creep in, I liked Barry but this had the potential to turn out a bit weird. I decided to give him the benefit of the doubt for now.

Despite the limited facilities he prepared an excellent dinner and then later before crashing out on the floor I ventured outside to gaze up at the night sky. Unencumbered from city lights or civilisation the sky was bursting with a billion points of light, the Milky Way resembling a thick fog that dissected the heavens. It was magnificent and truly awe inspiring. I stood there for quite a time after Barry had retired for the night. Such a spectacle stimulated my brain and put me in a reflective mood as I made a wish at every shooting star I encountered - and there were many that night. At first there was a sense of release from where and who I was. Mankind has for thousands of years pondered every thought that I held about the cosmos, there was nothing original in my head save for the simple fact that they were my reflections alone. I know everyone imagines the child of the Universe thing, who and what we are and why but that night I felt a deeper malaise. For some inexplicable reason my feelings of wonder distorted into feelings of pure terror as I became frightened, anxious and scared. I recalled Wordsworth's Prelude as he rowed, terrified, across the lake.

No familiar shapes remained ...

> But huge and mighty forms that do not live
>
> Like living men, moved slowly through the mind
>
> By day, and were a trouble to my dreams.

I had read these words years before but only now did I empathise as I hurried back into the house and closed the door. An eerie silence descended and I lay there until the early hours when finally tiredness took over and gratefully I fell asleep. This was not a good start and a complete turn a round to the day before when I had been so at peace but I had decided to seize the day and experience 'whatever emotion came along'. I suppose in my enthusiasm I overlooked the possibility of any negative connotation.

Barry arose early and for a laid back hippy was keen to get started; I was impressed. Morning had chased away the negatives and I jumped into the truck feeling very much the local artisan, when in fact I was a builder's mate; still, it made me feel cool. Arriving at Les Bregieres was somewhat surreal; various people just seemed to drift in and out. The house, if you can call it that, was an exotic mishmash of styles and ages of construction from classic stone Provencal to post modern ultra weirdness. Rooms had been built extending along a ridge, the only entrance being a ladder and then next to this was a sweeping stone staircase that went three floors up to master bedroom. Lounges, terraces and bizarre tunnels would connect the house parts together. The walls were decorated in eccentric patterns of inlaid coloured glass and opposite these were stark plain white walls and entrances with no doors. Barry's description of the house being wacky was spot on as I had no idea where it ended or began; it just went on and on and appeared to be growing of its own free will.

"So Barry what's the deal here, it's nuts. Have they got planning permission for all this?"

"I told you Phil, too much LSD," he said rolling his eyes like a spaced out hippy.

"You are dead right there."

"What exactly, are we here to build?"

We walked or rather climbed to the far side of the house, the hippy and his mate. Barry stopped and stood there pointing to a large two storey building and close by a group of white stuccoed oval rooms.

"We've got to connect that to that with a wall and then build a reinforced two storey tower between the two which will contain the bathroom."

"Whatever you say boss."

We began by moving stones and boulders as Barry pointed out the parts he'd already constructed, it was hard heavy work but it was in the sunshine and he was interesting company. The first morning flew by and at lunchtime we stopped for sandwiches that he'd prepared that morning. Various members of the household breezed over from time to time to look at the work. Barry explained that they were extremely wealthy but with a totally dysfunctional set up.

"Barry who's who in this house … I don't get it?" He took a deep breath and began,

"Phil pay attention. There is the husband Dave,

the guy I know, his wife and three kids but the husband has a girlfriend who lives in that bit of the house over there," he said pointing to my right. "She has a child from another marriage."

"Is that the teenager I saw earlier?"

"Correct. Now the wife Julie, also has a boyfriend who is very young and … wait for it … is the ex boyfriend of one of her own daughters." At this he raised his eyebrows in mock surprise.

"Okay …" I said slowly.

"Dave and Julie have one son and two daughters and an adopted Navajo Indian girl."

"What?" I asked, looking really confused.

"Stay with me man. It would appear that the reason why the boyfriend of Julie split from her daughter is because he found out that the two daughters are both lesbians."

"But one of those girls looks about fourteen."

"Yep I know, and over the next week you will see about thirty to forty people just come and go. Now, they are just friends. But, the entire family I have just described all live here together."

"Fuck me; if that's what drugs do to you, I think I'll stick to tea."

Barry laughed, leaned over and then lowered his voice to nearly a whisper.

"Phil you're a young good looking guy so be careful, those two daughters are real man eaters."

"Hang on, one of them is fifteen and besides

you said they're lesbians."

"That's right" he said lowering his voice, "but they're fucking dysfunctional lesbians.

I burst into laughter.

"Shit Barry I feel like a right boring fucker. I need to get a life."

He wasn't kidding when he said it was a weird set up, I decided early on to concentrate on the job and stick to Barry like glue. Who would have thought that my hippy friend was the straightest of the lot. The amazing thing about him was his capacity for hard work, he just didn't stop. The reason he'd come over to France was that he used to have a successful building company in the States which he'd just recently sold and Dave knew him and his excellent reputation and so flew him over.

At the end of my first day I was knackered but it had been illuminating to say the least. Barry was an odd kind of hippy in that he was remarkably capable and seemed able to turn his hands to most things quite easily so that nothing appeared to faze him and, more importantly, he really was a superb cook.

"Where did you learn to cook like this?" I said tucking into some amazing pasta.

"My Dad was a chef; he had a restaurant in San Francisco in the sixties. He was quite into different cooking styles and shit and I guess I just picked it up."

"You talk like he's not around any more."

"Yeh well he died about five years ago," he sighed in acceptance.

"I am sorry, he must have been quite young."

"Yeh, late forties ... drugs overdose."

"Shit, your Dad overdosed on drugs?"

"Yeh, that's why I quit, my brother was pretty strung out for a while too," he said opening a beer and swigging it back in a well practised movement.

"I can't really relate to that, I mean my family is what you'd class as *normal* I guess."

"Nuthin' wrong with normal Phil ... wanna beer?" He flipped open the top and passed me the bottle.

"Yeh thanks."

"You know after finishing up here I was thinking about heading down to Greece for the winter."

"It's a good idea, I know a few people who are doing just that; come to think of it if you get into the yachting scene you may bump into my friend Crazy John, you two would really get on" and, looking straight at him. "He's fucking nuts as well."

" 'Preciate the compliment Phil," he said with a broad grin, "but how would I recognize him?"

"Barry, trust me, if you met a hundred captains in Greece this winter you would know who I meant before you met him." Barry appeared slightly puzzled by this statement but I knew what I meant.

"Why don't we go together after the vendange?"

"That's a thought. If I can get enough cash together I may take you up on it."

"Cool, rock and roll man. Cheers! Yeh! Let's do that Greece thing," he said smacking his bottle against mine as he nodded his head.

'Hell of a nice guy', I thought to myself … totally fucking nuts though.

That night I crashed out on my mattress on the floor feeling completely 'bushed', as Barry would say but for some inexplicable reason I went straight into my anxious state of the night before and could not get to sleep. Normally I would have loved this kind of situation, working in a wacky environment with slightly off the wall people and staying at a house in a lush rural area of France surrounded by olive trees. But the whole thing really began to get to me, the house just had a bad vibe; and then, when I did finally sleep I would have terrible nightmares waking up in cold sweats feeling fearful and afraid. There were no curtains at the window, no locks on the doors, I suppose I just felt exposed and this was from a guy who had been sleeping on beaches and in rocky coves for the last few months. None of this made any sense; it's not as if its owner was a mad axe murderer or something. I mean this should have been a house with laughter bouncing of every wall and wit seeping from every crevice but it didn't. It was eerie, creepy and weird and each night darkness fell I had to battle these demons alone. Some people claim that a feeling of evil or evil itself is a figment of the imagination however one day I would learn that ghosts do not commit evil - only men.

The welcome relief of morning arrived once more and we set off to the village of Entrecasteaux to grab some supplies before we began work. Driving in the truck was great fun as Barry tore through the village streets completely oblivious of the mayhem that trailed in his wake. This was one yank who didn't give a dam what the French thought of the Americans.

"We liberated this country twice and our young guys gave their lives to save their asses, so if they don't like my drivin' … Fuck 'em." And this was from a peace loving hippy!

The medieval village was of course stunningly beautiful, this country is blessed with so many places such as this that after awhile you just come to expect it and have to stop yourself from becoming blasé. Interestingly the locals, who I imagined would be hostile to Barry, were completely the opposite; they treated him with respect and were helpful and courteous.

"Hey Barry, how come everyone is so nice to you?" I said as we raced through the cobbled streets in the sunshine.

"It must be my charm and good looks man." Maybe but about ten seconds later I discovered the real reason, as we walked into the local supplier of building materials. After the usual pleasantries Barry just opened up.

"Now Pierre, what the fuck was that shit you sold me last week?" This was said with a calm self assurance that belied the nature of the question.

"Pardonnez-moi Monsieur Barry but it was cement mix from our normal supplier," he said apologetically.

"Well you need to fire his ass, 'cos he's fuckin' with you."

"Oui Monsieur Barry. I have another type of cement I can recommend, it's the best quality."

The guy cowered as Barry leaned on the counter and pointed straight at him.

"Okay, but if this turns out to be shit to then it's *your* ass."

The guys ran around the shop and then began loading the truck. I was amazed. Barry was not aggressive, although it sounded fairly heavy to me; he was just firm and quite clearly on it. They respected him; it was as simple as that. It was my little sister Helen, who many years later explained the other side of the French character to me that was so evident that morning.

"Sometimes with the French you have to show them who's boss, a bit like a teacher at school. They primarily have to believe that you know what you're talking about and then if they mess with you, you tell them firmly just how it is … and don't take any shit." Forget the French; would you mess with my sister?

I suppose after working there a few months they had got to know Barry and exactly what he was like, and his expectations. He was clearly no ordinary hippy and on the way back I was intrigued to find out more.

"So Barry educate me a little on this whole hippy thing?"

"It's like I told you man."

"Yeh, so what went on, where did you live in California?"

America and the West coast in particular have always fascinated me, it is so completely different to Europe and I loved hearing about it.

"Well in 67, I was living in Frisco."

"Jesus, flowers in you hair and all that."

"You got it, peace, drugs and free love man," said Barry with a huge grin.

"What exactly is free love Barry?"

"Shit no one ever asked me that one before. Well you know the girls were pretty easy and spaced out, I used to like the olive oil parties the most."

"Talk me through that one," I said with barely conceived enthusiasm.

"You kiddin' you never been to an olive oil party?"

"Nope."

We arrived at Les Bregs.

"Let's get this stuff unloaded and I'll educate ya'll."

Moving about ten heavy bags took time having to manually carry it all the way to our work site. Next he demonstrated the secret to mixing cement to the right consistency with the correct balance of sand and water. After that and once he got the cement mixer going he proceeded to *educate* me.

"The organisers of the party would lay out sheets of like heavy plastic on the floor and then pour bottles and bottles of olive oil all over it. We would all be 'loaded' even before we arrived and then all the guys and girls would strip down naked, slide out onto the floor and have one big fuckin' orgy man. Yeh!"

"Now I *know* I haven't lived."

"Yep it was a lot of fun, still sometimes you had to watch out for where your head or your arse ended up - if you catch my drift."

We both laughed as we proceeded to pour the wet cement into the barrow and lug it up to the base of the tower. I found it fascinating that in the space of ten minutes I had learnt the social mores of an olive oil sex party, as well as how to mix a bag of cement. Fantastic.

Living and working with Barry certainly was a learning experience. He taught me how to build wooden 'forms' one minute and then explained the intricacies of 1970's economics and financial engineering the next. The wooden forms were needed for the concrete. Before pouring, Barry would make a lattice of connecting steel inside the forms and when ready we would fill it with wet cement and voila, a reinforced concrete wall. As for the financial engineering, let's just assume that today Barry is probably a Master of the Universe and no longer wears flowers in his hair.

Every so often as we laboured in the hot afternoon sun great music such as 'The Joker' by the Steve Miller Band or 'Ventura Highway' by America would play on the radio and Barry would be off singing his heart out, it was great fun. My time in Les Bregs was like that, hard work and fun in the day, long interesting discussions in the evening, followed by disturbed scary sleep at night. The strange thing was Barry loved Eric's house as it reminded him of the backwoods of West Virginia in the States where he used to live. Maybe it was just me.

However, one night Barry began an in depth discussion about Roswell, the supposed site of Alien landings in 1947. In those days I had never heard of it but Barry kept going on about a guy called Stanton T. Friedman who had conducted extensive research claiming this was an authentic event. I am a healthy sceptic but he was really into it and he scared me shitless. Needless to say by the time I went to bed and after scanning the heavens thoroughly, I was convinced that Eric's little retreat had been selected out of the whole cosmos for an alien abduction. My imagination was off and running and coupled with my negativity about the house it just made it a racing certainty that 'Beings' from another world had selected the hippy and me for tonight's entertainment. Petrified is not an adequate description of my feelings that night, every breath of wind or moving shadow in the silence of the darkness just grabbed me and made me feel sick. I lay awake the whole fucking night and the next day I told Barry he was not going to get much work out of me and petulantly informed him that it was 100% his fault. He understood and gracefully apologised.

"Hey listen man I didn't mean to freak you out. I know what a bad trip is like … I've had a few myself."

"Really, you felt the same thing?"

"Yeh … except mine was on LSD." I just laughed, I mean he was totally serious, but LSD, fucking hell, I just shook my head.

"Barry what is so great about all that shit you used to take?"

"What, you mean you've never dropped acid?"

"Of course not, I'm from Yorkshire," now Barry was laughing,

"What does that mean?"

"Listen my hippy friend, if you were brought up in Yorkshire, you'd know."

Watergate was a favourite topic for Barry, he was deeply political in his views on everything but they were a strange mixture of socialism mixed with a republican work ethic if there is such a concoction in America. Basically he was a hard working Yank with democratic principles but did not like State interference, yet he understood the importance of 'light touch' regulation and him being an ex-hippy just added to the blend. Consequently I was very surprised one day at lunch when discussing Watergate, and Nixon in particular, that he suddenly blurted out a rather odd declaration.

"So I guess Nixon was the guy you hated the most." I said as I reached for a beer.

"Nixon was a shit but I won't hear a word against him."

"Why's that?"

"Because Richard Nixon saved my life."

This is not the sort statement you hear everyday, so I was eager to learn more. Barry then quickly rolled up his right trouser leg to reveal a large deep scar.

"Jesus, did you get that from a building accident?"

"Nah, this happened when I lived up in the

backwoods in West Virginia."

"Is that 'Deliverance' country?"

"Well it's not the same place but yeh it's similar, I guess it's all part of the Appalachia Mountains." He put down his sandwich and proceeded to explain. "I moved there in 73 about a year after the Watergate break in. I was trying to get my head together after all my partying. I knew the only way I could kick my drug habit was to just escape into the wilderness and be on my own."

"Sounds amazing, a kind of get back to nature thing."

"You got it, anyways I had this shack that was high up in the mountains, no phone, no radio or TV and I lived there alone for over a year."

"Now I know why you're so relaxed at Eric's."

"Exactly," he said pointing a finger straight at me. "A friend of mine, Dave, a Vietnam Vet, lived about 10 miles away in big log cabin in the woods and he had TV and stuff and every few months we would get together and I'd catch up on things such as Watergate and other news. He had a truck too so he would get me supplies from the nearest town about 100 miles down river.

"Shit Barry, you were really out in the wilderness,"

"Yep," he said slowly nodding his head. "Anyways one day after he had dropped of some supplies I decided to go and chop some wood higher up in the forest. Dave said he'd see me again in 6 weeks. I rode up onto one of the ridges on my horse and then walked a small distance into a large clearing and started chopping. I'd been there about an hour when suddenly, just by chance, my axe skimmed of the wood and went straight into my leg cutting the main artery. Blood just poured out so I tried to stem the flow and tie a tourniquet around it," he paused, "I wasn't in pain I was just shocked; the only problem was I couldn't get to my horse, I couldn't move and I was bleeding real bad, so I just sat there and lent against a tree.

For a while I was in shock but slowly I realised that I was probably gonna die, so I kind a resigned myself to it, I lit up a smoke and decided to watch the sun go down over the trees and mountains. It was beautiful and quiet and … peaceful, you know. I didn't panic I just accepted my fate; this had been my life and I made my peace with that, besides I was in God's country and I was having my own personal religious experience. I slowly got weaker and weaker and after about 10 minutes or so, I passed out.

Anyways, what I didn't know was that when Dave had started back down the road earlier, he heard on the radio that Nixon had just resigned, the first President in history to do so. He knew how engrossed I was with the whole thing and so turned around and came back to my shack to tell me the news and then realising I had probably gone to chop wood, traced my tracks up the ridge and found my horse. It seems that just at the point I passed out he saw me and got to me in time. He put me in the back of his truck and called the Rangers on his CB radio. They immediately sent out a helicopter and flew me to the general hospital in about 20 minutes and that's when I came around about an hour or two later not knowing where the fuck I was. I opened my eyes and saw a beautiful angelic nurse and then lots of tubes and monitors and looking up, I noticed Dave and he just smiled and told me what had occurred *and* about Nixon. I said shit Dave; you saved my life, he laughed and replied, no Barry ... Richard Nixon saved your life."

I sat there opened mouthed, spellbound and sort of tingled. "Shit Barry, that's an amazing story."

"Yep sure is and I tell ya, that's a fuckin' *true* story man."

And with that, Barry jumped up, lit a cigarette and shouted, "Light up and live!"

That afternoon Barry had to go and pick up some materials from the village so I carried on with preparing more cement. The two 'straight' Lesbian sisters casually wandered over and asked if I could help them with moving a table. It was no big deal so I followed them up this odd ladder type structure and through an open window and found myself in their bedroom. The young one went into hyper provocative mode but I saw her coming a mile away and asked about the table.

"There's no table here Phil," she said giggling, "why don't you take an hour off and ... relax." Now in any normal circumstances this would be a situation that I would have thrived on *but* this was not normal and they were clearly very odd, my instinct said 'get out fast' and that's exactly what I did.

"Sorry girls, love to stay but I've got work to do."

On Barry's return I told him about their little ambush and he just laughed.

"Smart move Phil, they're jailbait."

All through the course of the week I noticed very odd goings on with their friends and family but I just stuck with Barry and gave them a wide birth. Life is very strange some times, I mean, there's Barry a free loving hippy and me, a young guy up for a good time and yet we both kept well away from the whole thing. Compared to that lot we were Bible Belt Christians.

The days of hard labour passed surprisingly quickly, it was intrinsically mundane but Barry was such an interesting guy that I didn't really notice. Sometimes I would just stop and look around and think about where I was and what the future may hold. My relationship with Dominique was confusing me quite a bit and I wasn't really sure what to do. My feelings for Jane never changed, she was my constant no matter what happened in my life and I just assumed that she would be there forever. I never thought for a moment that our bond could ever be broken by anything or anybody. So what was I doing? I felt bewildered - best mix some concrete, I thought.

Sadly our last night arrived and we decided to check out the local scene in the medieval village of Cotignac, famed for the huge cliffs that dominate the houses and tree lined squares below. It was a *thriving* Friday night and it felt like the proverbial dead parrot; it had ceased to be. After walking around for ten minutes we found the only bar in town that was open. The building had been there since the 1565 but I'm not sure if anyone had actually been in there for a drink since. There were a few tables, two faded strip lights and paint peeling of the walls. A crumpled poster of an exhibition in 1932 hung at the end of the drab bar and stale cigar smell permeated through the room. As we came in, two old guys well past retirement age nodded to us. It was deathly quiet and I half expected tumble-weed to blow through the door any second. But, the piece de resistance was its name; it was called 'The Modern Bar' or as Barry referred to it *'The Marderrn Bahr.'* He loved it because it was so dreadful it made him laugh. We moseyed up to the bar.

"We must look pretty strange to the locals?" I said.

"Sorry to burst your bubble man but somebody a lot stranger than us came in here a few years ago." I was intrigued as I realised Barry was off on yet another of his fabulous tales.

"Go on, *educate* me." I said as I ordered two *pression* beers.

"Eric, your Python guy, once told me that he came in here with some friends who were staying with him. At first nobody recognised these guys but slowly it dawned on one of the kids and then within ten minutes half the village was trying to get into the place."

"Shit, the owner must have loved Eric, I bet they had they had a busy night."

"You said it, the village had never seen anything like it … ever and apparently whenever Eric comes in now, it's always free beers all night."

"So go on Barry, who was it?" He smiled, had a quick swig of his beer, wiped the foam from his mous-tache and wandered over to the world's oldest Juke Box. He put in a few coins and as the music blasted out he turned to me and started singing and wiggling across the floor. It was 'Tumblin' Dice' by the Rolling Stones.

I laughed my head off and at the chorus both Barry and

I sang out together;

"You got to roll me and call me the tumblin' dice."

We had a few more beers before the night ended and returned home a bit legless to say the least but it had been fun, in fact the whole week had been a mix bag of many emotions and for that I was grateful. It was probably the first night that I actually had an unbroken sleep; maybe that was the answer; just get pissed.

We went back to Les Bregs the next morning to sort out some things and whilst there Barry showed me Dave's bedroom on the top floor of one of the houses. It was amazing with low arches and a magnificent view and bathroom, maybe there was method in their madness after all and I mentioned this to Barry.

"No way man, you build this much shit and just by default somethin' is gonna turn out good."

"He had a point."

Later after lunch, we got paid and then set out on our drive back to Dominique's.

"How do you think it's gonna go with your French babe?"

"Okay, good, she's great and I really like her and she is kind and beautiful and ..."

"Cut the shit man, I think she's fallen for you big time and I've only seen you two together once. So what's your problem? Don't tell me," he said looking over at me with both hands still on the wheel, "you got someone else back home I bet."

"Yep," I said as pondered my predicament.

"And she loves you too."

"Yep." This was torture.

"And I suspect that you *really* like the lady back home but neither of the women know about each other." I nodded,

"Yep. What can I say?"

Barry kept one hand on the wheel whilst lighting a cigarette with the other and then as he blew the smoke out he laughed. "Well my young Yorkshire friend, in the words of the famous unknown American philosopher, 'you, are fucked.'"

We both laughed. He'd nailed it in three words. I didn't know what I was going to do, so later we stopped and I called Jane. I told her about Barry and explained that I was going off to pick grapes for a few weeks. She was such an angel and wished me luck.

"So did you tell her about Dominique?"

"Of course not."

"Fair enough, listen man, I'll call you in a few weeks but I don't think you'll be goin' to Greece, I mean, you might end up fuckin' Aphrodite and then the Gods on Mount Olympus are gonna have your ass." He smiled to himself, most amused at the idea.

"Now there's a thought, the Goddess of Love. Wow."

Eventually the hilltop village of La Cadiere appeared and we realised this conversation would have to continue another day. Dominique looked fabulous as she welcomed us back, Barry stayed for an hour chatting politely about our week together and then we said our goodbyes.

"Thanks Barry I've had a great week." I said as we shook hands.

"Me too. You stay cool man, I'm sure you'll work it out. Listen, for what it's worth I think you're a pretty straight up guy, you're just a bit fucked up that's all." He paused for a second. "But then again, isn't everybody." We both laughed as he got into his old truck and lit yet another cigarette. I closed the door and watched him take off down the farmer's track in a cloud of swirling dust. Lynyrd Skynyard's 'Sweet Home Alabama' was blasting from his radio and I could just detect him shouting out the chorus. I smiled and uttered softly underneath my breath,

"Light up and live you crazy hippy."

CHAPTER 9
HEARD IT THROUGH THE GRAPEVINE

"Give me the luxuries of life and I will willingly do without the necessities."

Frank Lloyd Wright.

"I lurve your be-arrd," purred Dominique as she softly stroked the rough bristles on my face. I had not shaved all week and fortunately for me this proved a big hit with the 'artiste'.

"I think you look very sexy and cool."

"Does this mean I can still sleep in your bed tonight?"

"No, it means you can sleep in my bed now."

Returning from a trip or having spent time apart, most women, I am told, have to slowly bond with their man again. This can take a few hours or longer and then when they feel re-connected and have established their closeness once more, then they feel ready to make love. Men of course are completely the opposite. With a man the way he re-establishes the closeness of a relationship is by intimate sexual contact. These completely divergent views often cause tension when couples first meet. The man becomes anxious and the woman angry because both have strong beliefs that are pulling in opposite directions. I have always been fascinated by these sorts of emotional and physical conflicts and my personal view, rather than bottling up all the tension inside, is to try and state openly and honestly how you feel and why. Luckily with Dominique no such conflict existed, so supper had to wait.

My week at Les Bregs had been fascinating for many reasons but towards the end the comings and goings at the house just appeared to get a little heavy and weird and I was glad to leave. I now had some money and as Dominique had previously lent me a few francs it felt good to pay her back. We were now very comfortable together and it was with ease that we slid right back into where we had left off.

I thought and still think of Dominique as one of the kindest and most loving people I have ever met insisting that I treat her house as my home. She would play many songs from The Eagles, John Lennon, Fleetwood Mac and Crosby Stills and Nash, she loved them all and so did I. This wonderful music would resonate around the house and vineyards and be complemented by obscure lyrical French ballads, incomprehensible yet beautiful. She would work quietly in her studio painting her wonderful designs, undisturbed by me. I felt it was her own time alone with her work and I respected her privacy and her space. I understood that her creative force grew from the solitude she experienced in her studio and so I seldom interfered. The sun seemed to shine every day, if she needed vegetables or fruits she would walk directly into the fields by her house and pick whatever seasonal plants were growing there.

On too many occasions to count she would bathe me with luxurious fragrant soaps and natural shampoo that contained aromas that when released would intoxicate the air. The effect of the softness of her touch and her gentle voice are impossible for me to describe. Dominique's bathroom with its stone floors and delicate rustic design was from another age and in complete harmony with her mood and personality. In this dreamy state I would lie on the bed as she massaged oils into my skin. She had created the perfect idyllic existence and I was now sharing it with her. I felt grateful for this tranquillity and peace in my life and many times as I lay in the hammock listening to its sound I would just float away.

This abundance would last many weeks, it was a precious time for me and I hope it was for her. She was open about her feelings but sadly I could not be. This was not because of some emotional emasculation on my part but because the truth was far too hurtful. I knew that it would be grossly unfair for me to lie to her so in the end I said nothing. This was the missing piece of our lives together, the life we lived was wonderful, save for my inability to give to her what she wanted, needed and deserved - my love. The desire to be tender and loving to her was always there but not the love itself. Because our days that late summer were so magical perhaps we both accepted what we had and chose not to push for more, I don't know. When the vendange began the reality of work entered our lives and perhaps that helped to extend our time further. For the time being the response to her words, "Je t'aime" would go unanswered.

Monsieur Maurice or 'Le Patron' as he was known arrived one bright Monday morning on his tractor and invited me to "Montez!" I hung onto the back of his seat with one foot on the wheel arch as we raced through the vineyards to the first field of the day, the exhilaration as the warm wind raced through my hair was extraordinary. The feeling of connection as I watched other workers in the fields was very powerful. Dominique had told me that apart from an epidemic in the late 18th century vines had been cultivated in this region since 600 BC by the Phocaeans. This was living history, I could feel it and over the coming weeks I too would become a tiny part of this tradition and way of life.

I was to be a *porteur* and my job consisted of carrying overflowing buckets of grapes two and three at a time to the large container that was pulled behind the tractor. I believe in many areas the pickers would place the grapes into a large *pannier* that the porteur would carry but I never saw one. The La Cad' way was that the pickers would cut off a bunches of grapes with small clippers and then pile them into the buckets and I would race back and forth trying to keep up.

Apparently the owners have several meetings to decide on the exact day to begin and then once the date had been set, that was it and this vast flurry of activity would begin throughout the region, I hardly had time to breathe it was so frenetic; when people say this is hard work they mean it. We worked solidly for four hours in the morning and four hours in the afternoon with a two hour lunch break in between. Le Patron began with the customary introductions.

"Ca c'est Philipe, le porteur."

"Bonjour."

Fabulous, I now had a title which gave the impression I had been flown in especially from Paris for my extensive knowledge and expertise. There's nothing like a vivid imagination. It took at least ten minutes every day to shake hands and later on, kiss, all my fellow workers, but it was all part of the tradition and my understanding of it grew the longer I was with them. It's strange that we call it grape picking because nobody picks anything, its more cutting or snipping to be precise.

There were about eight of us in total, mostly women. Their skin was leathery, lined and ravaged by the sun reflecting the tough nature of their lives but they laughed a lot and were some of the happiest people I have ever met. They resembled movie characters but were real, it was fascinating. They even referred to themselves as *les paysans* , which although translates as 'peasants', does not have the same detrimental meaning as in the English version. The women wore headscarves and aprons and the men the traditional blue 'all in ones' with caps and ... believe it or not, berets. All day they were bent over and never let up, Christ they were tough. I admired them tremendously. A Tunisian guy, Ahmed would also alternate with Monsieur Maurice to drive the tractor. The first day they were polite, *"Mademoiselle Dominique est tres gentille,"* or they would compliment me on my hard work but by the second day the gloves were off and I was fair game. Dominique had warned me about their conversations but I was still a little taken aback when during the occasional breaks for water or cigarettes the old women would fire questions at me about my life in England and also more surprisingly, my life with Dominique. She was well known and so they were intrigued to know what this guy had that the local French guys didn't. Their English was as bad as my French, they were bold, bawdy and straight out of a Thomas Hardy novel or as they were French, Marcel Pagnol.

"How come you live *wiz* Mademoiselle Dominique?" asked one.

"Because he is like a bull, no." said another, who giggling, thrust her hips forward.

"Not every night," I paused and smiled ... "but most nights." Shrieks of laughter rang across the fields. Then one woman faked a small aside to the other with her hand hiding her mouth.

"Oui, I *zink* he 'as big one, like donkey."

I pretended to ignore what she'd said, walked to the tractor, opened the tool kit and came back with a hammer thrust down my pants. Even louder shrieks ensued and that was it, as far as they were concerned I was now one of them, I could do no wrong. After a quick ten minute break they would dive back into their work with incredible enthusiasm and chatter away at breakneck speed. Every now and then they would just sing and when they did it I would join in and sometimes, for a few brief moments I too was a paysan; it was an experience I would never forget.

One day the heavens opened but nothing stopped the work, it became very, very hard trudging through the mud carrying buckets with the women shouting "Allez Phillippe," but they kept their sense of humour and I kept going. The hum of the countryside, the rugged nature of the job and the wet grapes with their unmistakable odour all added up to an authentic mix of life in Provence. Occasionally I would have a go at the cutting myself and within ten minutes the bending over was so painful I went back to portering. It was much easier.

At first I found the lunchtimes odd because I would eat then return and do another four hours of hard labour but eventually I got the hang of it. The trick was to have a little snooze and then refreshed, off we would all go again. Dominique was brilliant, she would have lunch prepared and the hammock ready, I could not have asked for more and at the end of the day she would begin the bathing and almond oil ritual and my cup overfloweth.

We worked six days straight and rested on Sunday.

"Today we go to the beach and you rest your body," announced *ze* babe.

"Whatever you say."

"Yes, my friends will come too, you have met them, they live in Le Castellet."

"Ah yes, James Caan and Julie Christie."

"Who?"

"Sorry they just look like them." Dominique laughed, she was very quick.

"Ah yes, I will tell them that is what you call them, they will be most flattered."

So we all jump in the car and head to the beach, out come the towels, out comes the food, out comes the wine - and then off came everyone's kit.

"What's the story here Dominique?" I said with a puzzled smile.

"It is a nudist beach of course."

"Of course," I said stripping down, "thank God I've removed the hammer or it, could have been embarrassing."

"What do you mean?" said a confused Dominique.

"Oh nothing it's a paysan joke I have with the girls in the fields." Slowly she helped me undress and then whispered coyly.

"Ah, so now I am going to lose my lover to some sixty year old peasant woman?" I stood there naked and held my arms wide open.

"Sorry honey, too many pickers only one porter." She shook her head, smiled and looked over at James and Julie,

"He is impossible, no?"

I really did like her, she was great - so why the doubts? My life with her was beautiful but something was missing. I could see very easily how three people could get hurt here and two of them didn't deserve it and I was the reason. The thing I had buried was starting to stir, I pushed it back but Dominique was a woman and it would not be too long before she started to ask the obvious.

Another week passed and the pace of work quickened. Dominique had a little scooter and I would often rush back and forth to the fields on it swerving and dodging the other tractors as they all sped to the La Cadiere winery. I realized after a few weeks why the bawdy humour existed, it was such an exhaustingly monotonous job, it just kept you going. One afternoon the girls were giggling away at something and one of them was encouraged by the others to ask me a question.

"Philippe, tu connais une pipe?"

I thought she meant, do I smoke a pipe? So I replied, "Non."

"Jamais!"

"No," I replied, "I have never smoked a pipe." The girls seemed most concerned about this and they all stopped cutting.

"Ce n'est pas possible." They huddled together and asked again. "Une pipe. Jamais avec Dominique, jamais?"

I had never seen a group of women so concerned about a guy not smoking a pipe. I figured something must have got lost in translation so I pretended to light up a pipe and relief and laughter rippled through the vines.

"Ah qui Philippe, you thought we mean a pipe?"

"Well.., yeh."

"Non, non, non, *faire une pipe*. You understand." I didn't. She held up a small branch near her mouth and I realized she meant a joint,

"Ah qui je connais, a joint." They all smiled and nodded expectantly until I shook my head once more and said, "sorry, no."

All work now stopped and a few more workers joined us. What the fuck had I said?

"Philippe you must ask Dominique, *zis* is very important." She then put the branch in her mouth and moved her hand up and down; finally I got it but pretended not too.

"Oui, oui, la flute, do I play the flute?" Incredulity now turned to laughter and then frustration,

"No No No, Philippe."

Monsieur and Madame Maurice appeared, then Ahmed and half the fucking vineyard. This opportunity could not be missed. I explained that neither I nor Dominique had ever played the flute and could she please demonstrate what she means and, as God is my witness, there in the vineyards of Provence, a middle aged 'peasant' woman knelt at my feet and proceeded to simulate a blow job. I looked at all the people gathered around and smiled, "Aah ... a blow job." I said nodding my head. Yes, oui oui; Dominique gives me one everyday, tous les jours."

"Tous les jours. Tu a la chance, you are a very lucky man!"

I shrugged with feigned nonchalance. "No no, to an Englishman this is quite normal." Howls of laughter rang across the fields, the women thought I was extremely fortunate and the men thought I was a God. I don't think any of them would ever look at Dominique in the same way again.

About 3 weeks after we started the vendange for Monsieur Maurice we finally finished the last vineyard and I was knackered. Dominique and I and all the workers were invited to his house for a grand celebratory lunch. My life here just seemed to resemble one long incredible movie and here was yet another scene. If 'Manon de Source', which had not even been made yet, was playing I would have been in it. An enormous table was laid out under a large platane tree and in its dappled shade we whiled away a lively afternoon of laughter and song - I just kept pinching myself. Everyone had too much to drink and eat and at the end there were many toasts and thank yous and I of course was asked to make a speech. I have no idea what I said but everybody laughed when I thanked the women for their explanation of the "Kama Sutra Francais."

My friend Bobby and I had chatted on the phone a few times. He was still in England but had finally decided it was time to escape the damp clutches of rainy *Angleterre*. He had kept saying he might come out and join me and I really hoped he would but I never took much notice because there was nothing definite and besides he'd talked about coming over before and nothing had happened. Bobby was a real free spirit, you just never knew.

In an effort to motivate him I explained all about Dominique and her fabulous life. I knew he'd really like her meanwhile she said simply, "if he comes he can stay with us." She was just a cool lady.

It was now back to my lazy days of hanging out in the sunshine, Dominique mentioned that there may be more work in Signes which was about 20 miles away but it was work, so I had to consider it.

Our relationship continued as before until one morning as we lay in bed Dominique just knocked me sideways with a question out of nowhere.

"Phil, do you have a girlfriend in England?" I stalled.

"Why do you ask?"

She turned to me with her head resting on the pillow. "Because I think you do."

"Yes, her name is Jane." I decided immediately to be as honest as I could.

"Does she know that you are living with me?"

"No, I don't think so."

"And how would she feel if she knew?" I lay on my back looking straight up at the ceiling.

"Unhappy."

"And do you love her?"

"I don't know. Listen Dominique when I came out to France, Jane and I both knew the situation. I came here because I wanted to live a different life, to not live a normal existence and that had risks. It was always possible that she could meet someone else and so could I."

"And have you met someone else?" she said running her fingers through her hair.

"Yes."

"And do you love her?" she said now stroking my hair.

"I don't know."

She then got up and walked across the room and stopping by the door, turned to me, "I suppose I should ask you to leave … but I don't want you to. I want you to love me, the way that I love you. Thank you for being honest."

So now she knew. The truth was out that but now instead of hiding from her I was hiding from myself.

That afternoon a young friend of Dominique's called Leslie came over, she was about seventeen and gorgeous. We had met a few times before and she was very sweet and adored Dominique and would often help out with things around the house. We had a few glasses of wine and later on I decided to chill out with a relaxing bath.

"I shall come up in a minute *mon coeur*." said Dominique.

"Where are you going?" asked Leslie.

"To bathe him. Why don't you 'elp me Leslie?" She giggled and looked a little embarrassed.

"Okay." Well she wasn't the only one, I mean … crikey, however, every ball on the rise and all that. As they both gently washed me there were giggles and cheeky comments in French but I hung in there, so to speak.

"Leslie he as a very beautiful body, no?"

"Oui, Dominique." I think the poor girl was petrified and then of course came the almond oil bit. I am lying there completely naked and Dominique of course just carries on regardless but I suspect Leslie could see where this might be headed and unfortunately panicked a bit and half way through she made some excuse and left.

"That's a shame; that could have been a lot of fun," I said with a slightly miffed smile.

"Phil, don't be greedy I think you have enough women in your life already."

I didn't really have an answer for that one and even if I did I suspect I would have probably got a bit of a slap, so on this particular occasion I kept my mouth shut and just laid back and thought of England.

Later that evening, after a delicious supper, we jumped into her car and sped along the coast, the wind and cool night air swirling through the palm trees. She appeared more relaxed than normal. "I'm happy that I know about Jane because I always knew there was a problem and now I understand but Phil, you are living in Provence now with me." She smiled and turned up her stereo and Stephen Stills, 'Love The One Your With' came blasting out, we raced along at high speed with this exhilarating tune pumping out at high volume; this chick certainly had all the moves, she was very good. In only one day she had accepted with grace that I had someone else in my life, bathed and massaged me with a beautiful young girl, made love to me, cooked a fabulous dinner and was now taking me on a breathtaking drive along the moonlit Mediterranean to the sound of superb rock music - If she could have guaranteed Kevin Keegan banging in the winning goal against Brazil in a World Cup Final, I would have married her on the spot. Dominique seemed to be turning up the heat, she had got her man and she was going to keep him.

The next day the job in Signes was confirmed and she now talked of taking me to Martinique in the Caribbean for a holiday. This was all fabulous but for one small overlooked detail that had not surfaced amongst the grapevines. I had been away nearly five months and I missed Jane terribly. I appreciate this must all sound rather odd but that's what I felt and even though Dominique was a beautiful person in every way and I was genuinely very fond of her; I simply missed Jane.

Whilst on the subject of girl and boyfriends, meeting en ex-boyfriend of any girl I have known is sometimes a peculiar experience but meeting Dominique's ex was in a class of its own or his own, as it were. He was about 42 years old and therefore much older than her and the exact opposite to me. An immaculate dresser in English tweeds, suave, sophisticated, successful, an innate French charm, spoke about nine languages, flew everywhere first class, even around France and drove a Porsche. The only similarities, in my opinion, were that he was a good looking dude and cool. He lived in Paris and had an apartment in Sanary on the coast. One night he came for supper and even though their relationship had ended seven or eight years before, they were still good friends. Dominique used to live in Paris where the cool dude owned a nightclub, his name was Pierre Marc. I liked him. He wore his hair long, the way only middle aged French guys can, even when wearing a suit. His perfectly maintained moustache complimented his tanned and distinguished face. He was helping her set up a gallery for her paintings in Toulon. His English was so good he showed off with extensive vocabulary and anecdotes in different languages. The opposites between the two were obvious but when Dominique was younger I could see that he must have acted as her mentor helping to guide her career, a sort of Roger Vadim character; in fact I think he thought he was Roger Vadim.

"Dominique was always a free spirit and I knew Paris could never hold her," said Pierre Marc.

The French are brilliant at this ranging hyperbole, they do it constantly, it has no meaning but they love it.

"He is right, I live for the vineyards and my art is from the soul of the vine and the life it gives me."

The English translation of this is, 'I like living in the country because to me Paris is a shithole'.

It was fun listening to them; they were more like brother and sister.

"You always wanted to bring girls home in *ze* hope that I would sleep with them."

"It is a beautiful thing but you were not ready my love," he said with immaculate charm as he poured her a glass of wine.

I then chipped in for good measure, "Pierre Marc is right; I'm with him 100 % on that one."

"Yes, you are both the same in that you love women ... lots of women."

"Ha-ha, you see Phil, Dominique is an artist and the love of a man is very important to her but if she cannot have it, then she will find a man another man."

"I had better watch my step then or I'll be out the door." I said laughing.

"Yes," said Dominique waving a knife at me, "or one night I shall surprise you in *ze* bath." Pierre Marc thought this highly amusing.

"Phil, you do realize that a crime of passion is an acceptable defense in a French court."

"Cool it guys, I am getting nervous." I said holding both palms of my hands in the air in an act of surrender.

"Good" said Dominique, "You know Pierre Marc he is impossible, like you."

"In that case my love, he must be making you very happy." Smooth line, I liked this guy even more. When the evening was over he invited the two of us to his pad in Sanary to meet his new girlfriend.

"And how old is she?" asked a pouting Dominique.

"19."

"Pierre Marc you are disgusting." she said.

"Pierre Marc ... you, are a star."

"Thank you Phil, I can see you are a man of great taste. Bonne soiree."

That night, we lay in bed and talked a little about her life in Paris with Pierre Marc. She was very different to most girls I had met in my life and I was about to find out how different, when sometime later I awoke to find Dominique leaning out of the window and shouting out at the pitch dark.

"Fuck me what's going on!" I yelled.

"There is someone outside, a burglar I think."

"Shall I go down and check it out?" said Mr Brave.

"No." she said calmly and then in a very casual manner produced a small shotgun from behind the curtains and fired it twice out of the window into the darkness below."

"Jesus Christ!" I nearly had a heart attack on the spot. Instantly we heard the sound of some terrified individual tearing off down the track and then a scooter disappearing swiftly into the night. Dominique then coolly closed the shutters at got back into bed. Astonished, I asked rhetorically, "Fucking hell, you've got a loaded gun in your bedroom?"

"Of course, the farmer lent it to me for my protection; it was probably just young kids."

She really was a cool lady and to top it all off she then demanded I make love to her as well! I can honestly state that my performance that night was nothing short of spectacular, the consequences of anything less just didn't bare thinking about.

The flea markets or vide-greniers in France are a national pastime, it's like smoking, everybody goes to them and they all talk about how wonderful they are and of all the bargains to be had. I have visited my fair share and take it from me they are universally appalling. It's the King's new clothes; everyone seems to believe that they are going to unearth some ancient antique relic from 1350 AD - but what they actually get is shit. Dominique, being an artist was obviously a believer, though to be fair to her she used to look mostly at the furniture that she may be able to buy and then paint. I used to last about an hour, any more and I would have to sit down quietly and open a vein. A friend of hers, Jacques often accompanied us on these little trips. He was probably the coolest Frenchman I have ever met, long hair, goaty beard, good looking, dressed like a hippy and a lovely guy. He used to prep some of Dominique's work and permanently smoked a spliff; in fact I think he was pretty much 'out of it' the whole time I knew him. He once told me of a trip he did to China across Asia, in an old Citroen, on his own in 1972; we are talking cool. He was married to a girl called Marie who was a model working in Paris but I never met her because she was always away somewhere - until one day.

They both arrived on a late sunny afternoon; she too dressed like a hippy and was utterly gorgeous. We hit it off instantly and chatted for hours whilst Jacques and Dominique were doing their artistic thing. At one point we found ourselves collecting tomatoes in the fields near the house and began getting a little too friendly. Nothing actually happened but it was obvious to both of us that in any other time and place, it would have.

"I love Jacques and *j'adore* Dominique and I would never hurt them."

"I understand." I said kissing her gently, "Perhaps in another life?"

"That is very beautiful Phil, yes, in another life."

I only saw her one more time after that and it was very brief, she gave me such a wide birth I suspect I would have missed her in the next ten lives! Some women are very cool and controlled, they know danger when they are attracted to someone and she decided it just wasn't going to happen. A different woman could have made a different decision and that's why I can't understand people when they have affairs blaming the other party into coercing them. It's fifty-fifty you're both equally responsible, get over it. I admired her cool, bloody shame though, she was stunning.

My departure date for Signes was approaching fast and my reluctance was palpable, it would be for two to three weeks returning only at the weekends, the sleeping quarters were 'basic' and the money was lousy. On top of this were two further reasons for my reticence, the first was obvious, my life with Dominique and the second, Bobby was finally coming to join me.

I had now saved a little money but I had agreed to go and so off I went, Dominique gave me her car for the first day to take my stuff and I bid farewell. It was grey and overcast when I arrived in a field outside the village of Signes. Here I met a total stranger who instantly began ordering me around like I was a piece of shit. He then pointed to a disgusting shack where I would be sleeping with a bunch of bums whom I had never met in my life before. The person who had arranged all this was a friend, of a friend, of a friend of Dominique's, whatever, it was lousy. He then hands me a pair of clippers and said "allez, allez," no introductions, no bonhomie, no chat, I felt as if I had been press ganged into it. I was being treated like a nobody in a gang of nobodies. I attempted to explain to him that I had been hired as a *porteur* and not a picker but he treated me with utter disdain. This was not Monsieur Maurice and his family of paysans, this was dreadful.

I clipped away for about an hour whilst they were supposedly sorting out my role and on his return he just snapped at me to 'take it or leave it'. He was really nasty piece of work and I could see the others strangely frightened to say a word and slowly I began to realize why. It was obvious to me now that most of them were illegal immigrants and just did what they were told to do. Instinctively I knew I was in the wrong place. The purpose of my trip was many things but none of them was this, so I asked to see the guy in charge but again all I got was anger, disdain and rejection. I considered my situation whilst becoming more and more upset and then I noticed some guy pleading with me to calm down. "No trouble, no trouble monsieur." He looked petrified. I always know when something isn't right and this definitely was not right.

The time had come, I marched straight up to the prize bully, slapped his clippers in his hand and told him in my by best French to 'shove it' and I think he got the message because my walk to the car was accompanied by a torrent of abuse. As I drove off I looked back at the faces of the other workers and I felt desperately sorry for them, they couldn't do what I was doing, they had nowhere to go, they had no choice and slowly their heads went down and back to work. Again I felt I was in a scene from a movie but this was a movie I didn't want star in.

The skies cleared and so did the red mist as I made my way out of the valley. I gradually felt a wave of relief wash over me as I knew I had made the correct decision; if you know something is fundamentally wrong, then get out. I drove up high into the hills and on my descent was met with a breathtaking view of vineyards and forests. My relief now quickly morphed into euphoria as if I had been somehow liberated from some imaginary shackles. Suddenly the day was staggeringly beautiful as I raced through the trees, up and down along the twisting roads and sharp bends, faster and faster I went, my body was pumping blood round at an ever increasing rate, it was like some weird personally manufactured high. I felt literally delirious, even out of control and my whole body gorged on it compounding the feeling further in a cycle of exhilaration and joy and then, at the peak moment of pleasure, I lost control of the car. It shot straight off the road, crashed through a fence and slid forever down a slope heading directly into the forest below. Talk about a state change, I went from elation to terror in about one tenth of a second and sitting there wrestling with the wheel whilst sliding down an embankment was terrifying. The car was being buffeted about and I could hear the stones and ground scraping the underside of the car. Contrary to popular belief my life did not flash before my eyes; I was going so fast my life had been left at the side of the road and was still trying to catch up. Then, just before hitting the trees a rough track appeared out of nowhere and sliding across it the rubber bit into the ground and the car stopped. Bloody hell, two Mini's and two crashes in the space of five months – 'what is it with these cars?' I said absolving all responsibility.

With not a soul around I just sat there as the dust cleared, it was so peaceful save for my poor heart which was still pumping blood, adrenalin and a million other chemicals in an effort to preserve my own mortality. Mercifully neither the car nor I had received so much as a scratch. What a rollercoaster of emotions and what a morning, I needed to calm down, relax and get a grip. There was now an urgent and pressing need for a relaxing massage, a glass of wine, a restful hammock and a shag; luckily I knew of such a place. Gingerly I made my way along the track and after a bit of exploration ended up back on the road; if I had hit the trees I don't think I would have been found for days. A grateful young man then slowly made his was back to the arms of La Cadiere, the intermission was over and the cameras rolled once more.

"What has happened?" enquired the surprised

luvver.

"Nothing, I was jealous and thought I would come home early and discover you in bed with another man?"

She smiled. "You know to a French girl that is very romantic because it confirms your passion and love for me."

"What a nation, you're all bonkers."

"Ha-ha, what is this bonkers?"

"Oh, passionate, loving, romantic, that kind of thing," I said with a sarcastic smile.

"Yes, I see."

Oh well, ignorance is bliss and later when I told her of the mornings events she just shrugged and said, "I think you came back for me - and your friend."

"Well ... yeh." (Hello!)

After lunch and for some unknown reason I decided it was time to unwrap my drawing skills that hadn't surfaced since my early days in St Raphael. Out came the pencils, paper and drawing board from her studio and off I went. It was such a beautiful house I wanted to capture it in my own style as a gift to her. I spent the day sitting in a chair with Pillule lying at my feet; me drawing her house from the outside and her painting her pictures on the inside. What can I say?

That evening just after I had come inside for a shower, Dominique and I were sitting at her kitchen table and suddenly Pillule began growling nervously, I heard a shuffle outside and then a gentle knock. Dominique slid the bolt and slowly opened the door and there stood a tall, dark, handsome stranger. Actually that is a lie, it was in fact my best friend Bobby with a huge smile on his face, I was so happy I nearly cried.

"Hello you must be Dominique?"

"Yes, and you must be *Roberre*?"

CHAPTER 10

BOB

"People come into your life for a reason, a season or a lifetime."

Unknown.

I am fortunate to have had three relationships in my life with people who have genuinely beautiful souls, they are precious and rare, and Bobby is the only man I have ever known to be endowed with this special gift. Many years from now, Lucy his wife to be, would ask me a question.

"Is Bob as wonderful as I think he is?"

"Good lord no; he is much more wonderful than that."

And now framed in the doorway stood this precious soul. A man, unshaven with long dirty unkempt hair, smelly grubby clothes, fag hanging out of the corner of his mouth and looking all the world like a discarded tramp. Of course this appearance, as Dominique soon discovered, concealed an erudite mind and superb wit.

"Fucking hell wanker, I am gagging for a drink."

"You see Dominique I told you he was charming," I said pouring him a glass of my own hard earned Rose.

"Anyway Bob; how the hell did you find this place? You're fucking useless at directions."

"I see things haven't changed much. I've only been here two minutes and he's having a go at me. Listen Vasco da Gama at least I got here," said Bobby laughing and downing his first glass in one,

"Did you choose this wine?" he said looking over at me.

"Yes he did," said Dominique, "It is from one of the vineyards where he 'as been working."

"Really, that's interesting and quite possibly unique," he said as he sniffed the cork and sampled another sip, swilling it around in his mouth like a complete connoisseur.

"Why is that?" asked a confused Dominique.

"The words 'Phil' and 'working' combined in the same sentence. I think I need to phone his mum and dad and tell them the news, they'll be so proud."

All we did was laugh and to be fair so did Dominique. She instantly liked Bobby; most people do. At one point in the repartee he explained something to Dominique in French; her face nearly hit the floor. His French is so perfect it's uncanny.

"I 'ave never heard anyone, who is not French, speak so well."

"Thanks Dom. Phil taught me everything I know."

Dominique laughed, "*Roberre*, I have told him it

is terrible that his French is so bad."

"You're right but hopefully I have other qual-ties," I said with a smile whilst raising my eyebrows twice.

"Fortunately you do," she said kissing me on the cheek.

"Do you guys want to get a room? I mean I can always fuck off back to England."

"I am sorry *Roberre* I have been impolite. What can I get you to eat?"

"Oh give him anything, he won't care. Bob is the ultimate nice guy."

"He is very rude to you."

"No he's right actually. I'll have anything."

And then he said something else in French and she burst into laughter and replied, "Yes."

I had no idea what he said, save for Bobby now switching to a broad Mancunian accent with a stupid expression on his face. "I told 'er you were a twat."

Having no idea what he said, Dominique agreed. "Yes he is."

Her agreeing to something she couldn't possi-bly understand just made it more hilarious and espe-cially when she did it again when Bob asked me if Do-minique lived here alone.

"Does she live on her cocker?"

"Yes" she replied on my behalf.

We have always used language which is often

incomprehensible to anyone else, so these small inter-jections by Dominique just amused us even more. The speed of wit and switching of accents that Bobby can do is scary to most Brits so I felt a bit sorry for Dom, her new name, but she was up for the challenge and I could tell he really liked her. Pillule who'd been quiet up to now suddenly jumped up on my lap,

"Look Pillule this is Bobby Blue, the baby faced Brit."

"Ha-ha the dog is called a contraceptive pill, brilliant." said Bobby.

"What's he going on about Pillule?" as I cupped his chin in my hand.

"*Roberre* is right of course. Pillule is French for a birth pill."

"Really" I said laughing, "Well thank god your mum's taking them or we'd really be in the *merde*!"

During supper Roberre, as we now called him, told us of his journey. He had apparently hitched to Marseilles and then taken a bus to Toulon. Having no idea where La Cadiere was he wandered into a bar and asked the locals. Two PTT guys who worked for the French Post office were drinking pastis and offered to take him the twenty miles to La Cad in their Postman Pat van. From the village he walked down the hill, no-ticed Dom's small advertising sign at the end of the road and voila. This little vignette is much more remarkable than it sounds because his sense of direction in those days really was useless.

Later, whilst Dominique showered, I explained to him how my life had been here. The hammock, mu-sic, bathing, shagging, painting, working in the fields, the cool friends, her incredible lifestyle. Bobby listened patiently and as Dom resurfaced from the bathroom he said. "Fuck me Phil I think I've come just in time, at this rate you two will soon be putting flowers in your hair, dropping acid and dancing round the street naked."

By the end of the evening we were all pretty smashed but what a laugh.

In bed that night Dominique whispered, "I like your friend very much; but why aren't you as nice as 'im?"

"Because my soul is not as beautiful as his."

She smiled and stroked my beard, "Any man who can say that about his friend must have a small part of his soul that is beautiful too I think. Goodnight my love" and then she fell asleep. I was kind of hoping that the evening wasn't completely over but maybe she'd forgotten her pillule - c'est la vie.

Bob has always had a plethora of names. He was christened Robert by his Mum and when I first met him at the tender age of fourteen he asked that I only call him only that. I have called him anything *but* Robert ever since. However he has many others, Rob, Robby, Baby face, Roberto, the Bobcat, Bobby Blue and now Roberre. It would have been much easier if his mum had just christened him Keith.

The following morning by the time I got downstairs Dom and Bob were nattering away in French and getting on rather well. My devious mind had already hatched a plan. Bobby, for as long as I could remember, had always wanted to meet a cool bohemian French girl who went everywhere barefoot. He used to muse that there relationship would be so perfect that the only conversation that would exist between them would be.

"Roberre."

"Oui cherie"

"Ou est le chat? (Where is the cat?)

Je ne sais pas cherie.

"Je t'aime."

"Je t'aime."

It was such a big deal to him that when describing any girl at all it would always be in terms of, "Phil, I met this girl last week."

"Is she nice?"

"Yes, she's a total *ou est le chat*."

What was obvious to me, and now Bobby, was that here was the ultimate *'ou est le chat'* right there in the kitchen. Only problem being, she was in love with me - and we knew where the cat was.

It was clear that Dominique and I had a dilemma; the harder she tried the more I pulled back. I felt bad for her and even worse for Jane. I had considered leaving a few times before but when Bob said he was coming I thought I would wait. I phoned Jane from the village call box and it was impossible to talk. She knew Bobby was here but she didn't know anything about who I was living with, she just thought it was a bunch of people. I just felt shit. I was missing her terribly but if Bobby and Dom hooked up it would be perfect. As pathetic as it may sound I imagined a relationship between them, I believed they were just right for each other. I'm aware that this may have an echo of Jane Austin's 'Emma' but it was honestly how I felt; I am also equally aware that to presume on what Dominique may or may not feel is entirely inappropriate but people, and young men in particular, are just as likely as anyone else to dream up flights of fancy.

When Dominique went out that morning, Bob and I sunbathed on the grass adjacent to the cobbled driveway and discussed my scheme. This was strange, not because of the nature of our chat but because we were both completely naked. We did these odd things quite a lot and on more than one occasion were mistaken for a couple of 'woofters'. We always found people's reactions amusing and so we didn't give a toss.

"Phil this is a great idea but I'm not sure Dom's even remotely interested in me. She loves you and all she talked about this morning was you."

"I know but Bobby you're a great guy and she likes you already. I can tell."

"I don't know. You and your mad ideas, you're a fucking nut case,"

After about forty minutes Dom suddenly burns up the drive way in her mini and we're lying there starkers, giggling like a couple of schoolgirls. She gets out of her car, says, "Hi", and then goes inside and doesn't bat an eyelid.

"Told you she was cool." I said.

"Yes I know but I thought she might at least have clocked my tackle."

I am now in fits of laughter, "Maybe you should

stroll right in there like Oliver Reed in 'Women in Love' and ask her for a baguette."

"Nah, that's a fucking stupid idea"

"Why?"

"Because Alan Bates had a bigger wanger."

We are now laughing so much that neither of us can hardly breathe. The next minute another car shoots up the driveway and it is, of all people Marie, the model from Paris wearing an incredibly tight pair of white shorts.

"Bloody hell that's the chick I told you about earlier, you know the babe I got friendly with in the vegetable garden."

"What, the one who twiddled with your tomatoes?"

"Exactly, the one that missed out on my cucumber."

She also nods, does a quick glance and then races from the car to the house in about 3 seconds flat.

"She noticed it this time." I said to a Bobby, now doubled up with laughter.

"God knows what the conversation is between Marie and Dominique right now."

"I'd just love to be a fly on the wall on that one."

And at that comment Bobby was off, completely lost in an imaginary world of Marie and Dominique in the kitchen.

"Dominique you 'ave two beautiful specimens

in your garden this morning."

"Merci Marie, I 'ave already sampled one but not ze other."

"Maybe you should give it a try and I can 'elp by diverting Pheel's attention."

"But 'ow?"

"I can distract 'im with zees beautiful melons that I 'ave here."

"Let's do it now, quick, show 'im your peaches too and I shall ask Roberre to take me up the auto-route." And just as he said this, Dominique appeared at the door.

"Roberre!"

"Yes Dominique."

"This is it", I said to Bobby excitedly.

"Could you please come into ze house and help Pheel unblock the washing machine?"

Ah well, such is life but never mind I hadn't laughed this much in months and it was great to have him here. Later that day he asked me where the 'toi-lette' was because it wasn't in the bathroom.

"Oh yes, I forgot to mention that, it's outside in a little stone hut by the pond." About ten minutes later he returned, giggling away having discovered its secret.

"Jesus, the pond *is* the toilet!"

I smiled. "I'ts real country living here Bobby."

"Too true, still having said that, it's got a bazzing view."

"I know it's an incredible sight of La Cadiere isn't it? - Best not to look through the hole in the floor though."

"I'll say," said Bobby pulling a face, "not much mystery there."

After lunch we went with Dominique to a huge house near Le Castellet to visit a Domaine owned by a young guy who had taken over from his father called Pierre Bunan. What a place, just magnificent. I'm sure Pierre had a bit of a thing for Dominique, but then again so did half the neighborhood. They had over forty acres of vines and after a very cool afternoon hanging out we agreed to do a couple of weeks work. Now it was Bobby and I cutting grapes and portering, it was very different to before, because even though it was hard work, all we did was take the piss, I loved it. We had such a bond and so just slotted back into having fun almost immediately. There were many hard working Algerians as well as locals and we gave every worker a name or moniker. There was Supercut Ahmed, the quickest cutter I have ever seen, then Phyllis Diller, Zsa Zsa, Mohammad Ali, Porter man, One cut, Gomez, Babette, Osin, Ship Chandler, the babe, Doreen and many many more. Sometimes when the work got intense the women sing, "Allez Phillippe Allez Phillippe Allez." And Bobby and I would create fictitious competitions on who could work the fastest and then go into fantasies of working behind enemy lines in occupied France as under cover spies or RAF officers, with terribly posh accents. We just basically altered our mind set so that this tough job just became a children's game.

"I say Robo I think I just spotted Bally Jerry over the briny."

"Crikey Captain best keep close to the Frenchies or we'll get spotted."

"Still, dashed damned luck as we've agreed to meet Squidgy at zero 600."

Next minute Bob slips and falls over with his bucket and grapes fly everywhere.

"You okay Robo."

"Sorry Cap' thought I'd bought one from Jerry, I am spiffing thanks, just pan-caked on the undercarriage that's all." And on and on we'd go laughing and giggling all day long.

The more Bobby and I hung out together the more I tended to disregard Dominique. On our day off we all hit the beach and during the afternoon whilst Bob was sleeping Dominique came over all serious.

"Phil I 'ave to talk to you. I'm worried you are going to leave me soon."

"Dominique, I don't know what I am going to do tomorrow let alone next week. Why do you say that?"

"I see you are happy because Roberre is here and I am happy for you but last night when I walked across the bedroom, naked, you just looked at the TV and not at me. When we first met you would only have ever looked at me."

"I know." Then I smiled, "But you have to understand Liverpool were playing Man United and this is important stuff."

"I know you joke because you try to hide the truth," she said looking down at the sand. She was nearly in tears and I felt terribly sorry for her and then she said some thing I would never forget.

"I give you my 'ouse, my car, I give you my body, I give you my life and I give you my *lurve* … and all I want is your *lurve*."

"I know." I said quietly.

And then lifting up her chin towards me and with tears streaming down her face I kissed her. There was nothing I could say.

Over the next few days I tried to be a bit more attentive towards her and have more fun. On one occasion we finished work early as I had cut my hand quite badly and had to visit the doctors. It was all a storm in a teacup, the French love to give you ten different drugs even for a nose bleed; I was fine. The three of us decided to go and meet Pierre Marc in Sanary which is a beautiful little port that reminded me of a small unspoilt St Tropez. It looks similar but without the yachts or the money. We took many photos that to this day I have always cherished as a reminder of our time together.

Later that evening we went for dinner with 'the Coolster' Pierre Marc. It was of all things a Chinese restaurant but he recommended it and it was delicious. He still kept doing his brilliant command of English thing, although I could tell he felt slightly threatened, because every time he would switch to another language to show off an expression, Bobby would go with him. It was hilarious, especially when I told him politely that Bobby spoke more languages than he did. His best line came when we were ordering dinner and half way through, he lent forward in a semi pompous manner and announced:- "Beverages … are not included." I'm afraid Bob and I just lost it and started laughing and even Dominique was amused; poor Pierre Marc, maybe he wasn't so cool after all.

Bob and I attacked the last week of the vendange with a vengeance, we rode on the tractors and laughed at the usual bawdy humour but this time it was different because Bobby knew what they were talking about.

Before dinner one evening I recall Dominique rushing down the stairs looking slightly perplexed.

"Phil? Roberre is shouting something out loud in the bath."

"What is it?"

"I don't know, he keeps yelling, *Elaine, Elaine!* And then *Rob, Rob!*"

"Ah yes, he does that."

"Pourquoi?"

"Well if you really want to know," I said putting down my glass of wine and smiling. "The bathroom has great acoustics and he is trying to get the same pitch as Katherine Ross in 'The Graduate' when she shouts Ben! you know, in the church. He's re-enacting the whole scene by substituting himself for Dustin Hoffman so that he can imagine that she's shouting for him." Dominique gawped at me utterly askance, especially when I added, "it's simple really, I've done it myself many times."

Often Bob and I would ponder on topics ranging from the nature of true love to the indescribable magic of the Cruyf turn and whether if he actually did meet Katherine Ross would she love him at first sight or discard him on the scrapheap of life. These questions and many more would be dissected on nightly walks through the Provence night air, it was heaven and to have him here just contributed even more to the wonder of the place. I would discuss my feelings for Jane and my confusion with the whole thing, the situation with Dominique and what the fuck to do. Bob pondered, lit up a fag and then he was off.

"Look, if I could have my way I would stay here and live with Dominique forever. This is a fucking brilliant place and I love it as much as you do but we both know how you feel. Jane and you will be connected forever and nothing and no one will ever change that, no matter what happens. She gets really hurt by the things you do but to Jane all these incidents are just bumps in the road. She's above it all and you and her occupy a different universe to the rest of us. Nobody can understand why you behave like a twat but the fact it is you two will never leave each other and that's it, end of story."

"Wow, that's some speech - I need a drink."

"Me too, now what did I say again 'cos I can't remember a fucking word?"

Returning home one night Jacques and Dominique were having a drink and smoking a spliff. Bob as you might guess had no qualms and was puffing away instantly. When Jacques offered me a drag I of course refused.

"No point giving that to me, it'll only be wasted 'cos I don't inhale."

"'Ow come you do not inhale?" said Jacques utterly mystified.

"It's because he's a control freak." answered Bobby.

"I think you should try it once because that is what we say and do in France."

"Okay okay, it is against my principles but as I'm with a bunch of drug addicts I'll have a go." And I did, in fact I had several puffs and whilst everyone else was getting more and more wasted a bizarre thing happened - absolutely nothing, nothing at all. There I was inhaling away and zilch, bugger all. This amused them even more, the more spaced out they got, the more sober I became. I have no explanation for this, however after about an hour the room began to sway and I went outside to throw up. Feeling terribly ill I climbed, very carefully, upstairs to lie down. Slowly the room returned upright and I calmed down, Dominique and Bob both sat with me even though they were completely out of it. They were both giggling away as I explained my version of events. "You see guys my whole being just automatically rejects these foreign substances, my body is my temple and that's just the way it is." At this Bob just burst into uncontrolled laughter.

"Phil that guy you met, Crazy John, was right, you are full of shit." We all giggled away as I continued to talk bollocks for the rest of the evening.

The next day one of life's small but unforgettable moments occurred whilst assisting Pierre, Ahmed, Osin and some others with some work at a farm on the hillside. The sun was burning down and suddenly as we walked up a dusty rough track we noticed Osin up ahead of us. He sat on the oldest tractor in the world and was coming down the hill very slowly towards us. He was an Algerian about 32 years old but looked about

90. He had rough dark sun raddled skin, about three teeth, matted hair, a dirty old shirt and a fag end hanging out of his mouth. The trees formed an arch behind him as the sun filtered through. The tractor bumped and shook and suddenly he looked up, saw us, waved and smiled, his big wide grin exposing the gaps in his brown stained teeth. Bobby, pretending to do a voice over for some African charity, then announced in a low controlled voice laced with deference;

"You and your contributions have helped to buy Osin his tractor."

He'd nailed it in a single line whilst capturing a perfect image. To be able to make someone laugh as much as I did that day is a true gift that is impossible to value and something I will never forget.

On the very last day the heavens opened and we worked until dark, till the last grapes in the vendange of that year were picked. We were exhausted but decided to be 'rock men' and run the three miles back to Dominique's in the torrential rain. It was exhilarating for both of us as the rain lashed our faces in the darkness we finally arrived at the rough track to her house.

"There's something we have to do." I said.

He looked at me and even in the half light he could see I'd hàtched a plan, "What the fuck are you up to now?"

I walked in and suggested to Dominique that as a treat she should bathe Bobby, he couldn't believe I'd said it but she was cool and said why not. This was his big moment, it was now or never for Roberre. I made some excuse about having to dash out to the village and the stage was set.

An hour later I returned to find him sitting at the kitchen table smoking a fag and sipping a glass of Rose, "And where's Dominique?" I asked expectantly.

"Upstairs."

"And?"

"Sorry mate I fucked up, you know I'm crap at this kind of thing."

"What do you mean? She likes you, you like her, I'm out of the way, what happened?"

"Nothing, she bathed me all over and it was fantastic and when she got to my 'togger' she gave me the sponge and left," he said giggling.

"You fucking tosser, I gave you an open goal and all you had to do was bang it in." Now we were both laughing like little kids.

"I am just not like you," said Bobby, "I'm a lousy salesman; I couldn't close a fucking cupboard."

Maybe it was a stupid idea but you never know if you don't try. I still think they would have had a great time together; he's more French than they are and would have slotted in to their lifestyle in an instant. Dominique joined us and later and when we went to bed, I completed the task that he'd left undone. Dickhead.

The customary 'end of vendange party' arrived but as it was a Pierre Bunan affair it was a little more stylish than my other 'patron.' He had hired a fabulous restaurant on the edge of the rampart walls of Le Castellet. We had a scream and all got thoroughly plastered, only problem was quite a few of the local girls started to get very friendly with Bobby. Now normally this would be great news but some of these girls were, well, a bit older than girls and slightly more worrying was that Bobby was completely legless. I was becoming concerned that they might take advantage of him and then discard him later as a used toy boy and with him having no recollection of the event. I mentioned this to him as we staggered back to the car.

"Bobby shall I protect you from these older women and take you home?"

"You'll do no such thing. I want to be used, abused and discarded, it sounds fantastic." On the way down the steep hill they nearly raped him in the backseat. It was very dangerous, not the attempted rape, the intoxicated drive downhill. Actually it was very funny and quite harmless as he is utterly useless when he's drunk and later he staggered back all in one piece and none the worse. I was so happy that Bobby had experienced some of my time at Dominique's, she had welcomed him with open arms and maybe if things had been different our roles might have been reversed. I had now started to treat her poorly, maybe it was guilt, but I could no longer keep up any pretence, I was missing Jane and I needed to find work elsewhere.

My time here was done. We decided to leave, Bob would have stayed but I couldn't. Dominique even now treated me incredibly well, I had been terribly fortunate to find such a person. The next afternoon we went outside and sat down by the hammock, the poignancy of this setting was not lost on either of us as I looked back at her beautiful home.

"I am leaving." I said calmly.

"Why?"

"Dominique I can't stay here, I need work and I'm not being fair to you by staying. I would like to but I can't."

"It's Jane isn't it? You know you have treated her just as badly as you are now treating me. I have done *everything* for you." She sounded angry but I knew she was just upset and she had every right to be.

"What do you want me to say? I have never lied to you."

"Sometimes I wish you had … maybe just once. But you never did *and that is because of someone I have never even met.* You're right; you have not been fair to me. I love you but I've never had you." Tears rolled down her cheeks and I began to cry too. We held each other close

"Dominique we have had some wonderful times together and I will remember you all my life, it was just not meant to be." She calmed down and looked softly into my eyes and then said something else I have kept in my memory all these years.

"You do not love me, you have never loved me … it is my life here that you love."

We sat there for a brief second just looking at each other, the truth of her words could not be denied. Slowly she shook her head as acceptance slowly drifted across her face. It was a terribly sad moment for both of us as we realized our relationship that began all those months ago, on that balmy September evening, was now at an end.

It was a quiet night, she seemed okay and Bob was great and made her laugh and I think it helped soften the edges just a little. The next day Pierre Marc arrived, I guess for moral support and they chatted for an hour or so. He had to go to Nice and offered to drop us off in Cannes. Bob and I thought it a nice gesture and Dominique decided to come along too. What I did not expect was one of the scariest drives we've have ever had. He drove at 110 miles an hour the whole way in a very, very small car. He told us that he used to be able to do Paris to Marseilles in 5 hours in his Porsche. We didn't doubt him in the least but this wasn't a Porsche. We kept him talking in an effort to slow him down, it didn't work. I grabbed my hand rail, then Bobby grabbed his and then Dominique grabbed hers. It was crazy, mind you if Pierre Marc had grabbed his then I really would have been worried. We finally arrived, a bit frazzled and he dropped us off at Port Canto, "So this is where you came from," said Dominique. I laughed and she did too. We all said our goodbyes and I hugged her for the last time.

"Thank you … thank you for everything." I said as she gently stroked my beard.

"Au revoir my lurve."

The beautiful Dominique then climbed into the waiting car and left. I watched her go but just as the car left the port I saw her turn and look back over her shoulder; our eyes met for a fleeting second and she was gone.

CHAPTER 11
AIN'T NO MOUNTAIN HIGH ENOUGH

"You've got to jump of cliffs all the time and build your wings on the way down."

Ray Bradbury.

So now we were two Prisoners of the White Lines. Standing there on the edge of the port considering our next move was a little weird. I had spent so much of my time here and now I was back.

"Okay Butch what's the plan?" said Bobby lighting up a fag.

"Fuck knows I am making this up as I go along."

"You know it's funny, I have this vision that now you've gone, every eligible guy in Provence will be forming an orderly queue outside her house, thankful that the English twat has finally left." We both chuckled away at the image he had created; it was brilliant to have him with me. I guess our relationship has always been based on having a laugh and talking shit and we are still doing it today.

The very first thing I did was find a call box and call Jane. We had hardly spoken whilst I was in La Cadiere, and I knew she would be slightly guarded.

"So how was the grape picking?"

"It was fun, bloody hard work though."

"And how's Bobby."

"He's okay. Listen, I need to see you. If I get set up somewhere will you come?"

"Maybe, but if you're that desperate, why not come home now?"

"I am not ready yet."

"Why? Still too many distractions I suppose." I thought she was okay and being playful but then we hadn't talked for a while and out it all came.

"Well …" I began.

"Don't say anything. *Don't say anything*! I am fed up with this. Everyone at home thinks I am a fool waiting for you like some lovesick schoolgirl. When are you going to stop travelling and messing about and start treating me properly?"

"I don't know. This is really hard talking on the phone like this."

"Hard! *Hard!* How do you think I feel, not knowing where you are or who you're with or if you will ever come home?" She began to cry and my heart broke as I heard her sobbing on the phone. I wanted to reach in and grab her. The same dilemma of living a different life and being with her just swirled around in my head once more. What the fuck was wrong with me? Jane then repeated the same thoughts straight down the phone line.

"What is wrong with you? I can't keep waiting all my life and I won't."

"Angel I will never leave you, ever."

"You *have* left me. You're there and not here," she yelled.

"You know what I mean; you know I'll come back."

"I see and then I have to forgive you all over again. How many times will you be unfaithful? I am an idiot. How would you feel if I went out with other guys? All my friends have their boyfriends here at home with them. They're not gallivanting off around the world like you." She started sobbing again. It was killing me and I was running out of money and change fast. The pressure of the whole situation was crazy. This had all been building up inside her for a long time and she had every right to say what she wanted. I was guilty.

"Okay you're right. I don't want you to be upset; I want to make you happy."

"But you're *not* making me happy," she cried, "my mum keeps asking why I wait for you, why am I not going out with other guys?"

"Listen, listen angel, if I don't find a place where you can stay, then I will come home, *I promise*." She calmed down a little; Jane knew if I promised something then I would never break it. I may have odd values but one of them is that I will never break a promise.

"Do you promise?" she asked quietly.

"I said it. I mean it. I promise. The beeps are going. Will you come if I find something?"

"Yes but I hate you treating me this way, I wish I didn't love you but I do."

"Love you. Bye, I'll call soon."

"Bye … Bye." Beep … Beep…

I met up with Bobby in a bar across the road and he could see that I was a bit shaken up.

"Nearly lost her, huh."

"Yeh."

"Gotta be careful Phil. You lose her and you'll lose everything."

"Fucking hell Bobby, why am I such a dick-head?"

"Dunno, I think it's an art."

We checked into quite a reasonable hotel which I thought was going to be madly expensive but because it was November it was cheap. Later that night we met two German girls Claudia and Nicole and had a real laugh but only a laugh.

The next day we were walking down the street and bumped into Sarah, the babe. It was great to see her. We had a coffee in Café Roma on the Croisette, "So who's left in town?"

"Nobody, they've all gone to different places in Europe, some even went back to England." She looked quite sad.

"Shit, what are you going to do?"

"I don't know I've got no money left but I'll probably go to Paris."

"But what about you Phil, have you been with that French girl all this time?"

"Yep."

"Christ, that must be a record!" she laughed.

"You see Bobby this is the sort of bad press I get around here."

"What? As opposed to the good press you get in England,"

"Thanks for the support."

"He seems nice," she said looking at me whilst motioning to Bobby.

"Yes everyone thinks that but actually he's a twat."

We all had a good laugh and later said our goodbyes. Within ten seconds of her walking out of earshot Bobby asks,

"She's gorgeous, how come you never got together with her?"

"Dunno, she never seemed interested. I guess I wasn't her type."

"You must be losing your touch."

"Well, 'it's like I said Sundance ... over the hill."

We spent the next few days looking for work at the various yacht brokers. A pompous prick called Jeff told us of a guy who was interviewing for crew along the coast.

"Yes, try Villefranche and go and see Captain Van Vestering."

"Captain Van Vestering?"

"Yes, he's a hard man, but fair." said the pompous tosser.

We walked out of the office and then spent the entire day relating everything to a man who had a reputation of being 'a hard man but fair.'

"Can't wait to meet him"

"Who?"

"Captain Van Vestering."

"Really, what's he like?"

"He's a hard man but fair."

Arriving in Villefranche we checked into a tiny hotel by the port, it was a beautiful place.

"Well Bobby the time has come."

"What the fuck are you on about now?"

"This is it, the beard is coming off."

"You realize you might lose all your strength Samson."

"I know Delilah but it's driving me nuts."

Morning arrives and the shorn man and Bobby continue their search for the Captain.

"I tell you what Phil, he may have been hard and he may have been fair but actually I don't think the twat exists. I think he was a fantasy of Jeff the tosser."

To be fair we didn't really try that hard I think we both new the game was up on the Riviera for that year. We discussed going to Crete as many people had gone to Greece but really we just went round in circles trying to think of our next move.

Sitting on the prom in Nice we sang songs all day sounding fabulous. One of our over enthusiastic American cousins approached us,

"Are you guys professional, do you practice a lot, I mean guys, you're really good."

"Thanks very much," said Bobby sounding like Terry Thomas.

"Hey Bob maybe we've got something."

"Don't be ridiculous, he was as bent as a nine bob note."

We realized we couldn't keep hanging out here and had to make a decision otherwise we'd drift. The problem was we were having such a good time together that we didn't really care. However, the page was turning and as had happened so often in this journey, it came as a complete surprise when one afternoon, out of nowhere, Bobby came up with a brainwave. He doesn't have these very often but when he does they're usually inspired. He disappeared, made a phone call and came back with a smile on his face.

"Are you ready for this?"

"Get on with it tosser."

"Are you up for working in a restaurant in the French Ski resort of Val D'Isere for the whole winter, food, accommodation and pay included? We work every evening and ski all day courtesy of my friend Jeanin who's just bought a restaurant there."

"Brilliant, fucking brilliant idea, when do we go?"

"Now."

And so the adventure continued. I had never even thought about the Alps. Sometimes the obvious is right in front of your face. You spend all your time looking one way and the answer is already there just waiting for you to discover it. I mean, on a clear day, you can see the Alps from nearly everywhere in the South of France but we were too busy gazing out to sea.

We were both excited; I think we just knew it was right but Bobby hadn't finished, "Maybe you can rent a small apartment and Jane can come and stay too."

Told you he had a beautiful soul.

We were now re-energized, had a purpose and were fully motivated, all the ingredients necessary for success. Within 20 minutes of that phone call we were off, having done a complete 360 on our ideas and direction.

In the afternoon we hit the road and got a lift to the Frejus peage in a van with some kids who had just returned from Greece! I am not making this up, promise.

More rides and we are now lost in a world of Butch and Sundance for as we walk through villages people stare at us.

"Who are those guys?" we imagine them saying and then seconds later Bob's off on another tangent.

"Jean-Claude Killy must be shaking in his boots knowing the British Ski Team are approaching,"

"Yes, but do you think he knows I've never skied before?"

Bob shakes his head, "It's just a technical hitch, don't be negative."

"You know when you talk like that you remind me of Captain Van Vestering."

This surreal shit goes on for hours and remarkably we never get bored and never get tired as we trudge down the road in the middle of the night. It's 3 am and we have walked 5 miles to a motorway entrance with our heavy packs and feel like total rock imagining it's an SAS 'tab'.

"That's enough yomping for today chaps," says Bobby swinging his pack off all in one movement.

It was now bitterly cold and with a mistral blowing as well, bloody freezing. We were just thinking about what to do when I spotted what appeared to be a waiting room. I have no idea why there was a waiting room there but the door was open and it was warm and so in we went.

"I say Captain, dashed stroke of luck what?"

"Too true Chalky. Now shut the fuck up will you and go to sleep."

Morning came and we were just outside Aix en Provence. We got a lift and then marched on down a side road heading west. I briefly explained about Emile Zola and Paul Cezanne and before I'd finished Bobby was away with the fairies.

"You see Emile ze problem is, I just can't get ze trees."

"I know Paul but you must give it time and ze

trees will come to you, not in your 'ands but in your 'ead."

"Ah Emile, you are a true friend, 'ow do you know me so well?"

"Because I 'ave been shagging Hortense for months."

Bob instantly becomes a stupid football supporter from Manchester and starts pointing at me aggressively.

"Emile you are a twat and I'm gonna fuckin' have yer."

"Paul what iz this strange French zat you speak?"

"Listen yer short fat fucker, you're a tosser and that *Teresa Ranking* is shite."

"It's 'Therese Raquin'."

"No, it's shite."

I guess you have to be there but to us it's hilarious. Life though has decided on a wake up call and soon a perfectly ordinary couple stop and give us a ride; the only problem is they are perfectly *psychotic*. Being true psychos we weren't aware of it at first and they just behaved normally chatting away and discussing our trip with a pleasant nonchalance. But, ever so slowly he went faster, and then faster still. She had wiry black hair and a pointy nose and within about ten seconds had transformed herself into one of the three witches from Macbeth. It was fucking scary.

"Do you like to drive fast?" she said quietly and then accompanied by a manic laugh.

"Yes," said Bobby being calm, "sometimes."

"Good."

Now Banquo's ghost hits the pedal and we were off, much much faster than Pierre-Marc and with no control whatsoever. He overtook on blind corners and made every dangerous move in the book. Swerving and then breaking suddenly we just missed a lorry coming in the opposite direction. If they had been high on drugs it would have been bad but the problem was they weren't. This was real and they knew what they were doing. Bob remained calm and asked if they could slow down. Again, she turned in her seat and just shook her head. I swear to God I wouldn't have been surprised if it had swivelled all the way round.

"Vite, vite, vite," she screamed.

I was sweating profusely as this instantly re-minded me of my weird gay friends in St Raphael all those months ago. I thought oh no, not again, this is nuts. The driver never spoke, he was totally manic and deliberately began swerving and overtaking on the un-seen brows of hills. Other cars were blaring their horns whilst lorries pulled abruptly over to the roadside in swirls of dust. The more frightened we became the more she loved it, "Phil, she just told the guy in French that we were really scared and he said, 'Bien'".

"Look Bobby if we don't get out of here these lunatics are going to kill us."

Bob is just about the most laid back person I have ever met and so to see him frightened, scared the crap out of me. I've known Bobby all my life, since we were 14 years old and I don't think I have ever seen or heard him raise his voice but from nowhere he slapped his hand on the driver's shoulder and commanded him.

"Arrete! Arretez maintenant!"

I think the guy was nearly as shocked as I was. He slammed on the brakes and skidded to a stop, we jumped out and banged the doors shut. They sped off in a cloud of dust shouting expletives in an exact carbon copy of my gay nightmare. We sat there on the side of the dusty road in the now proverbial middle of nowhere and were pretty shook up.

"Fucking hell Bobby!"

"Shit, that was scary. I thought we'd had it."

"Me too she was a fucking nutcase. But Bobby that was brilliant, I don't know where you got that dominating command from but I'm glad you did?"

"Enter the Dragon."

"What?"

"Enter the Dragon; you know where Williams goes *'Bullshit Mr Han man!'* I thought of that and out it came."

At this we both burst into laughter and proceeded to re-enact nearly every scene in the movie which rather embarrassingly we can do even to this day. It relieved the tension and got us back to normal. Being typical bullies, the only thing they respond to is when someone bullies them back. What is wrong with people? I'm sorry, but I blame the parents, it's ridiculous. This is the second time I had come across madness or evil or whatever description one cares to choose. I always believed that these were isolated incidents in life and highly unusual. They are but one day I would learn that sadly they are not unusual enough.

Later we got a ride with an Aussie family who thankfully could not have been kinder or more generous and they restored our faith in humanity. In Salem we elected to take a train as I think we'd had enough excitement for one day. Here I said goodbye to the south of France as we left the warm Rhone delta and arrived 4 hours later in Bourg St Maurice in the middle of the French Alps at 10 o'clock at night. Unfortunately there were no buses so we hitched a ride up to a vast reservoir on the way to Val D'isere called Lac de Chevril. Here we were dropped off by a colossal dam known locally as Le Barrage. The drive up into the mountains had been amazing, fascinating and ever so slightly scary as we raced round hairpin bends on our climb into the Alps. The contrasts were striking when compared to the previous months. What a stunningly beautiful country. As we clambered out of the car the still cool night air hit us. It was cold; actually it was freezing, literally.

Nighttime in the Alps is extraordinary, the crisp snow and ice, clear starry skies, romantic ski lodges and crackling log fires. What a contrast to where we had just been, it was thrilling, save for just a few tiny little problems. Having just spent six months in the south of France I possessed no winter clothes, plus we were 6 miles from our destination which was 1700 feet above us, it was pitch dark, deserted and midnight.

"Okay Bobby where exactly are we going?"

"It's called Val Claret and is a village just underneath the glacier, near Tignes."

"Bobby this sign here says its 10 kilometers up there." I said pointing to the sign with one hand and a snow capped mountain with the other.

"Oops!" said Heidi.

"You and your directions, fucking hell," I said shaking my head. "So, what do you think?"

"Well I think we should have a fag."

"Yeh that should keep us warm, good plan."

Bob of course is now in total fantasy land. He had so many references from so many sources he hardly knew where to begin; this was going to be fascinating and quite possibly life threatening.

"Right I'll be Oates and you can be Scott." Here we were in a risky situation and he was having a kid's game based around Scott of the Antarctic. Then its '633 Squadron' and bombs away and all that just as we are crossing the dam. It's terribly silly and great fun.

"I guess it's up, then." I said assessing the north face of Annapurna.

We put on our packs and set off. The dam which was finished in 1952 is an impressive sight and the man made lake even more so but all we could think about was not wanting to get stuck on it all night. Within minutes we were warm and so I felt a bit more relaxed but we really had no idea how dangerous this could have been and this ignorance served us well. We plodded upwards and chatted away about football and girls and what the future may hold; the meaning of life, Jane Fonda and the entire world's knowledge. At one point he disappears off into the snow doing his Oates bit, I just let him go, fuck it. I refuse to play his silly games and besides I've got the rest of the team to consider as Amundsen has already got there first.

Not a single car passed. Some parts were really icy, especially near the man made run offs for avalanches and we could hear our voices echoing across the valley. There was lying snow in places but it was mainly confined to the high peaks at this time of year. We passed not one house or log cabin; it was quite simply a deserted mountain road. On our right was the steep mountain side and on our left a sheer drop into a silent black void. Our warm breath took off into the still night air and it was silent, save for our constant chatter and ribbing. The darkness created a tranquil feel as we believed we were the only ones awake but then again, we *were* the only ones awake, anyone with any sense was safely tucked up in bed. We climbed higher and higher, it was such an experience that we just seemed to keep on going, awestruck by the sheer wonder of the mountains that enclosed us.

At one point we rested and ignorant about the effects of altitude, were quite stunned at how quickly fatigue set in. But, at 24 years of age, fit and brimming with confidence and bravado we just kept going. It was a test of fitness and in less than two hours we made it to Val Claret and just felt brilliant. If a snowstorm or mistral had decided to arrive that night we could have been in jeopardy but fate was on our side and in the end it was simply an experience that we never forgot.

Arriving at 'Le Merle a Plastron' restaurant, wecrashed out, Edmund Hillary and Sherpa Tenzing had made it. Two weeks after this hike a snow storm did arrive and the road was blocked for two days.

Everyone knows that a bright sunlit morning in the mountains is beyond compare and if you don't know, well, you haven't lived and I suggest you go find out. Jeanin, our new boss spent the whole of the next day introducing us to everybody the same way.

"This is Phil and Roberre; they walked last night from Le Barrage!"

And everyone replied the same way, "Le Barrage, pas possible!"

He found this highly amusing; actually he found nearly everything amusing having the most infectious laugh of all time. He was cool with long fair hair, loved Bobby, loved to drink and was just an all round lovely guy. His girlfriend Astrid was completely the opposite, didn't drink, wasn't cool, never laughed and was a pain in the arse. Takes all types I suppose. Danny, a girl surprisingly, was the chef and Alain her husband assisted. Bob would be the waiter and me, the 'plongeur' or dishwasher; it wasn't sexy but I didn't care and some nights I did 'waiting on' as well to earn extra money. The restaurant was at the base of a block of ski apartments and did about 50 covers. It had a fantastic view and many nights Bob would find me sitting there in a half lotus gazing out over frozen landscape.

"Phil I'm off out, are you coming or what?"

"Hang on a minute; I'm just trying to locate my position in time and space."

"And?"

"Got it, let's go."

The number one problem was actually the dog called 'West' which was mad and kept eating everything, food ,tables, bags, socks, Bob's underpants - I mean to eat Bob's under garments you've got to be mad. Being early in the season it was quiet and so when Bobby told them I was an artist, they insisted I paint a huge sign to advertise the restaurant but as it was called 'Le Merle a Plastron', it took me all bloody day.

Very quickly we worked out that La Merle contained a few more secrets. The first was that unbeknown to Astrid and Alain, the piss head Jeanin was having an affair with Danny the chef. Second he wasn't just a piss head, he was a party animal extraordinaire and would normally not arrive back home until 7: 00 am utterly wasted. We suspected organizational chaos and that's just what we got.

I liked Val Claret because it was small and everyone new each other and although it was a purpose built ski resort; it had a village type feel to it. Tignes was the main centre and Val Claret the 'ski to your door' resort and one of the earliest of its type ever built. Mountains surrounded us on all sides: I loved it. There were lots of bars and nightclubs but they were very expensive and unless we got some kind of 'locals' pass it was obviously going to be expensive to stay here all through the winter. But, for the time being I enjoyed the contrast in comparison to the last six months and besides, I had some ideas already brewing in me for the future.

One night Danny asked if we would like to go skiing, we could borrow all their gear and their ski passes, "thanks but Danny there's hardly any snow."

"No not here, on the glacier."

"We ski on a glacier? I asked surprised."

Now, to a local this sounds completely normabut, to an ex Viking this sounds rather odd and

301

highly dangerous.

"What if I fall down a crevasse or shoot off the end?"

She just looked at me and thought I was mad. "Excuse me?"

Clearly I was missing something but as I had never skied before, I just didn't get it. Anyway the next day, with a special pass, the intrepid mountaineers set off. Bob was cool but I was convinced certain death awaited. The attire of the British Ski team, I am sure, is nothing short of fabulous but they would have passed out if they had seen us with our rag bag collection of ill fitting borrowed gear. Bob had skied before so he was to be my instructor and chief guide – God help us. The mountains have a truly uplifting feel about them and are both energizing and thrilling. I loved being above the tree line and soon realized that you can't tell the difference between a glacier and a normal piste; it's just white, no wonder Danny thought I was a head case. We took off and I was down the first slope and on my back before I'd left. Bobby was a superb instructor as all he did was laugh, especially when I clattered into a total babe or took out some dude who was giving it the full pose. I destroyed drag lifts because I sat down on them rather than being dragged by them; I know the clue is in the title, it's just that I thought they had some special affiliation to the gay community. On one occasion after a bit of a wobble Bob asked if everything was okay as a drag lift hauled us up the mountain.

"Yes cool."

"Good, now just take it easy Franz."

I said nothing for about two minutes pondering

my next move.

"Bobby there's something I have to tell you."

"What is it now?"

"I'm only on one ski."

"What do you mean?" He said looking down, "where the fuck is the other one?"

I pointed behind me, "About 500 yards that way - any ideas?"

"Yes, fuck off."

And with that he pushed me off the lift and straight into a tree. I just sat there laughing. This ski lark was going to take some time, some energy and I suspect a fair degree of skill.

Much of the day continued in the same vein and I would love to claim that I was a natural but I realized early on that my arse was going to take a hammering, drag lift or no drag lift. Nevertheless it was great fun and later we did an excellent job posing in the café on the side of the mountain; I guess we'd had a bit more practice at that.

La Mad Merle must have been France's worst restaurant, with minus 50 Michelin stars. It was utter chaos. When washing up, many times Danny would come into the kitchen having cooked the wrong sauce for a steak, stick it under the tap, put another sauce on and job done. She cooked endless fucking Osso Bucco, so much so that I have never eaten any since. Jeanin got a builder in to fit an extractor fan for the chip fryer, but then forgot to link it up and so every time someone ordered chips the whole restaurant would be filled with smoke. He never got it fixed. If someone complained he would just laugh, it was nuts. We had only been there a few days when one evening guests began arriving and Bob and I welcomed them in, lit the candles and offered them aperitifs whilst they perused the menus. The music was playing and you could see the light dancing against the icicles that hung above the windows. It really was a beautiful setting and the guests were obviously quite impressed and ready to order. The only trouble was we had no chef. Danny was having a lovers tiff with Jeanin and refused to come to work and Jeanin was still asleep in the apartment downstairs absolutely comatosed from the night before and we couldn't wake him. More people arrived. "Bob if you don't wake that nutcase you'll be doing the cooking. As you know I can do a mean Heinz tomato soup with a side order of toast but that's it."

Two seconds later he was back.

"Well I've woken him up. I just poured cold water over him."

"Shit. What did he say?"

"Nothing, he just laughed."

"And what did he say about Danny?"

"Kept laughing," said Bobby, giggling as well.

"Bobby where the fuck did you find these people? I thought we were supposed to be the young care free couple here, not the head chef and the owner. We've only been here a few days and we're running the joint."

At this moment I noticed a shadow lurking in the gloom, it was Jeanin, the monster from the deep in his underpants. "Phil," he whispers, "'ow many are in tonight?"

"About 40 so far."

"Okay, allez," he whispers again with his finger pressed to his lips and still quite clearly pissed.

Over the next two hours a short, long haired Frenchman, with no culinary experience, fag in mouth, a bottle of wine by his side and naked apart from his underpants cooks dinner for over forty people in a ski resort in the French Alps. To my astonishment at least half of them re-booked for the following week. A relieved Bobby turns to me and a laughing Jeanin, "Thank God they never looked into the kitchen and saw Billy Wizz and his sidekick 'West' the dog."

.   The Mad Merle Restaurant; what a bunch of nutters.

One afternoon we met some of Jeanin's contacts, it had to be the afternoon because none of his friends surfaced before 3 pm. Bob then helped me find what I was really searching for, it wasn't easy to get something reasonable and when we finally discovered it I was so excited I nearly burst. Ten minute's later I was in a phone box calling Jane.

"Hello."

"Angel it's me, guess what?" I said excitedly.

"I shudder to think, don't tell me, you are off to Madagascar."

"Nope"

"Oh stop it. What?"

"I've got us an apartment in a ski resort for a month, just for you and me."

"When, when?"

"Now! Book a flight and come now."

"Book a flight. What, just like that?"

In 1978 cheap flights to everywhere just didn't exist, so I knew it wasn't easy but I persevered. "You can do it." I said with conviction. I could tell she was all flustered. I had been away five months and now I was asking her to drop everything and come.

"Baby I want to come, I do, I do. Oh God you're impossible."

She started laughing and then sniffling and then all I could hear was her crying. We hadn't seen each other in such a long time but now she suddenly realized that not only was I asking her to be with me, I'd also kept my promise.

We hurriedly set everything up and somehow she managed to arrange a flight to Lyon on a last minute cancellation. How she did it, I'll never know but I think its called motivation. Luckily I had now saved a little money and as it was early season we got a great deal on the apartment. I just couldn't wait to see her. Bob and I went for a long walk around the resort that night. I loved gazing up at the stars, it was truly overwhelming and we became involved in a deep discussion about the future and what to do. When Bobby and I get talking it can go on for hours and we must have walked halfway up the mountain with no idea of where we were going. He is a truly incredible friend in that he sees into how I feel and then translates it, using wit and empathy, into a form of thought that I understand. I, on the other hand, analyze his depth of feeling by telling him that he's a dickhead. It seems to work. By the time we returned we had straightened out the future perfectly and had hatched a plan.

As I lay there in the darkness that night, a veil that had delicately covered me over the past five months slowly lifted and all became crystal clear.

CHAPTER 12

TOUCHING SOULS

"Love is the offspring of spiritual affinity"

Kahlil Gibran.

The day had arrived and I was bursting to see her. The excitement was unbearable and when the sun tumbled of the mountain peaks and lit up the day I was on fire. Confidence was now at an all time high and so I set my-self a challenge, I would hitch to Lyons Airport135 miles away and be there on time to meet her. A friend gave me a lift to Bourg St Maurice and then I walked for an hour downhill and as I had no pack it was a breeze but I didn't care anyway because I was floating. How many poets, writers and musicians over the centuries have tried to express what I was feeling? When I first began this trip I compared it to freedom, but I didn't know then what I now knew. Freedom is something you feel about yourself whereas love is what you feel about someone else. I was singing out loud as I accepted a ride to Albertville and then Chambery. In all this time away from Jane, the same recurring feeling would play over and over within me, I missed her. No matter what I did or who I met, I missed her. There had been a myriad of opportunities and situations that I enjoyed to the full and I had behaved selfishly on more than one occasion but the simple truth was I needed her in my life and I could never be complete without her.

Sometimes the words people say sound so much like clichés, glib and untrue, and love is a combination of so many different feelings and emotions that are often difficult to express. But for me, all I knew was that no matter what happened, I wanted to be with her. My life and hers were entwined even before we met and being with her was just a stage in a process that would go on forever. We could never be apart.

All was going well until the weather turned and in the space of an hour the clear blue skies turned into snow. Now I was cold and slightly worried this would slow me down but undeterred and highly motivated I cracked on and arrived near the airport with half an hour to spare. Unfortunately I then discovered that the exact the terminal I needed was still about 4 miles away.

I had waited 6 months to see her and I would not be late and leave her stranded. I start to run with my thumb out, half in panic and half in excitement. I scream at the cars. *"Why won't anybody stop?"* My heart is pounding fast and I am crying as I'm running, desperate to get there. I pray for someone to stop and then suddenly, somebody does. In 30 seconds flat I explain to a total stranger my exact situation and he instantly swerves, turns, and heads off to a completely different terminal.

"What are you doing?" I am now apoplectic.

"You were heading for the wrong terminal. *This,* is the right way."

I am speechless as he drops me by the entrance

and shouts, *"Go ... Gate 5 ... go my friend. Go!"* I don't think I have ever run so fast, knocking people over in my rush to get to her and as I circle a huge stone pillar she appears amongst the crowd and for a split second I stop and just stare, oblivious to everything except for a beautiful girl with long auburn hair and wonderful green eyes. Within seconds she notices me and smiles and then, at that exact moment in my life, I fell in love. When they say in the movies, it's like magic, it is and that's how you know.

As I put my arms around her waist my entire body tingled and when we kissed it was like kissing her for the very first time as we stood there all alone, save for each other.

She was radiant and glowing as I said, "Angel, I love you, I've always loved you."

She looked deep into my eyes, "I know, I've always known." And then she giggled, "I just wish you'd realised it a bit quicker, that's all."

We must have stood there for half an hour just talking and holding each other and when we finally boarded the bus to the mountains I asked, "We've been going out for four years, how come you know all this and I never did?"

"Maybe you weren't ready, maybe you're a bit slow," she said cheekily.

The bus was full of excited young people all on their way to the mountains for the winter season. We snuggled together blissfully unaware of the animated chatter of our fellow companions. All manner of rucksacks, jackets, suitcases and bags hung perilously from the overhead luggage racks. The heat from the passengers on the packed bus condensed onto the misty glass windows making it impossible to see outside but we didn't care; we could see each other. I just kept staring at her and holding her, and she just smiled as we talked about the first time I saw her at University and that time at breakfast and how we felt.

"Baby, do you remember the very first time we went out, we went down to the river and you sang to me."

"Of course." I said holding her tight.

"Well you had quite a reputation and everyone told me to stay clear of you, you know, 'he's big headed, likes women', all that."

"Yes, the usual bad press."

"Yes and it was true, you were like that *and still are*." she said laughing.

"But, I'd been out with a few guys who were all nice and charming and whatever, but not one of them and, as far as I know, not any of my girlfriends, have *ever* had anyone sing to them on a first date. And you were supposed to be this poser, this big head, all cool and suave and cocky. But you didn't care, you sang to me and it was funny and beautiful and silly but you didn't care."

I just smiled as I listened to her soft lilting voice. "Keep talking."

"I remember later as we walked along I asked you if you normally sing to girls on a first date and you said ..."

"I never have."

"That's right, that's what you said and then I knew, I knew you were different and I also realised that you must have felt the same about me because otherwise you would never have done that."

Her vivid green eyes just captured me and held me, there was this intense passion between us and it was electric.

"Are you saying that you fell in love with me that very first night?"

"Yes, it was if I had known you all my life." She then began to cry and then I cried - and it wouldn't have surprised me if the whole bus had been crying.

"Angel, do you know something, I felt the same way but I didn't believe it, until now."

"I know," she said still crying, "I know and that's why I've waited for you and that's what people don't understand and I don't care, *I don't care*," she was kissing me now, *"because I know, I know."*

I wiped her tears away and kissed her again, "And now I know too." Jane's soul was so beautiful, I could feel it then and I can feel it now.

As we climbed up into the mountains and the air became clearer I could see she loved the dramatic valleys and steep mountain gorges that were now encircling us. I began to tell her about my trip. She softly put her fingers to my lips, "ssh, tell me later, tell me after," she said with a smile so sexy I nearly had to stop the bus.

And that was the thing, Jane was attractive to me in every way, she was passionate and loving, sensual and romantic, silly and smart. I was so grateful to have her in my life, I could have lost her but now we were together. I told her a little about the hike up the mountain, the mad Merle restaurant, Jeanin and Danny and she told me of all the things she'd been doing, teaching, writing and reading. Having studied English at University she was a prolific reader and whilst I was away she completed nearly every classic piece of literature ever written and devoured countless novels. Jane was also deeply religious but in a very personal and unusual way. She never mentioned it to anyone; to her it was private, her relationship with God was hers. When we met people who talked of their religion, she said nothing, she was happy and contented and just as sure of her love of God as she was of her love for me. As we both had very loving close families she had been brought up like me, to be honest and open about our feelings; to us it was natural to express ourselves without fear of judgement or rejection.

We arrived in Bourg St Maurice and I suggested we hitch to Tignes.

"Well it better be all the way because *I'm* not walking ten miles up a mountain."

She had never hitched before but quite liked the idea of seeing and feeling what I'd been up to. We got a lift with a really nice guy and his girlfriend in a big Citroen DS. These cars were amazing; they were fitted out with huge comfy soft leather seats that felt like your favourite armchair. When the car slid round the twists and turns of the mountain roads the car would roll like a large ocean liner in a stormy sea. It was hair raising but fun and I could see Jane found it thrilling and cool all at the same time. She was also quite impressed with my little French chat with the driver's girlfriend in the front seat.

"I didn't know you could speak French, it's quite sexy," she said lifting one eyebrow.

"Oui, and you are very forward for an ingleesh girl who I 'ave only just met."

She wrapped one arm slowly around my waist and brought her lips close to my ear and whispered. "You have no idea." If we didn't get to the apartment soon there was going to be a seriously embarrassing international incident. Luckily we did, as he took us all the way to *our* apartment in Val Claret.

"By the way it's not always as easy as that." I said taking her bag inside.

"Mmm," she said pondering my last six months, "if all these different people picked you up, you must have got yourself into an awful a lot of mischief."

"Well you know. Anyway I was going to tell you that when ..."

She was shaking her head. "Not now angel." She stopped me mid sentence and kissed me so sensu-ally I nearly died. We lay down on mattresses, scattered with cushions that I had laid on the floor earlier that morning. Jane and I had always been very physical and passionate since the moment we first met but on this night, we made love. It is an expression so over used and so terribly misunderstood, I know people joke that women make love and men have sex and to a certain extent that's true but I have known numerous women who only ever have sex. I am afraid I can't personally vouch for men making love, all I can say is that night, I did.

Jane cried and I felt blessed that I had made her happy. This was real love and although we were young, I knew I would love her all my life and I have. I once asked her about heaven and what she believed.

"But how can we be together in heaven?"

"We will be but not in the way you think or can possibly imagine. All I know, is that it's beautiful."

As we lay there I had my music playing. Stevie Wonder was singing 'You and I', a song I would often sing to her and then, Marvin, Carly, Michael, John and we would drift away. Joni Mitchell then sang a special song that I must have sung to Jane a thousand times before. Many years later Prince would record a version that brings me and many others to tears every time we hear it. I don't know how he managed to take someone else's song and make it just as much his own but he did and if you have never heard 'A Case of You', then you must. When these lines came on we both cried as Joni explained in her own lucid way how we felt for each other, lying in the dark and enveloped by the rugged snowy mountains.

I remember that time you told me, you said

Love is touching souls

Surely you touched mine

Cause part of you pours out of me

In these lines from time to time

Oh you're in my blood like holy wine

You taste so bitter and so sweet

Oh I could drink a case of you darling

Still I'd still be on my feet

I would still be on my feet.

The individual silken threads of our souls had been so carefully woven together and entwined with such love that we could never be undone. I am always truly amazed at the sheer elegance and beauty of someone like Joni Mitchell. What a gift to be able to take two peoples tangled emotions and give them back all smoothed and perfect and still today when I hear this song, I always catch my breath.

In the night I lay there watching her sleep, my beautiful angel. I had missed her more than I could have possibly known. Some people go through their entire lives never experiencing this intense love; we were the fortunate ones.

After a blissful night, morning arrived and I went out early to buy fresh croissants and by the time I returned she had set up breakfast on a tiny table on the balcony overlooking the ski slopes. It was late November but still warm enough in our sheltered position to sit and sunbathe. We were sitting looking up at the drama of the mountain peaks and clear blue skies when she asked me to tell her about my journey through France. I felt nervous; I did not want to spoil the magic. I would tell her the truth but I was a mass of fear and trepidation as regards her reaction and her feelings. The thought of losing her now was beyond unbearable. I told her of

Crazy John, The Baron, Rob and Leo, Barry and Bobby, my gay mates, good and bad, the boats, the grapes and all the amazing things I had experienced.

"Now tell me about the girls," she said calmly.

I explained in minute detail every girl and every situation and she would interject constantly with comments or giggles.

"Fay sounded really nice, a bit like me," she laughed whilst flicking her hair from her face.

"She was, she reminded me of you a little; not as experienced of course."

To which she slapped my arm, giggled again and went "ssh."

God she was gorgeous, I kept going and when I told her of 'explode, explode' she just burst out laughing.

Jane was uniquely intuitive about me, she read me before I read myself and she could tell I was leading up to something. "I know these girls were fun and not important to you and so they are not important to me; now tell me about the girl who was." Her clear green eyes fixed on mine, not like some harsh interrogation but with love and understanding - "And how you felt."

"She was called Dominique; I lived with her for two months in her house amongst the vineyards. It was an idyllic existence and I loved the life she lived. She was an artist; she was beautiful, kind and considerate."

"Did you love her?"

"No."

"Did she love you?"

"Yes," and then I began to cry and so did Jane.

"Angel, Dominique was a lovely person but I could never love her because of you and she knew that and I hurt her terribly."

"And it hurts me that you could even give a small part of yourself to her." Again the tears ran down her face.

"But I didn't, I didn't and Dominique knew because she told me so."

I explained everything and how Dominique felt and I told her how much I had missed her. I even explained my idea of Bobby and her getting together and she laughed when I told her about his bathing experience.

"Sometimes you are more naïve than I am."

"Why?" I said laughing.

"Because that never would have happened; and you wanted me to come and live there too? What all four of us?" she said shaking her head, "you watch too many movies."

"Yeh, Bobby thought I was nuts."

"Yes and he was right."

A peaceful calm and quiet now descended across her face. "Tell me what she said to you and how she felt about you, everything." And as I did, tears once more streamed down her face; this was exhausting for both of us and terribly intense. "Keep going," she said and when I had finished she kissed me, held me and cried and cried and cried.

"Angel, I love you and she knew that."

"I know, I know, I am crying because you've hurt me and I am crying because you hurt her too."

"What do you mean?"

"Angel, don't you understand. If she felt even a tiny piece of how I feel for you, then I am upset for her. But there's a difference. You *are* here with me, it's true she never had you and I've always had you but she never knew what that felt like. These other girls want to be with you but they're not, I am. And I am crying because I feel sorry for them and sorry for Dominique but I am also crying because I am happy. You are here with me and you love me. *You love me*."

"I do love you angel, I ache I love you so much."

"I know."

And strange as it may seem we went inside and made love so passionately that we truly were, for just a brief moment, one soul.

Hours later there came a knock on the door. There was only one person it could be.

"Hi Jane, I see you two lovers are at it as usual, some things never change."

"Hello Bobby." Jane and Bobby had a lovely relationship; they were completely relaxed with each other. They were both beautiful souls and their common bond was that they both loved me.

"Phil has been telling me about Dominique."

"Ah, the French *loverr*," said Bobby.

"He tells me that he tried to get you two together and you were useless."

"Guilty," he said lighting up a fag, "and I suppose he told you about us sunbathing naked and that girl who fiddled with his tomatoes."

"What girl in the tomatoes," said Jane in mock annoyance?

"Oh yes, sorry, forgot about her." Bob and I burst out laughing and so did Jane when she knew the story. If anyone ever needed evidence of the beauty of honesty this was it, if there are no secrets then all that's left is truth. Now Jane could share our fun as if it was her own.

Later that day we visited the restaurant or asylum as it was now called and sat down to discuss our plans. Bobby would go to England to collect his winter clothes and return in a few weeks. Jane could help out in the Merle and I would stay on as *plongeur*. It was so early in the season trade was intermittent and so some days we worked and some we just hung out on our balcony. We had the most amazing panoramic view of the Grand Motte glacier and Jane acquired a deep golden tan from the reflected sunlight. Before Bobby left we went skiing again for a few days and Jane would wait in the bar on the slopes, reading her books and laughing at the spectacle of her cool boyfriend making a complete arse of himself. This was happiness.

After Bobby left, Jeanin decided that he wanted to extend the restaurant downstairs for the larger tour groups. Only problem was, he wanted me to help build it, me and my big mouth, I should never have told him about Barry and my building exploits. I had to construct wooden tables as well as help him install central heating

— total madness and guaranteed disaster. One day he was banging away and suddenly all hell broke loose and half the water in the building shot out of the pipes soaking us and flooding the entire basement.

"Shit Jeanin, the whole thing is going to collapse!"

"Aagh!" shouted the 'wet one' as all the pipes in the ceiling came crashing down. I waded through the water and helped him up and he just sat there and didn't stop laughing for the rest of the day. He was hilarious, totally nuts but a lovely guy.

Meanwhile Jane and I would have breakfast every morning outside as it was unseasonably warm and we loved it. Sometimes and especially after the water world episode Jeanin would get completely legless and not return till late and sleep in all day. This was perfect and allowed us to hang out together in the bright winter sunshine. This was really the first time in three years that the two of us had lived together as such and we loved it. Our life was simple, we had nothing but we were truly happy. Sometimes she would bathe me, just to demonstrate that she could do it better than 'your French luverr' and then half way through she'd throw the sponge at me teasing, "don't get too used to this." And sometimes I would bathe her, though that would prove a big mistake because I could barely get past trying to find the soap. We would chatter away late into the night about silly things and laugh and mess about generally. It was strange that Jane was now part of my adventure but I loved it and one night as we lay there she said "pinch me." And in the half light I could just see her beautiful face smiling and I heard her whisper, "it's real." Then she fell asleep in my arms. God, if only life could always be like this.

After a week the mad Merle was finished and our first tour group arrived.

It was *ze* Germans and a ski group of about 50 people and was complete pandemonium. They got an omelette and a piece of lettuce for some total rip off price. The chips weren't cooked, as usual, and it was embarrassing but Jeanin was so drunk he didn't care and just kept giggling. The next day they complained, but I don't think he even knew what they were saying he was so hung over. Jane and I earned a bit of extra money but really the whole job was badly paid and a waste of time. We persevered and one morning I got up early to prepare breakfast for the Canadian ski team. I had met them before and really liked them so I was happy to do it. The only problem was that Jeanin had organised it and cocked it up by getting the wrong day. How this guy earned any money in business I will never know. The only thing that mattered in the whole world was us. Walking in the snow at night was romantic but it also allowed us to wander for hours and plan our future.

We would talk about getting married one day as if it was the most natural thing in the world, which it was. We didn't get heavy about dates, there was no need to, we just knew it would happen. She'd discuss the type of house she wanted, how many children we'd have, their names and where we would live. We would argue about silly things and then laugh about it before we'd finished arguing. Jane and I could talk forever. I remember her Mum once saying to her Dad, "What do they talk about, they never stop, all I can hear is Jane laughing."

And that's how it was in our little mountain re-treat, chatting, laughing and making love, interspersed by the restaurant and the odd day skiing; it was effort-less and uncomplicated. We could see our future to-gether but there was one more thing I had to do first and Jane knew it.

"Are you going to stay here all winter?"

"That was the plan but it's not practical, I'm just not earning enough money to make it worth it."

"So will you come home with me?"

"Yes I think so, I haven't told Jeanin yet but I don't think he's that bothered."

She cuddled up to me as the wind kicked up the snow and blew it swirling into the air around us.

"And Bobby, will he stay here?"

"Yes, he can earn good tips as a waiter and he gets on great with Jeanin."

"And then you want to go away again don't you?" she said softly, just on the verge of tears.

"Don't cry angel."

"Baby I can't go through all this again, I can't." The wind was now biting cold as I held her close and sheltered her from it.

"Bobby and I have talked about travelling across America and it's something I have to do but this time I want you to come with me."

"Just like that?" she said half angry and half up-set. "Are you going to run around the world forever with me trailing behind or waiting for you at home? My mum's going to go nuts; she can't understand why you don't want to settle down and be normal."

"I'll never be normal."

"You know what I mean; she thinks I should marry a vet or something."

I just started laughing, she was serious and upset but I couldn't help it. "A vet, why a vet?"

"You know stability and security, someone who stays at home and looks after me."

"I know. Look, I have this freedom thing, bug, whatever you call it but it doesn't mean I don't love you and don't want to look after you, I do and I will. Listen angel, you know I want to marry you and be with you forever, you know that."

"You are impossible. What about what I want?"

We arrived at the apartment and sitting down I explained myself more clearly

"I told Bobby I will not go unless you come with me and I won't."

We talked till late and until we both understood exactly how we felt. "It's different now, I love you. Our lives will never be normal but we will be happy, I promise."

The next morning we had both thought it through and she had made a decision.

"Maybe it's good that I see the world, maybe I should take advantage of your wanderlust and see other places for my own reasons."

"So will you come?"

"I will but there is another reason," she said smiling.

"What?"

"I've got to make sure you don't run off with a blonde Californian babe called Sandy or Monica or God help us Joni Mitchell herself!"

She was so lovely and she made me laugh and I was ecstatic that she was coming on our next adventure. A week later Bobby returned and we briefly discussed our plans. We would return to England to work and save for our trip to the USA and he would stay and work the winter season here. We settled on late April as our departure date to America. This time we would all be prepared and organised. Jane would try and get a job in California and Bobby and I would travel across the States and meet her there. Nowadays people fly around the world with such nonchalance but in those days it was a dream and incredibly exciting for all three of us. I had been away from England for over six months and now I was heading back but with a new goal and renewed vigour. A few days later we said our goodbyes.

"Promise to write" said Bobby waving a hanky and taking the piss.

"I will my darling."

Alain dropped us at Bourg St Maurice station and we boarded the train to Lyons where we would change for Paris and home. Jane had done all the hitching she wanted to do and besides it was early December and bloody freezing.

As we travelled this now well trodden country, I thought back to all my exploits and all that had happened. I had begun with so many hopes and dreams and had outdone them all, 100 times over. I had lived for 6 months and was returning with £250, three times the amount I had left with. But, I had two other two much more important things, a rucksack full of memories and the woman I loved. I could never have imagined in a million years, on that sunny morning in Paris, all the experiences that I would have, nor all the wonderful people that I would meet. My gay friends in Cavalaire, Swarthy, Crazy John, sleeping on the beach, the party in Grasse, Graham, Rob, Martin, Leo, Sarah, the football match, Cannes, Hans and the Sirila, Pinky and Perky, the Saint Antoine, Harold Robbins and his exploding secretary, Barry, Eric's shack, both the mad rides with the nutters, fireworks, Monsieur Maurice, car crashes, picking grapes, the girls; all of them, Osin and his tractor, Pierre Marc, the dysfunction of Les Bregieres, Pillule, Jeanin, Danny, washing up, Skiing, our hike, Dominique, Bobby and my angel Jane. Who knew?

As the train pulled into Lyons Perrache station I took most of Jane's important stuff to look after as apparently the connection was sometimes a bit tight and I wanted to make sure that if we had to run she'd be okay.

Just as we pulled in I noticed our train to Paris was already on the next two platforms across from where we were. We would have to descend some steps to a tunnel, go under the tracks and come up on platform 6 just by the train.

"Come on, get ready baby, we've got to move it."

As the train slowed I opened the door and stood on the footplate which you could do on the older trains. I jumped, helped Jane off and then shot off down the platform with her right behind me giggling and running at the same time. A guy next to me said, "It's okay you've got plenty of time, it doesn't leave for another 5 minutes." I never, ever believe anything anyone tells me in a train station in Europe as they are always full of shit. I was bombing along into the tunnel and I could see Jane's hair bobbing up and down as she ran.

"Come on, keep up." I shouted as I ran through the tunnel. At the foot of the stairs I turned, "come on, come on." I leapt the stairs, two at a time and at the top of the steps I ran along the train, jumped on board and stood at the entrance holding the door open. Perfect.

But then at that precise moment I heard a whistle and the train slowly began to move. I turned again but this time she was nowhere in sight. Shit, where was she? The train was inching forward as my eyes scanned the crowded platform. Suddenly I saw her at the top of the steps, "Jane!" I shouted at the top of my voice and waving frantically, "Jane!" She saw me and ran and got close to the train, one carriage down from where I stood. "Jump on there - just jump on." But she was too tired and too frightened.

"Baby, I can't get on .*I can't get on.*"

My blood ran cold. The train was now picking up speed and I was panicking because it was now going too fast for me too get off. *Jane would be stranded here for another 10 hours all through the night and all on her own with no money, nothing.* And she realised it too as the train really began picking up speed.

"Don't leave me!" She shouted

And as she fell to her knees terrified she screamed again, "Don't leave me ... **Don't leave me**!"

Time seemed to stand still; people turned and stared in disbelief as her words took off down the platform racing towards me all the way into my heart and cutting deep like a dagger. I was petrified. But then, just as her words punched me, without thinking and out of sheer desperation, I jumped. I leapt straight out into an abyss, still with my rucksack on my back. I seem to float for a split second before hitting the ground hard, rolling and tumbling and finally crashing into the base of a pillar.

Startled passengers stood with gaping mouths and shocked expressions. I was cut to pieces, my shirt and pants ripped and blood coming from my elbows, hands and head. Incredibly no bones were broken even though I was pretty bashed up. Luckily my pack had taken a lot of the impact and the aluminium frame was now crushed and bent. I left my bag and staggered down the platform towards her; the train having now disappeared. When I reached her she was sobbing her heart out, I sank to my knees and wrapped my arms around her hugging her shaking body. I realised that all this travelling was too much for her and too frightening, she was only doing it for me. I loved her so much it hurt.

"You're always leaving me," she sobbed.

"Yes angel but I always come back. *I told you I will never leave you, never. No matter where I go or what I do I will never, ever leave you.*"

A French couple approached us holding my bag and asked if we were okay. I nodded, "merci." We must have knelt there for an awfully long time. She hugged me and wouldn't let me go; she was crying her heart out. Eventually we found a bench and after cleaning myself up we just held each other, shattered and exhausted from all the emotion.

Some time later, after checking on train times, I returned to find Jane just sitting there and I noticed she had a glow about her and to this day I have no idea why. She always had a presence but this was different and inexplicable, she hardly spoke, she just smiled and seemed almost serene. I was hers.

An hour later whilst enquiring about other trains to Paris, as there was nothing till the morning, another traveller asked if we were going to Calais, "yes, why?"

"Well they don't tell you this but in three hours time there's another train that by passes Paris and doesn't stop but goes directly to Calais. Because it doesn't stop, they tell you there are no trains to Paris."

"Unbelievable, thanks for your help I really appreciate it."

Now we only had a few hours to wait and as we were tired and hungry I said. "Let's leave our bags here and get something to eat."

"But I am not running," she said.

"I know angel and besides the 100 metres sprint is not your forte ... obviously."

She then wagged her finger at me pretending to tell me off and "if you say another word I'll jump on the only piece of your body that doesn't hurt."

"Now you're talking." I said enthusiastically.

"Ssh," she said laughing and so off we went hand in hand into the beautiful city of Lyon. The sun had disappeared but it was still light when we arrived at a small Italian restaurant. A chubby jovial Frenchman, rare in itself, sat us down at a table with lighted candles and soft calming music. He asked us about our trip and we told him off our little drama. He went away with our order and returned with a carafe of Beaujolais. "Sorry but I think ordered a beer and a coke."

"You did Monsieur, but I insist you have this instead."

I thought, well he's cool, why not? It was nectar and by the time we left we were just a little drunk when I requested the bill,

"No Monsieur, this is how you say - on *ze* house."

"I don't understand."

He looked at us both and with a warm smile said, "You are two young people in love and you bless my restaurant with your presence."

You see, sometimes the French talk a load of bollocks and sometimes they don't.

We slept nearly all the way back to England and as the ferry pulled into Dover, the same dark clouds as when I left, were there to greet me on my return. But I was a different man from the one who had left all those months ago. I was no longer imprisoned by the white lines on the road to freedom; I was released, Jane and I had overcome the restraints that had held me back and made me doubt. She was mine and I was hers and whatever road we travelled in the future we would always be as one. I had new goals, cherished memories and a profound unshakeable love. The heavy curtain of cloud and rain was now to me a veil, one which I could easily slip under unnoticed before slipping out again.

Later that day Jane and I said goodbye as we neared her home in Shropshire; she was happy and so was I.

"I think I'll hitch the last bit home."

"You really are impossible, you just won't stop will you," she said laughing.

"Well, I thought I'd finish how I started."

"Yes but if any girl picks you up between here and Knustsford and invites you back to her house - you just say *No!*"

I took off down the road a very contented young man and surprisingly enough a girl did pick me up who was on her way to the Lake District. I didn't consider it for a second, too cold and rainy up there.

She dropped me off, on the side of the motorway in the heart of the Cheshire countryside, "Are you sure you want to be dropped here, it's the middle of nowhere."

I smiled, "the middle of nowhere to someone is always home to somebody else."

I clambered up a steep bank hopped over a fence and walked across a frozen field left fallow for the year, jumped another fence and alighted onto a country lane. Within minutes I had arrived at my parent's house, the door was open and I strolled straight in. My mum heard the door, walked into the hallway and nearly had heart failure.

"Oh my God! Oh my God! Why didn't you

phone us? We'd have picked you up, how did you get here? You look so healthy; I must go shopping …"

"Mum take it easy I'm fine, I'm fine."

She hugged me, had a little cry. "Go into the lounge and see your father he'll be so happy to see you. Why didn't you phone?" She said as she fussed her way down the hall to the kitchen. I crept into the lounge, placed my pack on the floor and kissed my Dad on his forehead as he read his paper.

"Hello stranger," he said.

I sat down next to him as my mother brought me in a cup of tea. The log fire crackled as he slowly folded his paper and removed his spectacles just as he had done all those months ago. He took two puffs on his pipe and then turned to me and asked, "So, what have you been up to then?"

I smiled.

"Well …"

* * * * * * *

Made in the USA
Middletown, DE
11 September 2023